Voyageurs National Park

T0310034

Voyageurs National Park

The Battle to Create
Minnesota's National Park

Fred T. Witzig

Foreword by Elmer L. Andersen

University of Minnesota Press
Minneapolis • *London*

The University of Minnesota Press gratefully acknowledges the generous assistance provided for the publication of this book by the Hamilton P. Traub University Press Fund.

Published by the University of Minnesota Press
111 Third Avenue South, Suite 290
Minneapolis, MN 55401-2520
http://www.upress.umn.edu

Library of Congress Cataloging-in-Publication Data

Witzig, Fred T. (Frederick Theodore), 1925–
  Voyageurs National Park : the battle to create Minnesota's national park / Fred T. Witzig ; foreword by Elmer L. Andersen.
      p.   cm.
  Includes bibliographical references (p.   ) and index.
  ISBN 0-8166-4049-1 (hc : alk. paper) — ISBN 0-8166-4050-5 (pb : alk. paper)
  1. Voyageurs National Park (Minn.)—History.   I. Title.
F612.V6W85   2004
977.6'77—dc22   2003024484

Printed in the United States of America on acid-free paper

The University of Minnesota is an equal-opportunity educator and employer.

12 11 10 09 08 07 06 05 04   10 9 8 7 6 5 4 3 2 1

Contents

Foreword

Elmer L. Andersen

August 22, 1987, was a bright day at Voyageurs National Park. The sun was glancing off the ripples of Rainy Lake, making it a sea of diamonds. A large crowd in a festive mood had gathered for the dedication of Rainy Lake Visitor Center, the first visitor center in Voyageurs National Park, equipped so completely that a family could come without gear of any kind and have a Voyageurs Park experience. In addition to the visitor center, there was a dock and launches to take people out onto the water for a cruise around the islands, so they could get a real feeling for Voyageurs Park.

Fred Witzig has done a wonderful job capturing the story behind that accomplishment. It started in 1962 when a few people, including National Park Service director Conrad Wirth, son of Theodore Wirth of Minneapolis park-planning fame, toured the area. Those people decided that day that the area justified study for national park status. Twenty-five years later, in 1987, the job was complete: twenty years of planning, land exchange, state legislation, and other preparation to convince Congress to authorize and establish the park, and then five more years for the appropriation to outfit the park so it was ready to receive visitors.

Fred Witzig was in at the beginning. He must have kept careful notes because he has rendered a splendid service in recording things as they happened, in the way they happened, and with the cast of characters who caused them to happen. As I read the manuscript of his fine book, I kept wondering if he would mention this event or that event, and he always did; I wondered if he would give adequate recognition to this person or that person, and he always did. As one who was also in it from the beginning (and through all the details up to twenty-five years later), I can certainly recommend this account as the way that it truly happened.

As I sat in the crowd during the dedication program for Rainy Lake Visitor Center, I thought that two things seemed to be verified by the Voyageurs Park experience. First, people never lose when pursuing a worthy cause; there can be ups and downs, delays and frustrations, but persistence will eventually prevail. Second, substantial public improvements take time to accomplish. They do not happen overnight, and they do not happen with one sudden burst of activity. They happen when interested people devote themselves for a long time in tireless effort to achieve a worthy goal.

A hundred years from now people will be thankful for the preservation of this area as a national park. In the meantime, millions of people will enjoy the outdoor experience in a primitive area basically and carefully maintained to protect its inherent values while making its joys available to many.

Preface

Voyageurs National Park is situated at the western end of a federal recreational corridor stretching from Grand Portage on Lake Superior to International Falls at Rainy Lake. This region of unusual natural beauty, with its many lakes and streams, was the French voyageurs' preferred route to the North American interior during the fur-trading days of the eighteenth and nineteenth centuries. The region, therefore, has natural and cultural attributes that prompted late-nineteenth- and early-twentieth-century American and Canadian citizens to look for ways to shield this valuable heritage from the often destructive consequences of traditional settlement and development.

Although early conservation leaders saw the *entire* corridor as a natural unit deserving of protection, it was the area from Crane Lake eastward to Lake Superior that first came under the cover of public control. This segment of the border lakes region was included within the boundaries of the Superior National Forest in 1909, and within a decade, forest administrators had made their first assessment of its recreational value. From that date forward, repeated efforts have been made through internal U.S. Forest Service management decisions, presidential orders, and congressional legislation to define and refine the management policies that govern what is now called the Boundary Waters Canoe Area Wilderness (BWCAW).[1]

Meanwhile, much of the area from Crane Lake westward to International Falls passed into private hands, and its natural resources were thoroughly integrated into the industrial resource economy of the region

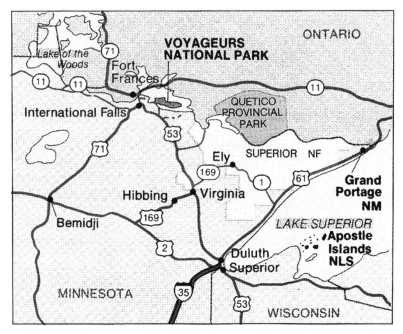

Vicinity map of Voyageurs National Park. Courtesy of the National Park Service.

and the nation. Nevertheless, conservationists continued to look to the time when this westerly segment of the border lakes region would come under a federal management policy similar to that of the BWCAW. Seeing this linkage with the BWCAW and the entire corridor zone is essential to understanding the efforts to secure legislation for Voyageurs.

Most who participated in the campaign for Voyageurs were not aware of the long-sought quest for continuous public control of the maze of lakes, islands, and streams along the Minnesota–Ontario border. Their motivation was the opportunity to secure a national park for Minnesota and to bring a portion of this border area into the "system" of national parks. Most would have shared the philosophy expressed by Charles Lindbergh in remarks made at the 1973 dedication of his boyhood home in Little Falls, Minnesota: "In establishing parks and nature reserves, man reaches beyond the material values of science and technology. That is why I say that parks symbolize the greatest advance our civilization has yet made."[2] They would have agreed as well with novelist-historian Wallace Stegner, who wrote that the national park was "the best idea we ever had."[3] But they soon found that "park-making" is not easy.

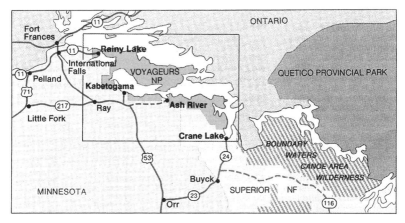

Voyageurs National Park. Courtesy of the National Park Service.

Creating a national park where land ownership had evolved into a complex mix of private and public holdings made land acquisition policy a significant issue throughout the campaign for the park. And for more than fifty years local residents had become accustomed to essentially unrestricted recreational use of private and public lands in the proposed park area. They were stunned at the prospect of losing these advantages of proximity to an area that had suddenly been described by the National Park Service as having "national significance." It was in this environment that the legislative battle for Voyageurs began. Both sides had to endure periods of bureaucratic inertia and wrangling and interminable, unexplained delays of reports, public hearings, and responses to questions germane to the controversy. And both opponents and supporters alike were often frustrated, albeit for different reasons, with the cautious demeanor of the congressman who was carrying the park legislation in the House of Representatives.

This study of the legislative history of Voyageurs identifies and explains the central issues involved in the lengthy debate over this park. The time frame is 1962 to 1975, when the secretary of the interior certified that all the conditions in the congressional act authorizing the park had been satisfied, and he formally established the park as a unit in the National Park System. Archival documents from the Minnesota Historical Society, Voyageurs National Park, the Midwest Regional Office of the National Park Service in Omaha, the Legislative and Congressional Office of the Department of the Interior in Washington, D.C., records of the Superior National Forest in Duluth, newspaper files of the Northeast Minnesota Historical Center at the University of Minnesota Duluth, personal interviews, and my personal files were used in preparing this account.

As a participant in the quest for the park, I was familiar from the beginning of the debate with the central issues that separated the opposing groups. My vantage point was close to the events in time and space, and this has been a distinct advantage in writing this story of the twists and turns leading up to the legislative phase and then following the convoluted legislative path to final approval by Congress. As an academic committed to objective scholarship, I sought to treat the issues, events, and personalities associated with the controversies in an impartial manner. I trust the reader will see that this was accomplished.

Acknowledgments

I credit Eliot Davis, the superintendent of the Grand Portage Monument, for stimulating my interest in Voyageurs National Park. I first heard of the potential for a national park at Kabetogama during a talk he gave in 1965 to a small group at the Duluth YMCA, and later I became a participant in the campaign for congressional authorization of the park. The exposure to and interest in the politics, personalities, and procedural maneuvers during the legislative process caused me to undertake the legislative story.

I am deeply indebted to the University of Minnesota and the National Park Service (NPS) for providing assistance with expenses during the early years of my work. In 1978 I received the first of two grants for travel and expenses from the Graduate School of the University of Minnesota. The second grant was awarded in 1984 and coincided with a sabbatical research leave in 1984–85 that enabled me to devote more time to the project. In 1989 the NPS provided a grant for expenses to research the files at the NPS Midwest Regional Office in Omaha, the archives of the Minnesota Historical Society in St. Paul, and the archives at the Voyageurs National Park headquarters in International Falls. This grant also allowed me to reach and conduct interviews with individuals who played key roles in the campaign for congressional approval of the park.

Many individuals were helpful over the life of this project. I am particularly grateful to Mary Graves, cultural resource specialist at Voyageurs National Park. Mary was my valuable and principal link not only with the NPS (especially with the Midwest Regional Office) but also with the superintendent and staff at Voyageurs; she also carefully reviewed all of the written material, edited the original manuscript, and made helpful suggestions along the way. And through it all she exhibited remarkable patience and good humor! I am also deeply appreciative of the professional assistance and encouragement of NPS historian Don Stevens at the NPS Midwest Regional Office in Omaha. He frequently offered opinions and suggestions based on his professional training and his own experience writing similar documents for other units in the system.

Beth Kwapick, executive secretary of the College of Liberal Arts, University of Minnesota Duluth, rescued me in the latter stages of the project by agreeing to integrate changes into the final form of the manuscript and prepare it for the publisher. Patricia Maus, administrative director of the Northeast Minnesota History Center in Duluth, contributed immeasurable assistance on numerous occasions by locating archival documents and other materials related to the Voyageurs story. She also provided study space and assistance with duplicating materials. Clifford Alexander, associate professor emeritus in Industrial and Technical Studies, University of Minnesota Duluth, offered invaluable assistance and incredible talent in his work with the maps for this study. Mary Lou Pearson, historian for Voyageurs during the 1970s, conducted numerous interviews with park staff and local citizens. These were extremely useful in researching this history. Barry Mackintosh, historian with the NPS in Washington, D.C., explained the objectives and the format of legislative histories and encouraged me to research the Voyageurs story. Dr. Roy O. Hoover, professor emeritus of history at the University of Minnesota Duluth and coeditor with Professor Neil Storch of *Upper Midwest History,* helped with the publication of an earlier paper on Voyageurs and then encouraged me to go forward with a detailed study of the events leading to its establishment. Donald Eng, former deputy supervisor at Superior National Forest and supervisor of national forests in South Carolina (and a good friend), explained through many conversations over the years the issue of federal land use and management in northern Minnesota. Interviewees and other individuals who were helpful include Elmer L. Andersen, Archie Chelseth, Roger Williams, Lloyd Brandt, Martin Kellogg, Myrl Brooks, Judge Edwin Chapman, John

Blatnik, Sigurd Olson, U. W. Hella, John Kawamoto, Dale W. Olsen, Joan and Larry Olson, David Zentner, and Thomas Zogg.

Finally, I am deeply grateful to my wife, Lois, who always encouraged my work and exhibited remarkable forbearance and patience through the life of this project.

Introduction

Legislation authorizing the secretary of the Department of the Interior to establish Voyageurs National Park in northern Minnesota was signed into law by President Richard M. Nixon on January 8, 1971. This action occurred almost eighty years after the Minnesota Legislature, in April 1891, approved a concurrent resolution requesting that the president create a national park in Minnesota by "setting apart a tract of land along the northern boundary of the state, between the mouth of the Vermilion River on the east and Lake of the Woods on the west...."[1] (Much of that territory identified in the 1891 request was incorporated in the final legislation authorizing Voyageurs National Park.)

Although the legislature's request was never acted upon by Congress, conservationists would continue to press for some form of federal protection for the forest and water resources of northeastern Minnesota and especially the border lakes region. Their persistence was buttressed by a growing national awareness that much of the nation's natural resources were being pillaged and squandered with little regard for future needs. The federal government finally recognized this public concern for more careful management of these resources. In a dramatic departure from the previous practice of generous land disposal policies, the Congress enacted the Forest Reserve Act on March 3, 1891. This legislation authorized the president to establish forest reserves on lands in the public domain.[2] Significantly, the Minnesota Legislature's request for a national park followed by one month the congressional action on forest reserves, and by five months the establishment of two national parks, Sequoia and Yosemite.

The sentiment for forest land conservation through reserves and parks, which was the basis for the legislature's action, was not popular in the wooded lake region of northeastern Minnesota. Its inhabitants saw the region as one with a resource base that clearly distinguished it from the other emerging economic regions in the state. Pine forests, minerals, and water were the dominant resource assets, and the region's entrepreneurs wanted a free hand in their development and utilization. Examining a map of presettlement vegetation supported the regional claim of uniqueness. Such a map reveals a state divided into three broad environmental zones: a fertile prairie region in the southwestern half of the state; a pine forest and bog region in the northeast; and a mixed forest-grassland transition zone in between.[3]

As late-nineteenth-century settlement progressed across the state, it became evident that agriculture would be the dominant land use in the prairie and transition zones, while mining and lumbering would prevail over the northeastern third. Human adjustments and adaptations to this varied pattern produced distinct regional economies with their attendant economic and political philosophies. In addition to these regional contrasts was the reality of an expanding urban region around the twin cities of Minneapolis and St. Paul. For an ever increasing number of its residents, the "North Country" represented the state's prime outdoor recreation area. The rapid depletion of the wood and wildlife resources of northern Minnesota and the absence of a resource management program were major concerns for many Twin Cities residents.

At this point in the state's economic history, logging interests were engaged in a highly profitable enterprise removing timber from the pineries of northeastern Minnesota—an activity restrained only by the status of the marketplace at the moment. Influential business leaders as well as politicians who were eager to protect the lumber interests from unfriendly government regulation vigorously opposed any regulatory measures that threatened to interfere with this lucrative practice. For their part, the timber industry made certain that workers and residents who were dependent on the local logging activity understood the logic and "advantages" of the system as it operated at that time. This was dramatically illustrated in December 1891 when a public meeting was held in Duluth to discuss the national park proposal still being advocated by the Minnesota Forestry Association. The chairman of the meeting expressed the prevailing local sentiment when he stated that the park pro-

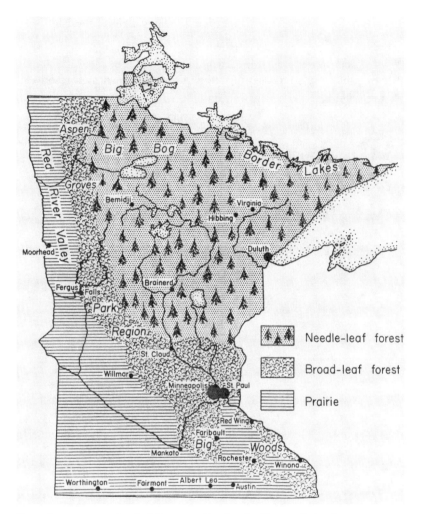

Presettlement vegetation in Minnesota. Reprinted with permission from
John Borchert, *Minnesota's Changing Geography* (Minneapolis: University of
Minnesota Press, 1959).

posal was a "scheme to deprive Duluth of its tributary territory. There is
a concentration of political influence in St. Paul and Minneapolis which
is always manipulated against the rest of the state."[4] In obvious agreement with this sentiment, the Duluth Chamber of Commerce, another
strong defender of "regional turf," announced its opposition to the park
proposal several days after the public meeting.[5]

Another national park proposal was advanced eight years later, in
1899, when the Minnesota Federation of Women's Clubs campaigned

for a national park in the area that eventually became the Chippewa National Forest.[6] Again, northern Minnesotans saw the meddling hand of the people from the "south" who were attempting to impose their values as they related to the utilization of the region's natural resources, thus interfering with the established practices in northeastern Minnesota.

It is evident from these and other similar accounts that even before the turn of the century, legislation advocating preservation or restraint in the use of the natural resources of northeastern Minnesota would be met with suspicion and opposition from business and political leaders in the region. This was especially true if the proposals involved a federal agency. Although a number of arguments were presented as justification for such opposition, two were most frequently and forcefully advanced: that these proposals were inspired by outsiders, primarily Twin Citians; and that these proposals were "land grabbing" schemes of the federal government. Both of these arguments were employed often during the early part of the century, in the 1930s, and again in the 1960s to blunt the efforts of advocates for national park status for any border lakes segment.

The first official step toward public control of the border region was taken with the establishment of the Superior National Forest in 1909. In the same year, the provincial government in Ontario established the Quetico Provincial Forest Reserve along its forest and lake boundary with Minnesota. (The Quetico Reserve became Quetico Provincial Park in 1913.)[7] Although the 1909 boundary of the Superior National Forest encompassed much of the border lakes region east of Crane Lake, it did not include Crane Lake. Nor did it include the four larger lakes to the northwest—Sand Point, Namakan, Kabetogama, and Rainy—which are now included within Voyageurs National Park. Nevertheless, the establishment of the Superior National Forest introduced the potential for comprehensive federal protection of the wilderness values along the entire border lakes region from Grand Portage on Lake Superior west to International Falls.

Even before the Superior National Forest was established, the unique scenic values of the border zone were recognized by conservationists, including Christopher C. Andrews, Minnesota's first forest commissioner. In 1905 he submitted a request to the General Land Office asking that public land along a major segment of the border waterway be withdrawn from sale. Several years later, in 1909, these lands were included in the boundaries of the newly established national forest.[8]

In 1917 the U.S. Forest Service (USFS) conducted a major study and review of its recreational facilities. This study, which followed by one year congressional action creating the National Park Service (NPS) within the Department of the Interior, sought to advise the USFS as to how *it* might identify and administer its recreational facilities. Some historians have suggested that the timing of the study was more than coincidental with the establishment of the NPS. They also record a growing uneasiness among high-level USFS administrators regarding the congressional practice of creating national parks out of scenic USFS lands.[9] In part to stem this kind of land transfer, the USFS embarked on a systemwide program involving evaluation of especially scenic areas under its jurisdiction. The intent of the studies was to determine if the management policy in these areas should focus on aesthetic values as opposed to more traditional utilitarian uses.

One area to come under this review procedure was the boundary waters region of the Superior National Forest. In 1919, Arthur Carhart, a landscape architect employed by the USFS, came to the region to assist in the development of a recreational plan for the national forest and especially for the boundary waters area. Carhart's plan, completed in 1921, represented a radical departure from past practice because it advocated a management policy that would facilitate the "enhancement, preservation and development of the canoeing features of the Superior National Forest."[10] Recent research emphasizes that Carhart's plan was not a wilderness plan as we understand the concept today. Rather, it envisioned facilities (chalets and hotels) at strategic locations to accommodate the many tourists who may wish to "withdraw from civilization's complexity without having to sacrifice too much of civilization's comforts."[11] In this way he was apparently borrowing a technique of the NPS at that time, which was to promote attendance by providing access to the scenic areas in many of its western parks. However, the importance of the Carhart plan really resides in the fact that for the first time the USFS seemed willing to entertain formal plans that highlighted the *recreational* values of national forests.

The first internal test of the USFS plan to protect wilderness values in the Superior National Forest came shortly after the adoption of the

Carhart-inspired recreation plan for the Superior. During the 1920s the nation embarked on an extensive road-building campaign supported by congressional action that provided federal funds through what were called "good roads" bills. Communities and tourist associations in northeastern Minnesota campaigned strenuously for a share of these funds and supported road projects that led to and were constructed within the Superior. Staff foresters believed an expanded road network would facilitate management and, especially, fire protection within the forest and thus lent their support to the road expansion effort. By 1923, conflicting road plans for the region resulted in bitter controversy between conservationists, who backed a conservative approach including a complete ban on roads in wilderness areas, and local resort owners and tourist associations, who backed a more extensive road system. Many conservationists who were close to the situation, like members of the Minnesota division of the Izaak Walton League, finally concluded that the best way to guarantee a roadless status for the border lakes region would be through the enlargement of the Superior National Forest. Although encountering difficulties and frustrations with USFS bureaucracy, conservationists still saw the single-agency *federal* management of the area as the best hope for long-term protection of the region's natural resources. Therefore, they supported congressional legislation advanced by Representative Charles Fuller of Indiana that would have enlarged the Superior to include much of the border area from Rainy Lake to Grand Portage on Lake Superior.[12] Although the bill was dropped in 1924 for lack of support in Congress, its objectives survived in later proposals made by individuals and organizations who continued to work for placement of the entire region under federal control—preferably through expansion of the Superior National Forest.

The road controversy continued until September 1926, when the secretary of the Department of Agriculture, William Jardine, issued a policy statement that sought not only to resolve the road issue but also to clarify the Agriculture Department's position on wilderness recreation management. The secretary "settled the controversy on September 20 by approving the construction of certain roads which he regarded as the minimum necessary for the protection of the national forest. At the same time he emphasized the desire of the department to keep as large a part of the forest as practicable in wilderness condition and stated that at least 1,000 square miles containing the best lakes and canoe routes would be kept free of roads."[13] The policy statement did not ignore the fundamental purposes of a national forest—production and utilization of timber using scientific methods—but it did recognize, in a more formal way, the growing significance of recreational values in the management of forest lands.

A year before Agriculture Secretary Jardine's directive establishing a roadless primitive area within the Superior National Forest, a far more serious threat to the wilderness border zone appeared in the form of a flood control and power development plan for much of the canoe country along the Minnesota-Ontario border. The scheme, advanced by E. W. Backus, president of the Minnesota and Ontario Paper Company, called for damming Rainy and Namakan Lakes and for building storage dams at the outlets of a number of smaller border lakes to the east. Water levels would have risen eighty-eight feet in some places, and virtually two-thirds of what is presently included in the Quetico-Superior canoe wilderness would have been destroyed.[14]

Conservationists were stunned by the implications of the project. In spite of their earlier and relatively successful efforts at protection of this resource, they now realized that they could expect *repeated* threats to the pristine character of the border waterway. Also, the westerly section of this region, from Crane Lake to near International Falls on Rainy Lake (now within Voyageurs National Park), was not included in the Superior National Forest and was subject to future private development that might destroy its primitive qualities.

Seeking to respond to these realities, a new conservation coalition, the Quetico-Superior Council, was formed in 1927. The members of the council, meeting for the first time on January 28, came from groups centered around the American side of Rainy Lake and the Twin Cities, and included officials from the Department of Agriculture, who were used as resource people. Ernest Oberholtzer, from the village of Ranier on Rainy Lake, was the chief architect of the council's program and served as its first president.[15] Oberholtzer spent most of his adult life at his island home on Rainy Lake a few miles east of International Falls. Born in Iowa in 1884, he left his native city, Davenport, to study architecture at Harvard, graduating in 1908. Later he came to Rainy Lake to recover from the effects of rheumatic fever and to fulfill a desire to learn more about the wilderness environment and the Indian people of the Minnesota-Ontario border lakes area. Oberholtzer saw his leadership role in organizing a movement to protect these resources as a necessary response to ward off what he believed to be a ruinous scheme endangering the physical and cultural integrity of the region.[16]

The Quetico-Superior Council quickly attracted the support of a variety of conservation groups, including the Izaak Walton League of America and the Minnesota Conservation Association. The council launched a coordinated effort to alert the public to the fragile nature of the area and to promote the adoption of a sustained-yield management policy for the entire region that paid due regard to its scenic and social values. Central to this plan was "achieving continuous public ownership along the international boundary from Rainy Lake east to Lake Superior."[17]

To forestall future threats to the area and to move toward the goal of public management, in 1928 the Quetico-Superior Council proposed a plan for an International Peace Memorial Forest, honoring the veterans of World War I, that would be administered by policies agreed upon by the appropriate governmental agencies of the two nations.[18] The proposal, which encompassed a much larger area (the entire Rainy Lake watershed) than the existing Superior National Forest and Ontario's Quetico Provincial Park, clearly recognized the geographical unity of the area. Although the plan was never formally adopted as proposed, it served as a useful mechanism for discussion, mediation, and international cooperation, and it also helped focus attention on the one remaining segment of the border lakes region on the U.S. side that was still to be brought into public ownership: the Kabetogama Peninsula and the lands adjacent to Namakan, Sand Point, and Crane Lakes. Credit for keeping the goal of wilderness protection alive for this international forest and lake country must go to Oberholtzer. He worked for more than twenty-five years to get his International Peace Memorial Forest protected by treaty, but his goal was never fully realized. However, his vision of a protected waterway along the international boundary *was* realized. He explained his proposal in an article published in 1929 in which he stated his aim "[that] park-like conditions, free from logging, flooding, draining, and all other forms of exploitation, be established and maintained on all visible shores of lakes, rivers, and islands under public control."[19]

For Oberholtzer, public control always meant the USFS. He had no problem with the USFS and its commitment to commercial forestry so long as that activity was excluded from scenic areas better suited to wilderness recreational use. And so to prevent further damming of lakes and streams and to assure protection from further damage to wooded shores, islands, waterfalls, and rapids in the border waterways, the Quetico-Superior Council, under Oberholtzer's leadership, began working with members of the Minnesota congressional delegation to formulate protective legislation. Legislation written to achieve protection of these resources was sponsored in the U.S. Senate by Minnesota Senator Henrik Shipstead, and in the U.S. House of Representatives by Congressman Walter Newton from Minnesota.[20] The bill was introduced in 1928, and after considerable debate, it was passed and signed into law in 1930. The Shipstead-Newton-Nolan bill was the first major piece of regulatory legislation approved by the U.S. Congress for Minnesota's wilderness border waterway. Within three years of its passage, the Minnesota Legislature enacted legislation applying the same general principles to state-owned land within the area.

The Shipstead legislation, sometimes called simply the Shipstead Act, conserved for recreational use the natural beauty of shorelines on all federal lands "which border upon any boundary lake or stream contiguous to this area, or any other lake or stream within this area which is now or eventually to be in general use for boat or canoe travel."[21] To carry out this principle, it forbade logging on all shores to a depth of 400 feet from the natural waterline and forbade further alteration of the natural water level in any lake or stream within the designated area of the Shipstead Act. The beautiful shorelines of Rainy, Kabetogama, Namakan, and Sand Point Lakes, now within Voyageurs National Park, were subject to the provisions of this act and represent dramatic testimony to the wisdom and forethought of the charter members of the Quetico-Superior Council.

Following passage of the Shipstead Act, Oberholtzer and others on the Quetico-Superior Council intensified their efforts to bring more of the border lakes region under public control. To achieve this objective meant expanding the holdings of the Superior National Forest, including acquisition of the Kabetogama Peninsula. They soon learned that this would not be easy because opposition to the Quetico-Superior program was building, especially within the state's Conservation Commission. Oberholtzer first learned of this when he met with Governor Theodore Christianson in November 1930, shortly after the governor had lost his bid for reelection. Christianson told Oberholtzer that he felt his loss was due to his having expressed himself in favor of the Quetico-Superior program and the Shipstead Act.[22]

Floyd Olson, who succeeded Christianson as governor, had little contact with the advocates of the Quetico-Superior program during his first term. However, during his second term, opportunities to consolidate holdings within the Superior and achieve the long-range objectives of the Shipstead Act and the Quetico-Superior program began to appear when the Roosevelt administration made available substantial funding for its conservation programs.

One objective of the New Deal conservation agenda was the purchase of cutover lands that could then be placed under the management of the USFS. Oberholtzer and an associate on the council met with Governor Olson to explain the opportunities available and seek his assistance. They told him that other states were taking advantage of the new programs, but in Minnesota his Conservation Commission was blocking efforts to enhance consolidation and expansion of the federal forest holdings in the Shipstead-Nolan areas of the state. The explanation for this blocking action was simply opposition to further expansion of the federal forest. As a matter of policy and practice, the USFS was reluctant to go ahead with such purchases in the face of opposition by state government authorities. Governor Olson, now wishing to improve the position of the Quetico-Superior program, replaced several members of the Conservation Commission, and in a reversal of state policy the commission invited the USFS to resume its consolidation program. Olson's untimely death in 1936 removed the only governor in that decade who had shown any significant support for the program. But the depletion of federal funds toward the end of the 1930s greatly reduced the opportunities for realization of the Quetico-Superior plan for expansion of federal administration along the border lakes corridor through westerly expansion of the Superior.

The state's anti-federal attitude continued into the early 1940s during the administration of Governor Harold Stassen. This time it directly affected the Kabetogama Peninsula, the future site of Voyageurs National Park. In a further display of "states rights," the legislature in its first session in the 1940s passed legislation "providing that there should be no further federal purchases of land in the state of Minnesota without the consent of the Governor.[23] Stassen did not have to wait long to use the authority granted in this legislation. The USFS had been meeting with owners of land on the Kabetogama Peninsula and adjacent areas for some time and had put together purchase arrangements to extend federal ownership into thousands of acres of cutover land in what the USFS called its Kabetogama Purchase Unit. When they approached the governor for his approval of the purchase arrangements, he told them their proposal was not in the public interest and turned them down. Oberholtzer later termed this a serious defeat for the Quetico-Superior program. Not long after rejection of the USFS purchase plan the Minnesota and Ontario Paper Company took options on more than 50,000 acres of peninsula land. In a journal article in 1944, Oberholtzer wrote in prophetic fashion that the company thus became "the final arbiter of what is to be done in this region."[24]

CHAPTER ONE

The National Park Service in Northeastern Minnesota

The Early Years

The Quetico-Superior Council's proposal in 1927 for an International Peace Memorial Forest in the Rainy Lake watershed helped focus attention on the remaining forested lands and the disposition of the extensive area of cutover lands in northeastern Minnesota. The council, under Oberholtzer's leadership, had assumed a lead role in shaping policy for publicly owned land in this region. As the economic depression of the 1930s deepened, local units of government saw vast amounts of privately held land disappear from the tax rolls. Practically all of the large landowners within this area permitted their land to go tax delinquent. Many townships and communities continued to carry the cutover lands on their rolls as delinquent—hoping for a land boom that would increase assessed valuations once again.

But as the decades wore on, it became obvious that for them, the legacy of the lumbering era was an impoverished area beyond the capacity of small governmental units to revive. The Quetico-Superior Council, although recognizing that exploitation had greatly reduced the natural resources of the region, maintained that the basic character and possibilities of the area remained, and that the best way to realize its potential was through federal control and management. For the council that meant working through and with the U.S. Forest Service (USFS), an agency within the Department of Agriculture.

Throughout most of the 1930s and into the early 1940s, the policies of most of Minnesota's governors had the effect of blocking further expansion of federal ownership into the cutover areas. Some of the pressure to resist federal ownership allegedly came from state forestry personnel who feared for their jobs if the federal forests were expanded.[1] However, many private owners, and local and county governments as well, took a more pragmatic course and actively sought federal purchase of delinquent land within their jurisdictions. For them, federal expenditures for employment and improvements as the lands came under forest restoration programs and the assurance of payments of 25 percent of all revenues generated on USFS lands were the preferred option. Placing these lands in state forests, frequently described as "paper forests," would simply not produce the revenues that came with federal purchase.

The actions of the board of commissioners of St. Louis County, where most of Voyageurs National Park is located, are a good example of the thinking of local units of government in the 1930s. In 1933 and again in 1937, the St. Louis County Board passed resolutions addressed to the governor, favoring federal purchase of its lands in the Kabetogama area. The resolutions noted the economy of administration and the benefits to the county and state if these lands were placed under USFS management.[2] (In the 1960s, the board's reaction to the proposal for a Voyageurs National Park in the same general area was quite different. The St. Louis County Board, on every vote related to the park proposal, was nearly unanimous in its opposition.)

Occasionally, during discussions about future ownership and management of cutover lands, reference was made to some portion of these lands being placed under the control of the National Park Service (NPS). The only reference to anything approaching a formal proposal is in correspondence between the USFS regional forester in Milwaukee and Supervisor R. V. Harmon of the Superior National Forest in late summer 1937. In a memorandum to Harmon, the regional forester said that representatives of the NPS planned to visit the Superior for the purpose of conducting examinations of the "Primitive Area" (now part of the Boundary Waters Canoe Area Wilderness [BWCAW]). He said they would be examining this area to determine its suitability for a change of status from the national forest system to the national park system.

The USFS apparently regarded the NPS visit as a serious matter because the regional forester requested that the Superior National Forest supervisor prepare a report on the subject areas and that the NPS visit the chief forester's office in Washington, D.C. He asked that the report emphasize the USFS's plan for management of the area from a recreation standpoint. This would maximize the report's usefulness to the chief forester if he were confronted with legislation recommending transfer of USFS land to the NPS.[3]

Harmon's report, completed in 1937, carefully explained how the USFS's management policies for the Superior were more advantageous to the local communities and county government than the more restrictive policies of the NPS. Harmon titled his report "Superior National Forest vs. Superior National Park."

This same title was used a year later in published notices announcing a public debate in Duluth between Sigurd Olson, representing the Quetico-Superior Council, and Hanford Cox, who represented the Minnesota Arrowhead Association. The latter is an association of resorts and commercial establishments catering to the tourist trade in northeastern Minnesota. Olson, a Wisconsin native, was at that time dean of the Ely (Minnesota) Junior College and gaining a reputation for his knowledge of the natural history of the Minnesota-Ontario border lakes region. He told the group that he was not then nor had he been at any time in favor of a national park for this area, and that the policy of the Quetico-Superior Council was always to work for public control through the USFS.[4] Although Olson accepted the explanation that the program committee's use of Superior National Park as the title for his speech was unintentional, the choice of that title may well have been deliberate. The concept of a national park in northeastern Minnesota was no more popular in the 1930s than at the turn of the century. Nevertheless, the USFS treated all rumors and references to national park proposals very seriously.

In May 1941, the assistant chief of the USFS wrote to the regional forester in Milwaukee regarding an office visit from an official of the Weyerhaeuser Timber Company. The official told him that a "Minneapolis group is instigating a movement to have a part, if not all, of Superior National Forest converted into a national park."[5] He asked the Milwaukee office to look into the rumor to determine who was behind such a move, how far they had gone to that date, and what was the attitude of local people who would be affected by such a change of status. In sum, it is fair to say that references during the 1930s and 1940s to a national park for the border lakes region—though desired by some—never matured into formal proposals.

The NPS was very much involved in the state during the New Deal years of the 1930s, not in promoting a specific proposal for a national park in Minnesota but rather working with the state's park system to evaluate the state's recreational resources and upgrade established park units. Under the emergency relief program adopted during the first one hundred days of the Roosevelt administration, the NPS was given the responsibility of conducting and supervising the work of the Civilian Conservation Corps (CCC) in the nation's state parks.[6] Two individuals, who would later play significant roles in securing legislation authorizing Voyageurs National Park, were key people in the CCC program. Conrad Wirth served at the national level, and U. W. "Judge" Hella worked at the state level in Minnesota.

Wirth came by his interest and knowledge of public parks as the son of the superintendent of parks for the city of Minneapolis and would eventually become the sixth director of the NPS (1951–64). In April 1933, he was given the responsibility of organizing and administering the state parks work program of the CCC for the NPS. Because of previous cooperative efforts between the NPS and many of the state park systems, it was deemed the logical federal agency to coordinate the CCC work with the states.[7]

In Minnesota, the NPS hired Hella, a young civil engineer, to serve as engineering foreman for CCC work in the parks. Hella was born in Cloquet, Minnesota, and received his engineering degree from the University of Minnesota. Known to most of his associates by his nickname "Judge," Hella was assigned to the Omaha regional office of the NPS for a brief period in the mid-1930s. There he gained valuable experience with park administration and the intricacies of shaping public recreation policies. In 1937, he returned to Minnesota to supervise the preparation of the *Minnesota Park, Parkway and Recreational Plan,* which was part of a nationwide study program on parks and recreation. In this capacity he developed a thorough knowledge of the Minnesota state park system and a good working relationship with the NPS.[8] Hella was named director of Minnesota State Parks in 1953 and served in that capacity until 1973. During those years he earned the reputation as a respected state official and was certainly the most knowledgeable person on parks and recreational resources in the state. His opinion on such matters was highly regarded by legislators, NPS officials, and prominent conservationists. When the campaign began in the 1960s for legislative support of the Voyageurs proposal, it was Hella and his friends on the Minnesota Council of State Parks who helped organize the citizens groups and associations required to carry the campaign forward.[9]

In 1957, Hella asked the NPS to return to the state to assist in updating the 1938 *Park, Parkway and Recreational Plan,* which the NPS had helped prepare. As part of their work in Minnesota, Hella asked the NPS to include an evaluation of the Northwest Angle area to determine its qualifications for national park designation.[10] For years many Minnesotans had thought the Northwest Angle should be accorded national recognition by the NPS, and Hella felt this to be an opportune time to do a thorough evaluation of the site. After study of archival records and site fieldwork, the NPS concluded that the Northwest Angle did not qualify for NPS recognition.

Meanwhile, research work and site analysis for the revision of the 1938 report continued across the state during summer 1958. The work required the survey team to evaluate a number of areas thought to have some potential for state park or recreation area designation. The last stop in the team's journey took them to the Kabetogama Peninsula east of International Falls. The team reviewed previous studies and reports of the area and also cruised the shoreline for a closer look. On the evening of the last day, the survey team gathered in the Rex Hotel in downtown International Falls for dinner. During after-dinner conversation among the survey party (which included Hella, NPS planners Evan Haynes and Chester Brown, and Bernie Halvor, a recreation planner from the State Parks office), the subject turned to the merits of the Kabetogama Peninsula for state park designation. (Hella recalled that Dr. Norman Baker, a leader on the Minnesota Council of State Parks, had long advocated a state park on Kabetogama, and that the local state legislator Ed Chilgren was also favorable to the idea.)

The discussion continued at the Rex with participants recalling the spectacular scenery that they had seen that day along the Rainy Lake shore. At some point in the conversation, Haynes suggested the peninsula might actually have national park possibilities. Its relative isolation kept development to a few cabin sites on both the Rainy Lake and Lake Kabetogama shores of the peninsula. The picturesque rocky shorelines resembled the scenes along many of the lakes to the east in the Boundary Waters Canoe Area. The discussion produced a consensus that national

park designation for the Kabetogama Peninsula should be explored further and that some indication of local sentiment should be determined.
Before the conversation ended, Hella called a prominent local businessman and close personal friend, Wayne Judy, to come and join them.
Judy, an Iowa native, had moved to International Falls in 1935 to be
closer to the hunting and fishing opportunities he and his wife enjoyed.
Judy taught vocational education in the high school for several years
and then opened a successful sportsmen's services business. Judy, responding to Hella's invitation, brought along the secretary of the International Falls Chamber of Commerce, and after hearing of the national
park suggestion, Judy agreed to seek local support for the park when
definitive plans were developed for public review.

Hella, recalling the meeting some years later, said that Judy was warned
that "he could expect bitter opposition and personal abuse in a supporting role." Mindful of the warning, which proved to be prophetic,
Judy nevertheless agreed to seek local support for a possible national
park.[11] Judy, at considerable sacrifice to his business and himself, became
the key contact for the NPS in the International Falls and Rainy Lake
area. He also helped organize the Voyageurs National Park Association
(VNPA), a statewide organization that was at the center of the long
campaign for Voyageurs.

During the middle and late 1950s, Minnesota's Eighth District Congressman John Blatnik began to receive inquiries from constituents regarding the release of the Bureau of Land Management (BLM) holdings
in the Rainy Lake area. These lands had been withdrawn from sale in
1928 as part of an agreement with Canada to maintain stable water levels
on the border lakes. In July 1958, the NPS advised Blatnik and the BLM
of the recreation survey underway for the state and asked that they
delay decisions on release requests until the survey was completed.[12]
The BLM complied with this request, and in 1959 the director of the
BLM again informed the NPS that they would continue to withhold
these lands.[13]

The BLM and NPS requests were the first indications of federal interest in the recreation potential of the Rainy Lake area. Blatnik's small
role in the withdrawal of the affected lands was just the beginning of
the many recommendations and decisions he would be required to make
involving eventual land ownership and jurisdiction in this section of
Minnesota's border lakes region. But this was "home territory" for him,

and he could rely on his early experience and associations with its land and people. Blatnik was born in 1911 to immigrant Slovenian parents in Chisholm, Minnesota, a small town on the Iron Range about 100 miles south of the Canadian border. After high school he studied chemistry and education at Winona State Teachers College. He later taught in Chisholm and worked for a time with the CCC program in the Superior National Forest. After serving with the Army Air Force and the OSS (Office of Strategic Services) on assignment in Yugoslavia during World War II, he returned to Minnesota and began a political career that took him first to the state senate and then, in 1947, to the House of Representatives as Minnesota's Eighth District congressman.[14] In this capacity he would eventually be drawn into the struggle for congressional authorization of Voyageurs National Park.

Evan Haynes, chief of the NPS Recreation Resources Planning unit, returned to Minnesota in July 1959 to make a reconnaissance survey by boat and air of the Rainy, Kabetogama, and Namakan Lakes area. In his report on this field trip he wrote, "the peninsula and islands constitute a combination of beauty and extensive wilderness hard to equal these days." His recommendation was that the area be seriously considered for designation as a national park, essentially reaffirming his observation of the previous autumn.[15]

Between mid-July 1959, when Haynes wrote this report, and fall 1961, NPS personnel made frequent visits to Minnesota for the purpose of completing the task of updating the 1938 parks and recreation plan for the Minnesota Division of State Parks and to conduct further study and analysis of the Kabetogama-Rainy Lakes area to determine its suitability for inclusion in the National Park System. Coinciding with this federal activity was heightened interest at the state level in the Kabetogama Peninsula as a worthy addition to the state park system.

Early in 1961, Clarence Prout, Minnesota's Commissioner of Conservation, sent a memorandum to all directors in his department stating that he was withdrawing from sale specific parcels of state lands on the peninsula pending completion of a study by the Minnesota Division of State Parks of the area's qualifications for state park status.[16] In July 1961, rumors about a state park in the International Falls area prompted the manager of the International Falls Chamber of Commerce to contact Hella for clarification. In his reply, Hella cited particular interest in 5,000 acres of mainland and islands in the Black Bay region because of its scenic and historic values. The Black Bay area was closest to the mainland on the west, and one can speculate that the acreage was more in the range of the state's ability to develop and manage than the entire peninsula, which was about 75,000 acres. Hella also said that he would be coming to the International Falls area in early August along with an NPS representative to look over the area.[17]

In September 1961, Hella sent a memorandum to Governor Elmer L. Andersen, providing information on the department's recently completed long-range (ten-year) plan. In this same memorandum, he also spoke of the NPS interest in the Kabetogama Peninsula as a potential site for a national park that would "include the shoreline fringe leaving the bulk of interior lands for commercial forest development."[18] There is no evidence that the NPS ever considered limiting their interest on the peninsula to the shoreline. This declaration did not rule out conversations on the subject, but the events of the previous two years clearly indicate that the NPS was interested in the entire Kabetogama Peninsula as a unit within the federal system. NPS policy at that time required that parks be large enough to maintain a reasonable balance of plants and animals as part of the natural setting and, at the same time, allow for public use.

Also at this time, NPS personnel were careful in official correspondence to refer to the Kabetogama Peninsula as having *potential* as a national or federal *area* rather than a *national park*. Minnesota officials always referred to national park status for the peninsula, but not all NPS people were at this time convinced that it qualified for this designation.

A major move toward clarifying federal intentions for Kabetogama came in October 1961 in a report from Howard Baker, NPS Midwest Regional Director, to NPS Director Wirth. Baker's report described a field trip completed earlier that month by state and NPS personnel that included Conservation Commissioner Prout, Parks Director Hella, and naturalist-writer Sigurd Olson. The field party agreed that "Kabetogama had potential as a national area and recommended that the director authorize full-scale studies of the area."[19]

Before Baker left Minnesota, he visited Governor Andersen and told him of the recommendation for further studies. The governor, who was already enthusiastic about national park possibilities for Minnesota, was told by the regional director that it was all right to say publicly that the NPS was *considering* a national park in Minnesota, but no specific location should be mentioned.[20] On October 27, 1961, NPS Director Wirth sent a letter to Baker "authorizing advanced studies of the Kabetogama-Rainy Lake section, Minnesota."[21] Previous experience with bureaucratic inertia prompted Governor Andersen to quickly initiate a campaign of persistent pressure urging the NPS to follow through with these studies as soon as possible. He began his campaign—actually the beginning of a ten-year effort to secure authorization of Voyageurs—by contacting several Minnesota congressmen, including Walter Judd and Albert Quie, asking them to write letters to Wirth expressing support for a national park in Minnesota and for quick completion of studies required to accomplish that objective.[22]

Andersen, a successful businessman and political and civic leader, was born in Chicago and spent his boyhood days in Muskegon, Michigan. He moved to Minneapolis as a sales representative for a Michigan company, earned a business degree at the University of Minnesota, and went on to eventually purchase a small adhesives company, the H. B. Fuller Company. The Fuller Company is now listed in the Fortune 500 list of American companies. He began a career in politics by winning a seat in the state senate in 1949, and in 1960 he was elected governor. His interest in the national park campaign was consistent with his long-standing involvement in civic and cultural affairs in the Twin Cities and around the state.[23]

Director Wirth's action authorizing advanced studies for Kabetogama quickly shifted state energies away from the Kabetogama Peninsula's value as a state park. Governor Andersen's administration turned instead toward total cooperation with the NPS with the ultimate goal a national park for Minnesota. Aside from top state officials and some members of the congressional delegation, there was little public knowledge of these activities on the Voyageurs project until the summer of 1962. It is safe to say, however, that with advanced studies underway and the state's commitment to cooperate with the NPS, the work to establish the nation's thirty-sixth national park in Minnesota had begun.

CHAPTER TWO

Developing a Proposal for Voyageurs National Park

With NPS Director Conrad Wirth's authorization for advanced studies in hand, NPS personnel began laying the framework for detailed field investigations of the Kabetogama area. The scope of the study was outlined in a June 21, 1962, memorandum addressed to Midwest Regional Director Howard Baker from Assistant Regional Director Chester C. Brown.[1] The objective of the memorandum was to provide background information to Wirth, who was scheduled to visit northeastern Minnesota during the last week in June. Wirth was to be the honored guest of Governor Elmer Andersen at the dedication of Minnesota's newest park, Bear Head Island State Park near Tower.

Following the dedication, Andersen and Wirth would be joined for a reconnaissance journey of the Kabetogama-Rainy Lakes area by naturalist and writer Sigurd Olson; Russell Fridley, director of the Minnesota Historical Society; U. W. Hella, director of the Minnesota Division of State Parks; and George Amidon, a senior official with the Minnesota and Ontario (M&O) Paper Company, the largest landowner on the Kabetogama Peninsula. Arrangements for this three-day event were made in the governor's office and were planned to acquaint and impress Wirth with the beauty of the area and, more importantly, to publicly announce the NPS's interest in the Kabetogama area as a potential site for a unit within the National Park System.

The memorandum prepared by the assistant regional director turned out to be more than just an informative piece for his superiors. Careful study of its contents reveals some important concepts and opinions about

Kabetogama based on over twenty years of NPS experience in the region. As we have seen, the NPS was no stranger to northeastern Minnesota. It had assisted the Minnesota State Parks Division in its initial park and recreational plan (1939) and returned again in the 1950s to help with the updating of that plan. The Brown memorandum shows that the NPS did not view the Kabetogama Peninsula in isolation but rather, as Brown observed, "an integral part of the total northern Minnesota border complex—the voyageurs' route, if you will. In our study, we hope to recognize this, pointing our report specifically at the general Kabetogama area perhaps, but making complementary recommendations on other portions of the border country."[2]

The memorandum is also specific in designating for *detailed study* the "whole area east of International Falls to the Quetico-Superior/ BWCA region including Kabetogama Lake, the Kabetogama Peninsula, Namakan Lake, Sand Point Lake and Crane Lake."[3] Thus it is clear that national park planners saw an excellent opportunity to complete a federal recreation corridor from Lake Superior to International Falls. The Crane-Rainy Lakes section was the last large missing segment in that corridor.

The reference in the Brown memorandum to the voyageurs' route also recognized the historical significance of the border lakes region. In this they were strongly influenced by Olson, northern Minnesota's most outstanding authority on the "voyageurs highway" and an articulate advocate for public control of the entire border waterway region. Olson was better known at the time as one of the strongest advocates for wilderness. He was a charter member of The Wilderness Society and was its president when the Voyageurs bill made it through the congress.

The Brown memorandum also stressed that the study area included some scenic, geologic, archeological, and ecological features and characteristics not then included in the National Park System and that the water-based orientation to recreational opportunities would also give it unusual status within the system. However, Brown also expressed some reservations about the Kabetogama area's qualifications for national park status. The stability of the water levels of all the lakes in the proposed study area—Rainy, Kabetogama, Namakan, Sand Point, and Crane—is to a greater or lesser degree affected by two dams that were built at Kettle Falls early in the century. Brown, in noting this alteration of natural conditions in his June 1962 memorandum, said it raised some concerns for him in considering the area for national park status. John Kawamoto, the NPS's key planner for Voyageurs, said that later on this situation presented a problem for other park officials as they moved toward a formal position and proposal for the park.[4]

Some thoughts regarding NPS management of the Kabetogama area can also be found in Brown's memorandum. The suggested management strategy assumed a federally managed area stretching from Crane Lake to and including the Kabetogama Peninsula and recommended the national park formula for development. It stressed the importance of limiting access to just two sites—Crane Lake and Kabetogama Lake—and proposed a development and interpretation strategy that would "encourage leisurely enjoyment by water and by trails . . . arrive by car, park it, and lock it up."[5] Finally he envisioned an area that would fill the recreational opportunity gap between the wilderness experience of the canoe country to the east and many commercially developed lake areas in northeastern Minnesota.

In retrospect, Brown's report was an important document because it reveals the earliest thinking of the NPS planners regarding issues and questions that would become so important in shaping final proposals for Voyageurs National Park: the Kabetogama area's physical and cultural amenities, its strategic position in the emerging federal recreation corridor along the Minnesota-Ontario border, its potential as a "recreational alternative" in the region and the state, and the uncertainty of park planners regarding its categorical place as a unit within the National Park System. It would be almost two years before the NPS shared many of these issues and concepts with the general public.

On June 28, 1962, the *International Falls Daily Journal* carried a front-page report on the Kabetogama trip hosted by Governor Andersen for Director Wirth and other NPS and state officials. This was the first official public acknowledgment that state and federal officials were seriously interested in seeing the area become a national park. The article included excerpts from a press release written by Governor Andersen in which he announced a "consensus" of opinion that the Kabetogama Peninsula was an enormous recreational resource to a great degree still in its natural state. "It should be made available for use by more people while preserving its wilderness character for posterity."[6] On this and other occasions, Governor Andersen never hesitated to express his respect for and confidence in the professional expertise of the NPS.[7] His statement also noted that a national park in the Kabetogama area would add historical, recreational, and wilderness values not then represented in the National Park System. Recognizing the area's strong ties to the French voyageurs and the fur trading era, the statement concluded with a suggestion, generally attributed to Sigurd Olson, that the park be called "Voyageurs Waterways National Park" and that federal, state, and private parties "should cooperate in detailed and comprehensive studies to determine whether a national park should be established in this area."[8]

NPS planners were preparing for comprehensive studies in the Kabetogama area even as Governor Andersen and his guests were enjoying the beautiful scenery on Rainy and Kabetogama Lakes. On June 28, one day after the excursion led by Governor Andersen, Director Wirth, Midwest Regional Director Baker, and Olson flew over the entire border lakes region. What they saw convinced Baker and Wirth of what Olson and others on the Quetico-Superior Council had maintained for years— that the "entire complex of the Voyageurs Waterway from the Northwest Angle to Grand Portage should be tied together through a coordinated program. . . ."[9] This meant, of course, public control over most of that area by federal agencies along the border waterway from International Falls to Lake Superior.

The study team from the Midwest Regional Office of the NPS worked in the Crane Lake to International Falls area from July 30 to August 10, 1962. For part of that time Minnesota State Forest division staff and K. W. Udd, a staff person from the Superior National Forest office in Duluth, accompanied them. Udd was invited because much of the study area from Crane Lake to Kabetogama Lake fell within what was officially designated a National Forest Purchase Unit. Udd said that the National Forest Reservation Commission authorized this unit in 1956 with prospects for formal inclusion within the Superior National Forest at a later date. An earlier state policy opposing expansion of the Superior had been set aside, and considerable acreage within the purchase unit had already been acquired through trades and purchase agreements between the state and the Superior National Forest.

In late summer 1962, personnel at the Superior National Forest fully expected that the westerly boundary of the forest would soon be extended to include these lands. Upon returning from his trip with the NPS study team, Udd prepared a report that noted that the NPS was not confining its study to the Kabetogama area but had expanded its range to include lands already in the Superior and other potential USFS lands as well.

Udd's report regarding the geographic extent of the NPS study alarmed USFS personnel and especially George James, the regional forester in Milwaukee. James immediately expressed his concern in a letter to the NPS's Midwest Regional Director in Omaha. In his letter he said, "I was under the impression that this area of interest [National Park Service interest] was outside the adjusted National Forest Purchase Unit boundary west of Crane Lake.... We are surprised and perturbed to now learn that the study under way at the present time includes a portion of the area already within this adjusted National Forest Purchase Unit boundary extending down to and including the Crane Lake area."[10] He went on to say that the *Development Program for the National Forests* sent to Congress and the president in 1961 clearly spelled out USFS concerns for the protection, public use, and recreation environment of lands managed by the USFS. He closed by asking for a meeting with NPS staff before they scheduled any further work in the Namakan-Crane Lakes area.[11]

Regional Director Baker informed Director Wirth of the conflict with the USFS and suggested an NPS response that would urge delaying action of extension of the boundaries of the Superior National Forest into the Namakan-Crane area "until the study is completed and there is then the opportunity to weigh the several resource use potentials against the overall public interest."[12] Perhaps looking for some assistance from a neutral party in arbitrating this matter, Baker's letter continued, "Since this area involves federal interests crossing departmental lines as well as state and local interests, it appears to fall within the sphere of the Bureau of Outdoor Recreation (BOR)."[13] Newly established in April 1962 as a coordinating agency, the BOR played a minor role in the formulation of plans for Voyageurs and no significant role in dealing with the interagency squabble over USFS lands in the initial NPS proposal for Voyageurs.

Developments in fall 1962 quickly revealed that the USFS would have nothing to do with a delay in extending the boundaries of the Superior National Forest to include the Namakan-Crane Lakes area. Instead, USFS staff began to plan an offensive to protect what they felt were their legitimate rights and interests in the area. Historically the creation or spatial expansion of national parks often ate into surrounding national forests, and the proposal for Voyageurs was seen as no exception. To the

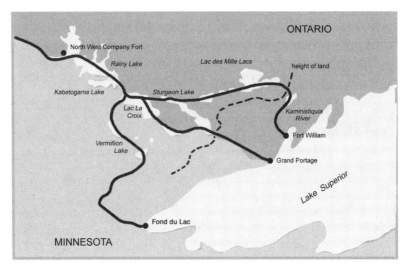

Voyageur routes between Lake Superior and Rainy Lake. Courtesy of the National Park Service.

USFS, this proposal, if adopted, would represent yet another violation by the NPS of the territorial integrity of a national forest. The staff at the Superior National Forest realized they would have to move rapidly if they were to prevent such an incursion into the Superior.

Ironically, just as they prepared to do battle with the NPS and defend their interests in the Namakan-Crane area, they learned that at its fall meeting in Hawaii, the Advisory Board on National Parks, Historical Sites, Buildings and Memorials had voted to submit a formal recommendation to the secretary of the interior that stated that the Crane Lake–Rainy Lake region was "superbly qualified to be designated the second national park in the Midwest."[14] (Isle Royale in Lake Superior became the first national park in the Midwest when it was authorized in 1931.)

In language that captured one of the fundamental objectives of the Quetico-Superior Council more than thirty years before, as well as describing a remarkable and strategic opportunity for the NPS, the Advisory Board declared, "With Grand Portage National Monument at the gateway of the region, 200 miles to the east, and a National Park at the West Entrance, the two areas of the National Park System would hold between them the Boundary Waters Canoe Area of the Superior National Forest and the adjacent Quetico Provincial Park of Canada. They would stand as inviolate bastions at either end and give added protection and significance to the entire complex of waterways on both sides of the border."[15]

The Advisory Board's recommendation on Voyageurs came after considering Director Wirth's report to them on NPS studies of the entire Minnesota-Ontario border waterways. Wirth's report emphasized the more detailed study of the Kabetogama Peninsula and Namakan-Crane Lakes area that the NPS was now advocating as the site of a new national park. (A policy decision had apparently been made late that summer to drop reference to the site as a "national area" and call it a "proposed national park.") Governor Andersen and Sigurd Olson had made it clear that they would support only a *national park* proposal. Significantly, in what was a departure from normal procedure, the Advisory Board made its recommendation in the absence of a completed draft proposal. That proposal was still in preparation and would not be ready until March 1963. It is quite possible that the Advisory Board was aware of the pending westerly extension of Superior National Forest's official boundary to include the Namakan-Crane area and that they wished to get their position on the record before that event occurred. It is also true that without the draft proposal on the park and details regarding the pending enlargement of the Superior National Forest, they could rely on briefings and explanations on both matters from one of their colleagues on the board—Sigurd Olson.

Another boost to the Voyageurs cause came from Governor Andersen in a speech at the Rex Hotel in International Falls on September 19, 1962. In a story reported the following day in the *International Falls Daily Journal,* the governor, who was campaigning for reelection and traveling with a Republican state candidate's caravan, gave a progress report on the national park proposal.

Unaware of the deepening rift between the two agencies over the NPS intent to include the Namakan-Crane area in its proposal, Governor Andersen said that the two agencies were working together to "get a plan going for the Forest Service to exchange land with the National Park Service."[16] He said that consolidating land ownership was a necessary first step in securing a national park for Minnesota. Following that would come NPS recommendations to the National Parks Advisory Board, which in turn would recommend to the secretary of the interior and then to Congress for authorization.

In fairness to the governor, it would have been impossible to provide details about the process for gaining approval of a national park proposal in a brief campaign speech. Nevertheless, the speech did give some insight as to what the governor and other park advocates saw were the logical steps along the path leading to final approval. For some, what transpired over the next few years to distort that path was wholly unexpected.

As November 1962 began, the NPS could take a measure of satisfaction that their recommendation for a national park along the border lakes region had the strong support of the governor of Minnesota, the Minnesota Department of Conservation, and some prominent conservationists in the region, and the recommendation of the National Parks Advisory Board. But any hopes for early congressional action on their proposal were significantly diminished by three events that occurred before the year was out.

The first of these events was Andersen's defeat for reelection to a four-year term as governor. The race between Andersen and Democrat Karl Rolvaag was so close that a statewide recount was ordered—a procedure that took nearly five months. Rolvaag was eventually declared the winner in March 1963.[17] Although both candidates favored the establishment of a park at Kabetogama, Andersen's support was predicated on firsthand knowledge of the natural resources of the region, its cultural significance, and the firm conviction that its preservation was in the national interest.[18] Losing his bid for reelection was a serious blow to the park cause. It meant that Andersen no longer had the power of the governor's office in his quest for a national park and was required to continue his efforts on behalf of the park as a private citizen. He assumed a leadership role in the movement for national park designation and for its authorization by the Congress. Without his organizational skill, his ability to energize park advocates during the long seven-year campaign, and his dedication and enthusiasm, there would be no Voyageurs National Park today.

The second event that worked against speedy authorization for Voyageurs was the emergence of determined USFS opposition to the relinquishing of lands in the Namakan-Crane Lakes area to the NPS. This became apparent during a November 15, 1962, meeting in Duluth attended by NPS and USFS personnel along with the commissioner of conservation and the state parks director for Minnesota. It was the meeting Regional Forrester James had asked for in late August. During this conference, NPS Assistant Midwest Regional Director Chester Brown presented the NPS plan for the entire border lakes region. The proposal included the Namakan-Crane Lakes area in a proposed national park stretching from near International Falls on Rainy Lake to the Vermilion River gorge near the river's entry into Crane Lake.

L. P. Neff, supervisor for the Superior National Forest, responded by noting that the Namakan-Crane Lakes section was already appropriately managed by the USFS and saw no reason for its inclusion in the proposed national park. Neff's position, of course, was contrary to Brown's, which was that the entire stretch of the proposed park be managed by a single agency. As the meeting broke up, Brown asked the USFS to send him their management plan for the Namakan-Crane Lakes segment so that it could be appended to the NPS report on Voyageurs, which would be completed in early 1963.[19]

In the weeks following the November 15 meeting, the USFS went on the offensive to protect what it felt were its legitimate interests and mandate in the Namakan-Crane Lakes area. Forest Supervisor Neff and his staff were determined to retain control of their holdings in the area by countering with a recreation plan of their own. In a letter to the regional forester, Neff emphasized that the fight to retain the Namakan-Crane Lakes area under USFS management would be difficult mainly because of the lack of USFS development. He proposed an aggressive course of action, including reordering budget and planning priorities so as to complete a five-year development plan as soon as possible and to put administrative personnel in the area no later than May 1, 1963. He further urged the USFS to "do everything possible to have the unit proclaimed as part of the National Forest as soon as possible."[20]

Neff's position was supported by the report of a special task force assigned to look into the matter. The task force leader said that moving the forest boundary westward to include the Namakan-Crane Lakes area would be the "most positive action that could be taken to strengthen our position." (He also suggested that the BOR be called in to review the proposal given the conflict between the two federal agencies rather than "letting the National Park Service roll along with their proposal.") And because the largest landowner in the proposed area was the M&O Paper Company, he suggested contacting M&O to remind them of the "long-term future prospects of what might happen to this entire stretch of country with respect to future availability of timber products and that the national position of the wood industry has generally been to disfavor further extensions of federal ownership and reductions in areas available for multiple use management."[21]

The file copy of the task force report found in the Superior National Forest office files has the following handwritten comment, which actually became the official position of the USFS regarding the NPS proposal for Voyageurs: "I think we cannot afford to be 'against' a national park in Minnesota and I think we should go slow in attempting to scotch the Kabetogama proposal. Believe our best bet is to hold fast to our line at Junction Bay on Namakan and stand on our management of this area."[22]

Anticipating early presidential action on westward extension of the forest boundary to include the Namakan-Crane Lakes segment, Neff's call for quick action on a recreation and management plan was approved at the regional level and rushed to completion in early 1963. It was a hastily prepared plan that included several new roads providing two access points to the south shore of Namakan Lake and another to the northwest of Crane Lake.[23] Such road penetration was just the opposite of the NPS proposal to develop a water-based park with highway access at only four locations throughout the entire park.[24] Nevertheless, the commitment and energy displayed in preparing the plan were unmistakable evidence that the USFS had no intention of giving up their claim to the Namakan-Crane Lakes area.

Forest Supervisor Neff and his staff did not have to wait long for federal action on expansion of the Superior National Forest. On December 28, 1962, President John F. Kennedy signed the executive order incorporating the Kabetogama Purchase Unit (Namakan to Crane Lake) within the official boundaries of the Superior National Forest. This action represented the third major obstacle to quick action on the NPS proposal for Voyageurs. The Namakan-Crane Lakes segment, now securely within the forest, could be included in future planning. Through this action, USFS officials had already realized their principal objective, which was so clearly stated in November by Neff and again in early December by Bacon, the task force leader: get official action on the boundary extension as soon as possible!

Sometime in mid-1963, the USFS abandoned its hastily prepared Namakan management recreation plan in favor of one more sensitive to the wilderness character of the region. This plan, titled "The Crane Lake

Recreation Area," stressed the primitive nature of the unit, expressly prohibited public roads or the use of motorized vehicles, and encouraged the use of powerboats as the principal means of access to scenic areas and prime fishing locations.[25] In fact, the overall recreational objectives of this revised plan were essentially the same as those proposed by the NPS for the same area as part of its proposal for Voyageurs. This similarity with the NPS plan was deliberate. The USFS was determined that higher officials and, eventually, the general public see their proposal for the Namakan-Crane Lakes area as one that effectively complemented the NPS plans for the Kabetogama area, thus making it unnecessary to include it within the proposed park boundaries. This determination to hold fast to the newly won addition to the Superior National Forest became all too apparent to the NPS and Voyageurs proponents during the first months of 1963.

Governor Andersen, concerned that the vote recount might go against him, sought to move the park proposal forward while he still retained the power of the governor's office. In January, he asked his conservation commissioner to contact the regional offices of the NPS and the USFS regarding progress on USFS land transfers that were required to meet the recommendation of the NPS proposal for Voyageurs.[26] Andersen realized that given the mix of land ownership in the proposed park, timely resolution of the land exchange and transfer questions would greatly facilitate early authorization of Voyageurs. Unfortunately, Andersen was not encouraged by the responses to Commissioner Prout's queries. The agencies' answers were revealed by their actions.

Having stated their positions at the November 15 meeting in Duluth, the two agencies proceeded to follow paths consistent with those positions. The USFS began the new year with the Namakan-Crane Lakes segment now solidly within the boundaries of the Superior National Forest, and the NPS continued to work toward completion of its draft proposal for Voyageurs, hoping to get some accommodation from the USFS so that it could include the Crane Lake unit in its plan. However, the NPS's task was made far more complicated by an interagency agreement made on January 28, 1963.

Debate centering on the establishment of a new national park seldom takes place without reference to past issues or controversies involving similar circumstances or questions of policy. Voyageurs National Park was certainly not an exception. At the time planning began for Voyageurs, serious disagreements over management jurisdiction between the NPS and the USFS were occurring in the Cascade Mountain region of Washington State. There, a bitter interagency wrangle had developed over USFS territory proposed for a North Cascades National Park. Such disagreements were, of course, not new, but they were inevitably confusing to the public, who found it hard to understand how two agencies both charged with the responsibility of managing and protecting public lands could engage in such acrimonious jurisdictional disputes. Because these "family" squabbles were also proving embarrassing to the Kennedy administration, something had to be done.

So it was in the course of the debate over North Cascades National Park that the top administrators in the two affected departments came forward with an agreement that they believed would alleviate the situation. On January 28, 1963, the secretaries of the Department of Agriculture and the Department of the Interior sent a letter to President Kennedy that spelled out their agreement. The press quickly dubbed the agreement the "Treaty of the Potomac." In the secretaries' statement to the president they said, "Neither department will initiate unilaterally new proposals to change the status of lands under the jurisdiction of the other department. Independent studies by one department of lands administered by the other will not be carried on. Joint studies will be the rule."[27] The joint studies clause indicated a willingness to moderate the departments' competitive spirits and negotiate differences—a process requiring that both parties agree to meet at the table. The agreement was put to the test at Voyageurs.

When Judge Hella received a copy of the agreement, he wrote to Sigurd Olson noting his disappointment with the accord. "It, in fact, entrenches the Forest Service more firmly in the recreation business in a major way and at the expense of the National Park Service. Obviously, the Kabetogama proposal will now end up as a recreation area under the dual administration of the two services."[28] In his reply, Olson, who was closer to policymakers in the NPS, said, "The National Park Service has no intention of giving up its hopes for a Voyageurs National Park in Minnesota. It may be necessary to whittle down our acreage some, but it also may be possible in view of the agreement between Agriculture and Interior to work something out. I do not intend to go for any joint recreational area and I am sure no one else feels otherwise, including Governor Andersen."[29]

Governor Andersen, continuing his quest for information about the status of the Voyageurs proposal, asked key administrators from the two federal agencies to meet with him and his conservation department staff in St. Paul on February 8, 1963. What he learned from that session was not at all encouraging. Regional Director Howard Baker explained the NPS proposal, using a map that showed the proposed park extending from Black Bay on Rainy Lake to the mouth of the Vermilion River at the south end of Crane Lake.[30] USFS Regional Forester George James took exception to the inclusion of the Namakan-Crane Lakes area in the proposal and proceeded to reaffirm the USFS stand against any intrusion into the Superior National Forest.[31] He also stated that there could be no discussion of land exchanges until legislation authorizing the park clearly defined its boundaries. (This reference to land exchanges pertained to scattered parcels of USFS land on the Kabetogama Peninsula.) James came to the meeting knowing that the USFS position had been significantly strengthened by the recent executive order extending the Superior's western boundary and also by the "Treaty of the Potomac" aimed at avoiding jurisdictional disputes involving competing recreational management proposals.

Andersen expressed irritation that the USFS boundary adjustment was made without his being informed. Then, addressing both parties, he stated that his primary objective was to secure a proper national park for Minnesota and that in pursuing that goal the *national* interest should prevail over agency objectives. But as the meeting progressed, he could see that the USFS would not budge on the Namakan-Crane Lakes area, and so the governor turned to Baker and suggested that the NPS accept a "compromised" area if in return Minnesota would get a national park. Baker replied, "In order to propose an adequate national park we must include the Namakan-Crane areas."[32] He also said that the Advisory Board had already endorsed the proposal with the Namakan-Crane Lakes segment included, and he felt compelled to submit the full proposal in its first draft to Director Wirth on March 1.[33]

This report titled *The Voyageurs Route and a Proposed Voyageurs National Park* circulated internally at the NPS, and copies were sent to the USFS and state officials in Minnesota. It dealt with the entire border area from Lake Superior to the Northwest Angle and contained a special section proposing a Voyageurs National Park. That section included USFS lands in the Namakan-Crane Lakes area, thereby fulfilling Baker's

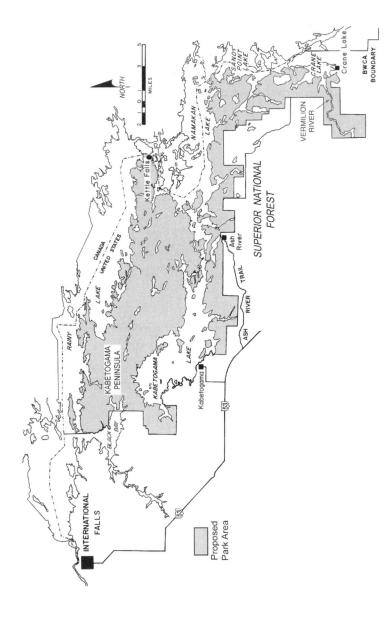

Initial proposal for a Voyageurs National Park, March 1963. The recommendation for a park was included in a National Park Service report, "The Voyageurs Route and a Proposed Voyageurs National Park." The report was never published and circulated internally at the National Park Service; copies were sent to the U. S. Forest Service and state officials in Minnesota.

strongly felt obligation to present the full report. The USFS predictably objected to the part of the NPS proposal that incorporated USFS land within its proposed boundaries.[34]

The interagency squabble as to how to present the Namakan-Crane Lakes area in the official Voyageurs proposal was kept within the two departments except for the governor, some top staff people at the state level, and a few Minnesota conservationists, most notably Olson. In the absence of public knowledge about the proposed park, rumors and distortions about Voyageurs began to circulate in the International Falls area, and the delay did not help Governor Andersen in his quest for something substantial that he could carry to the public for their support.

In International Falls, local businessman Wayne Judy, an early supporter of a national park for the border area, became concerned over ill-founded rumors and local misunderstandings about the park and expressed these concerns in a letter to Hella in St. Paul. He wanted the governor and NPS people to meet in International Falls in late April and conduct a public information meeting.[35] (Unfortunately for Judy, other park supporters, and the citizens of the International Falls area, more than one and a half years would pass before such a meeting took place.)

Meanwhile, Governor Andersen along with a few others close to the issue sought to resolve the differences between the two federal departments. Miffed by the slow pace of events and possibly facing defeat in the vote recount, he tried his hand at speeding things up. He knew that the untimely extension of the Superior's boundaries and the subsequent jurisdictional dispute over the Crane Lake area could go on for many months. He therefore decided to work through the NPS for a solution. Early in March he called Director Wirth and repeated the suggestion he had made to Baker at the February 8 meeting in his office. He suggested to Wirth that the NPS "try to reduce the dimensions of the proposed park to the limits of the Kabetogama Peninsula."[36]

A few weeks after Andersen's March 1 conversation with Wirth, unmistakable evidence that the USFS was not going to budge on the Crane Lake issue was contained in a late-March letter to the director from the USFS Chief Edward P. Cliff. Cliff said that it was his understanding that the NPS proposal for Voyageurs would include the Kabetogama Peninsula and adjacent lands. He endorsed that proposal and stated that the USFS would cooperate by transferring any USFS lands in that area to accommodate the NPS and its proposal for Voyageurs National Park, but any lands east of that were in the Superior National Forest. In the same letter the chief forester explained that the USFS would be developing a management plan for the Namakan-Crane Lakes area that would "complement" the proposed national park at Kabetogama.[37]

Before the end of March, a meeting was held in Washington, D.C., to discuss the impasse over inclusion of the Namakan-Crane Lakes segment in the Voyageurs proposal. Attending the meeting were personnel from the Bureau of Reclamation, NPS, and USFS, and Sigurd Olson from Minnesota. In a letter to Interior Secretary Stewart Udall summarizing the results of the meeting, Olson said they had decided to "go ahead with the park proposal for the reduced area, and that in any legislation drafted, should be a statutory provision for a joint study of the controversial area."[38] Given the USFS intransigence on the Namakan-Crane Lakes issue and pressure from prominent supporters in Minnesota, the NPS felt compelled to prepare a revision of the preliminary draft that would not only comply with the provisions of the "Treaty of the Potomac," which required joint studies in such cases, but would also mollify the USFS.

In a revision dated September 1963 and again circulated in-house, the NPS recommended that the "Namakan-Crane Lake area within Superior National Forest containing scenic and natural values of national significance be designated a *study area* to be jointly studied by the USFS and NPS to determine the most practical means of assuring that the values found in this area are adequately preserved in the public interest."[39] The few park advocates in Minnesota who were aware of the USFS-NPS dispute considered this proposal a compromise and wished to move on. But some, including Olson, who advanced the proposal in a letter to Udall in May 1963, were disappointed with the turn of events.[40]

In his letter, Olson recommended going ahead with a park proposal that identified a reduced area (Kabetogama Peninsula) and stated that authorizing legislation should contain a provision for a joint study of the controversial area. Olson believed that a required future joint study of the contested area would lead to preservation management policies close to or the same as those that the NPS would develop for a national park on Kabetogama. But his close identification with the initial planning for a park extending from Crane Lake to Rainy Lake revealed his strong preference for the concept of a single-agency administration. He wanted NPS officials to stress the physical unity of the "voyageurs high-way" in the revised report and even wrote the introduction to the report, incorporating the unity theme and the need to complete the protective measures for the voyageurs' route along Minnesota's border lakes region.[41]

For its part, the USFS was no doubt pleased to see that the revised draft for Voyageurs excluded the Namakan-Crane Lakes section. How-ever, they took exception to the joint study recommendation, and they were offended by the claim, implied in the request for a joint study, that the USFS's management would not adequately protect and preserve the scenic resources of the area. Therefore, in its final draft, released to the public in September 1964, the NPS removed the offending implication regarding USFS management standards and softened the language rec-ommending a joint study.[42] Even this language bothered the USFS. The official USFS response to the NPS was contained in a letter from the Chief Forester Edward Cliff to Director Wirth just before the report was released to the public. In his letter he expressed the opinion that reference to a joint study was unnecessary and then noted his prefer-ence for cooperation on an informal basis regarding the management strategies for the Namakan-Crane Lakes area. He also objected to maps in the report that highlighted the proposed study area.[43]

The NPS addressed the chief forester's concerns in a revision to the 1964 report dated September 1965.[44] Although this 1965 report was never formally produced for public use, it did reveal a revision of national park policy: complete abandonment of the notion that the Crane Lake area would someday become a part of Voyageurs National Park or an area jointly managed with the USFS. Future reports on Voyageurs would show a park *restricted* to the Kabetogama Peninsula and the adjacent lakes Kabetogama and Rainy.

Over two years had passed since Governor Andersen had written his statement announcing NPS intentions to do detailed field studies for a proposed Voyageurs National Park. The 1964 report described a much smaller and, according to some park professionals, a less meaningful park than originally envisioned. The general public was never aware of the maneuvering that took place between the two federal agencies over the disposition of the Namakan-Crane Lakes segment. For the next five years all the literature, audio-visual material, and speeches devoted to the promotion of the park proposal carefully excluded any reference to the area southeast of the Kabetogama Peninsula. The USFS continued to develop its plans for the "Crane Lake Recreation Area," and the official position of the NPS was to work for the establishment of a national park whose territory lay wholly outside the boundaries of the Superior National Forest.

The NPS pullback over the Namakan-Crane Lakes issue was clearly a victory for the USFS. Unlike similar situations in the West, the USFS in this instance was able to prevent the transfer of lands for the purpose of achieving a NPS objective. The only way the NPS could restore this territory to its original proposal would be through congressional legislation. The delays between 1962 and 1964 proved costly to any hopes for quick approval of a Voyageurs National Park.

There is no question that pulling the Namakan-Crane Lakes area out of the proposed park boundary troubled park professionals and supporters who were best acquainted with the area. Some, like Judge Hella, director of state parks, feared that removal of this section weakened the proposal for Voyageurs and that the NPS might even settle for a national recreation area. In a memorandum to the conservation commissioner, he stated, "I doubt that Kabetogama Peninsula by itself will qualify as a National Park and I believe that we would have little to gain if it were established as a National Recreation Area—a National Recreation Area would command no more attention than would a major State Park in this region."[45] Hella's concerns turned out to be prophetic as public debate over Voyageurs progressed during the 1960s. The concept of a national recreation area as a more logical management strategy for Voyageurs was frequently offered by public officials at both the local and national level, and it would always be vehemently opposed by leading advocates for the park.

CHAPTER THREE

Delay and Frustration

In early March 1963, when Wayne Judy made his appeal for a public meeting on Voyageurs National Park at International Falls, he, along with most other park supporters, was unaware of the interagency controversy over the territorial extent of the proposed park. This dispute and the realization that the earlier field studies did not yield the kind of detail needed for a suitable report caused the NPS to shy away from public hearings in spring 1963. They did, however, schedule a briefing session for the benefit of the new governor, Karl Rolvaag, and other state officials.

George Amidon, representing the M&O Paper Company, the largest landowner on the Kabetogama Peninsula, and Sigurd Olson attended the meeting that took place in late April in St. Paul. Both became important participants in the lengthy debate over authorization of Voyageurs. Amidon, born in southeastern Minnesota, graduated in forestry from the University of Minnesota in 1936. After several years with the state forestry division, he became director of the Forestry Division for the M&O Paper Company, where in the 1940s he developed the first long-range forestry program for the Kabetogama Peninsula. According to newspaper accounts of the April meeting, Regional Director Howard Baker described the purpose of the proposed park and also announced the NPS's intentions to hold a series of public meetings around the state so that citizens could learn about the park and raise questions concerning details of the NPS plan for Voyageurs.[1]

Although Baker set no dates for these meetings, one can assume that the NPS had late fall or early winter in mind, because a revision of the park proposal was expected in September. It was evident that the NPS needed some time to work things out with the USFS and also to get answers to some important questions certain to be on the minds of residents, particularly those living near the proposed park. For example, the NPS realized that staff would be hard-pressed to answer questions about wildlife management because they lacked specific information about the ecology of the Kabetogama Peninsula.[2] For a more comprehensive assessment of informational needs and also for a current "reading" on the park issue in northeastern Minnesota, the NPS turned to Eliot Davis, superintendent of the Grand Portage National Monument and the NPS's "key man" for the Voyageurs project in Minnesota.

Davis spent a week in early June 1963 traveling throughout the proposed park area and talking to residents, state foresters, conservation officers, resort owners, and other business people. His report was remarkable for its clarity and objectivity, and, especially, for its candor. Compared to the several hundred documents pertaining to the earliest years of the Voyageurs story, the Davis report can be regarded as the most useful statement on the kinds of information the NPS would need if it wanted to be successful with its proposals for the park. Davis was especially candid in his assessment of local feelings regarding a national park in the Kabetogama area. In Davis's direct manner he said, "They don't want one!"[3]

The straightforward style of the Davis memorandums may have been unusual for interoffice communications, but it evidently caught the attention of those responsible for planning Voyageurs. Davis warned his colleagues that they would need to find answers to a lot of important questions before trying to sell the park locally. He said park planners should move quickly to fill some vital information gaps before meeting the public in open hearings in the fall. In his report, Davis made the following observations, summarized here:[4]

- Not one single person is in favor of a park in a truly altruistic sense. They are in favor or against it because they have some "iron in the fire" that will make or lose them a dollar, or they will lose some privilege they now enjoy.
- The proposed park is not canoe country—canoeing can be dangerous. (He saw only one canoe in his travels through the park area.) Power-boats will be required for access.

- The NPS does not have firsthand knowledge of the area. No one from the NPS has ever been over the Kabetogama Peninsula on foot.
- Archaeological fieldwork should be done regarding Indian cemeteries, and the protection of Indian artifacts will be necessary.
- Some trappers make a living in the area, especially trapping beaver.
- Land values in the park area are inflated, but this is not obvious by looking at the tax assessment records. The M&O and the state are no longer leasing land that makes private holdings more valuable. "The worst shack on Kabetogama will be worth 100 times what it would cost in International Falls, and no one will want to sell when he gets a life lease and even then it's going to be a tough job."
- The Kettle Falls Hotel is a ramshackle firetrap but has significant historic and strategic value. There is no relation between the actual building value and what it will cost to purchase the place.
- In his conversation with Sigurd Olson, Davis mentions the possibility of a recreation area instead of a national park. [Olson let it be known that he was absolutely opposed to a national recreation area, and it should not ever be mentioned again—it must be a national park.]
- Land acquisition costs will be greatly increased by the cost of purchasing resorts and especially Jeno Paulucci's lodge on Kabetogama. [Paulucci was president of the Chun King Corporation in Duluth.]
- "The Sand Point and Namakan Lake areas should be included in the park. But the Forest Service has their foot in the door, and unless Mr. Udall [secretary of the interior] can pry Mr. Freeman's [secretary of agriculture] shoe out of the crack, we are going to have a smaller park."
- State foresters cannot be relied upon to help much with ecological studies. "Fine men but most are not college graduates and have come up through experience and self-study. They are multiple-use men—to them a park is wasteful of wood and wildlife. Their jobs are at stake if a park is formed and they can't get jobs with other agencies except on the basis of experience. Forest Service has no room except for college trained men. . . ."

Davis recommended that before the NPS tried to sell the park locally, it should have the answers to several questions, and he recommended the following actions:

- Conduct a comprehensive ecological survey of what is there now and what changes can be expected over the next fifty years. Determine what impact fluctuating water levels on the park's lakes have on the ecology of the area.
- Conduct a survey of historical and archeological sites.

- Conduct an economic survey including a tax study to determine the park's impact in the surrounding area.
- Complete a study of all lands and leases and an inventory of all structures.
- Complete a recreation survey and plan including access roads.

Davis said, "We shall be questioned frequently about our plans and we should have something to sell such as the Forest Service plan for Crane Lake and Namakan. This has had a powerful effect in consolidating this new section of the National Forest and stimulating interest. If we go ahead without a plan we bring confusion and indecision rather than calm, purposeful administration that builds immediate confidence."

Hindsight shows that Davis was accurate in his assessment of the kinds of information required to meet the challenge of local public hearings on Voyageurs. But to acquire the information would take months of background research, including an economic impact study, land ownership analysis, assessments of wildlife populations, and a determination of the kind of wildlife management policies that would be appropriate for the proposed park. It was evident to the NPS by late summer that public hearings and a formal printed proposal and report for public distribution could not be completed in 1963. Also much of the required information for reports and public hearings would have to come from Minnesota's state agencies just as a new administration was settling in at St. Paul. I could find no instance where state officials or their departments deliberately stalled or interfered with the NPS's efforts to acquire data required for its research during the nine-year period leading to congressional authorization of the park. However, I think it safe to say that the transition periods between administrations may have resulted in brief but unavoidable delays in the progress of the project.

From the time the NPS began serious study and planning of Voyageurs until the park's final establishment in 1975, it dealt with four different state administrations. Each change brought new personalities and administrative styles as well as contrasting organizational structures to the state's park effort. At this point in the legislative history of the park the new administration was led by Governor Karl Rolvaag, a Democrat who narrowly defeated Republican Governor Elmer L. Andersen. Rolvaag, a Minnesota native who graduated from St. Olaf College, was a highly decorated veteran of World War II and served as lieutenant governor from 1954 to 1962. Rolvaag, who campaigned in support of a Voyageurs

National Park, assigned the task of coordinating the park effort to Commissioner of Conservation Wayne H. Olson. Olson had held several positions in the state attorney general's office between 1955 and 1962, including chief deputy attorney general in 1962. Olson replaced Clarence Prout, a career forester, whom Rolvaag appointed to the post of director of the Forestry Division.[5]

After the NPS announced its support for a park on the Kabetogama Peninsula in 1962, local residents and landowners in the proposed park area adopted a wait-and-see attitude. However, by late summer and fall a year later, what goodwill existed between the NPS and local residents began to slip away. And NPS planners were not careful about keeping their supporters informed. Records of correspondence between park advocates and the NPS show a decided reluctance on the part of the NPS to level with them regarding the primary reasons for the delay in completing the report and their decision not to schedule public hearings for late 1963.

For their part, park supporters were naive about the process and procedures for gaining legislative approval for a national park. In their own enthusiasm for a park, they believed that a general plan and an NPS recommendation for a national park would be sufficient. Many were successful professional people, and their own experience as visitors to the nation's western parks had convinced them that the NPS could be trusted to manage the Kabetogama area in the same professional manner.

As the months went by, however, even supporters close to the park project became impatient. There were not many of them at this time because no formal organization for promoting the park proposal had yet been formed, and a number of prominent leaders lived outside the park area, in downstate Minnesota. But they continued to have confidence that the NPS would come forward in a timely fashion with details about the proposed park and how it would mesh with the existing social and economic patterns of the area. By fall 1963, however, it was obvious that many of the people who resided near the proposed park did not share the same confidence and enthusiasm for the NPS that the "outsiders" had. Park advocates saw for the first time the emergence of strong anti-park sentiment in and around the communities adjacent to the proposed park.

Olson, the new conservation commissioner, was also dismayed by the delays in Washington, D.C., in completing the first Voyageurs report for the general public. He wrote to Midwest Regional Director Baker in late

August expressing deep disappointment to learn that the project might be delayed until the following year. Baker replied that a September public meeting was not possible. The report was scheduled to go to the printer in the second week of September, but printing, checking, and review by officials, including Interior Secretary Udall, meant that release of the plan could not occur until early November. Baker also said they were still doing land and construction cost estimates.[6]

Elmer Andersen did not have the kind of information Olson received from Baker during the first week of September—information that essentially placed the publication date for the first formal report by the NPS on Voyageurs well into 1964. Operating on earlier information regarding publication dates, Andersen told the press that the report would be ready in October and that it would recommend a national park at Kabetogama, thus assuring "the preservation of a significant portion of our great wilderness canoe country."[7] However, a month later, viewing such announcements as stalling tactics and troubled by references to "wilderness" and "canoe country," a number of citizens showed up at a meeting of the International Falls City Council to express their opposition to a national park on the peninsula.

The small group appearing at the council meeting proved to be a precursor to public opposition—organized and unorganized—that would be expressed about Voyageurs over the next six years. In his response to the citizens assembled at the council meeting, the mayor of International Falls appealed to them, and the general public, to keep an open mind on the proposal and asked the city clerk to write a letter to the NPS requesting public meetings on the issue.[8] The following day the editor of the daily newspaper also called for a public meeting with the NPS "before we either condemn or sanction a national park in our area. It is apparent that it is this lack of definite information that is giving rise to much opposition to the plans for a park. Until the government announces specific plans, it might be wise to withhold judgement, lest too much premature opposition kill an asset that most any community in the nation would give its right arm to have established in its back yard. We should reserve judgement until the facts are known."[9]

In early December, Amidon, vice president of the Woodlands Division of the M&O Paper Company called the Minnesota Department of Conservation regarding the need for a public hearing to offset rumors circulating about the park proposal.[10] By year's end, the situation was so bad that one conservation officer was moved to write to the state parks director that "there is little question but that the possibility for local support on the subject proposal is fast deteriorating and perhaps has already passed the point of recovery.[11]

Opposition to the proposed park continued to build in the early months of 1964. In the absence of an official printed report detailing the purpose and objectives of the park and the processes and plans for achieving those goals, the public was left with the difficult task of trying to sort out rumor from fact. Some public officials added energy and encouragement to the opposition movement, making it even more difficult for the average citizen to take a position on the issue. Many county officials, including members of the boards of Koochiching and St. Louis Counties, where the park was to be located, quickly took an anti-park stance. It became obvious early in the discussions and debate that official bodies from both counties would never endorse the park and, indeed, would prove to be strong allies of those individuals and organizations opposed to the park through the 1960s. The NPS's contact for Voyageurs, Davis, brought this fact to the attention of the regional director on several occasions beginning with a memorandum in January 1964: "From what I have been able to learn the purpose of the [county] board is to see how a park can be prevented rather than established."[12]

The interagency jurisdictional dispute over the Namakan-Crane Lakes area, as noted in the previous chapter, was a major stumbling block in producing a preliminary report for Voyageurs. The NPS and the USFS exchanged correspondence throughout spring and summer 1964—all concerned with arriving at mutually acceptable language for describing the future disposition and management of that area. But NPS planner John Kawamoto, the official with the longest identification with Voyageurs, recalled additional factors contributing not only to the delay in completing the initial report but to winning local support for Voyageurs' legislation.

As previously mentioned, the largest landowner in the proposed park (two-thirds of the Kabetogama Peninsula) was the M&O Paper Company located in International Falls. From the beginning, Andersen and other supporters hoped for a land exchange arrangement that would bring these private lands under public ownership for donation to the federal government for the park. The process they proposed was relatively simple: M&O would exchange their Kabetogama holdings (which were mostly logged over) for state forested land outside the park. The state could also make some exchanges with the USFS to add more federal lands within the proposed park boundaries.

Kawamoto also believed that in the case of M&O lands, going from private to public ownership in the manner just described was the most expedient way of meeting land acquisition goals for the NPS.[13] Amidon had participated in the early meetings with Governor Andersen, NPS officials (including Director Wirth) as well as other state and federal officials as they laid the groundwork for the park proposal. Amidon, always the spokesman for the M&O on matters related to the park proposal, remained on good terms with Andersen and many other park advocates throughout the controversy over Voyageurs. He knew that the key to a successful proposal was to find an expeditious and mutually acceptable way of shifting the M&O lands to the NPS.[14]

A locally based company at the time, the M&O initially gave the impression that the land acquisition issue could be worked out. However, according to Kawamoto, park officials detected a change in the attitude of the M&O toward Voyageurs in spring 1964. That M&O's position was shifting is evident in a letter to the NPS in which Amidon cited rising local opposition to the park. In it he said, "The local opposition concerns our company and will influence our decision as to whether we will consider an exchange of company lands on the peninsula."[15]

Kawamoto believed that negotiations were already under way early in 1964 for a buyout of the M&O by the Boise Cascade Corporation and that Amidon's lukewarm attitude really reflected Boise's philosophy, which turned out to be much less friendly to the NPS. He also felt that Amidon's detailed knowledge of early plans and discussions on Voyageurs with the NPS and state officials gave Boise an advantage in later public hearings on the park.[16] Wayne Judy, International Falls businessman and the strongest park advocate in the area, was acutely aware of the impact that M&O's position on the park would have in the community. In a letter to Wayne Olson, Governor Rolvaag's commissioner of conservation, Judy wrote, "As you know, in our one industry town we have what is known as the 'Great White Father,' the M&O paper company and, on the surface at least it seems as if they are opposed to the park and their employees are reluctant to express themselves otherwise."[17]

Another problem for park proponents was the charge by opponents that Voyageurs would simply represent an extension of the BWCA. About the time the park's preliminary proposal was ready for public distribution, Congress passed the Wilderness Act on September 3, 1964. Also, a special BWCA review committee appointed by Agriculture Secretary Orville L. Freeman was holding hearings in northeastern Minnesota, gathering information for its recommendations on management of the canoe country. Before the year was out, the committee recommended a larger no-cut zone in the BWCA and made other recommendations that upset local advocates of multiple use.

Proximity to the controversial BWCA would prove to be a distinct disadvantage in promoting the cause for Voyageurs National Park. Kawamoto, as well as others associated with the park movement, observed that many people confused Voyageurs with the BWCA. The assumed linkage of Voyageurs with the often quarrelsome events and issues in the BWCA was detrimental to progress on the park proposal. Kawamoto later observed that quite often some decision or event favorable to Voyageurs seemed to "come out after something had occurred at the BWCA and we tended to take the brunt of the public's ire against bureaucracy and a few other things. So when the Park Service proposal for Voyageurs came out, even though we said boats, motorboats, would be able to use the lakes because of the large bodies of water and so forth, no one believed the Park Service...."[18]

Internal disagreements and procedural problems in the NPS also contributed to the long delay in completing the initial proposal for Voyageurs, and they continued under a new director. George Hartzog, associate director under Wirth, took the helm of the agency in January 1964. A seventeen-year career professional, he was recognized in the NPS as an activist director with a good working relationship with his boss, Interior Secretary Stewart Udall. During the "Hartzog years" (1964–72) five new national parks were added to the system—Voyageurs, North Cascades, Guadalupe Mountains, Redwood, and Canyonlands—and over sixty other units including national monuments, lakeshores, historic battlefield sites, recreation areas, seashores, and wild and scenic rivers.[19] Several months before assuming his new position Hartzog had declared his support for the NPS policies on preservation in management decision making and pledged to uphold the high standards for acceptance into the system. In that light when he reviewed the Voyageurs proposal, he raised questions about the area's qualifications for national park status. His concern, and that of other professionals in the early studies on Voyageurs, related to the fluctuating water levels on the big lakes in the park. In response, Kawamoto said, "These were natural lakes, but the water level had been raised through the construction of the dam here at International Falls and the dam at Kettle Falls. So I remember that . . . we had to discuss with him [Hartzog] the fact that the water levels were raised, but we were still dealing with natural conditions in a sense that it didn't change it that much."[20]

Some park professionals were also concerned that the area was not in pristine condition—it had been logged and some logging was under way at the time the park was under discussion. Also, the park's relatively small size and location adjacent to sustained yield forestry activity could make it difficult "to maintain natural conditions. They would be spraying for one reason or another and we would not, obviously, allow that within the park, and then we became what might be the breeding grounds for something."[21] Kawamoto said that the questions about the area's qualifications were finally resolved by agreeing "to look beyond today, perhaps say a hundred years from now or beyond, and [look at] what conditions this area would be [in] if set aside as a national park, the contention being that it would be rather unique by that time. . . ."[22]

Another factor contributing to the delay in completing the preliminary proposal for public inspection was the NPS's failure to keep Congressman John Blatnik properly informed about studies and plans for a park in his own district. Only rarely has an NPS unit been approved by Congress without the local congressman's endorsement. According to Kawamoto, park officials continued their contacts with former Governor Andersen and state officials in Governor Rolvaag's administration, but did not involve Blatnik in these early stages of planning for Voyageurs. At the time the first NPS studies were under way, Blatnik was already in his fifteenth year in Congress. A thorough and disciplined man, he was always careful to know what was going on in his district. Being left out of "the loop" in the initial NPS planning was a serious blunder by the NPS. Kawamoto believed that this was not intentional but was due to procedural errors and inexperience with the implementation of "new area studies" for new projects.[23] But the fact remains that Blatnik was offended by the oversight, and this helps to explain his less than enthusiastic public support in summer 1964.

Institutional inertia plagued the Voyageurs proposal as it has many other government programs including creation of a number of national parks. For Voyageurs, inertia frustrated the quest for funds and research personnel to conduct an economic impact study of the proposed park. Eliot Davis urged such a study in June 1963, calling it essential if the NPS hoped to "sell" the proposal to people in northeastern Minnesota. In September of that year, Sigurd Olson was looking for state funds to pay for the study, and in October the NPS said *it* might find funds for such a study.[24] Eight months later the NPS offered $4,000 to the University of Minnesota College of Agriculture in St. Paul to do the study, but the offer was rejected by the dean, who said the amount was insufficient to fund the study.[25]

Finally the NPS turned to the University of Minnesota-Duluth campus, and on June 29, a contract was made with Richard Sielaff, chairman of the Department of Business and Economics, to conduct the study for the budgeted amount.[26] The study report, completed on December 1, 1964, was never seriously challenged as to its accuracy during the entire public debate over Voyageurs. It was unfortunate that it took more than a year to engage the research team to complete the study. It would have been useful to NPS personnel at public hearings and in meetings with public officials, particularly when confronted with assertions that removing Kabetogama lands from the tax rolls would be harmful to county taxing units. The study's findings did not support such assertions.

Taken together, the time-consuming bureaucratic maneuvers, procedural errors, and interagency squabbles almost proved lethal for a project that was seen by many of the state's top officials, a number of leading conservationists, and many other citizens as such a logical proposition when it was first advanced in 1961.

Impatient and tired of waiting for the long-promised NPS proposal for Voyageurs, the Koochiching Sportsmen's Association sponsored a public meeting on August 27, 1964. The meeting featured a panel of local business and professional people, most of them opposed to the notion that a national park on Kabetogama was the best thing for the area. The restless and angry crowd of about two hundred people heard repeated claims that the park would be just another federal land grab, an extension of the BWCA wilderness area, and removal of valuable land from the tax rolls.

Amidon, representing the M&O, said that his company would base its decision on public opinion and the final boundaries proposed by the NPS and that "the paper industry is fundamentally opposed to the locking up of large areas for single use."[27] This was the same position the timber industry was taking in the West, where the industry and the USFS were fighting about expansion of park lands and wilderness designations. It was also an indication that the M&O was beginning to reflect the philosophy of the Boise Cascade Corporation, whose formal merger with the M&O was only a few months away. The day after the meeting, the local newspaper scolded the NPS for failing to provide the public with solid information about its plans for Kabetogama and noted that in the absence of such information formidable opposition had developed. "If park representatives were present and said little, it was because they had little if any factual information to present and it is this lack of information from the Park Service that has given rise to the opposition."[28]

The NPS finally announced a public hearing schedule for Voyageurs in early September 1964. Three meeting places were identified: International Falls, Duluth, and Minneapolis. A later announcement said that the long-awaited report on Voyageurs would be available for public comment in time for the meetings, but the NPS was careful to note that this would be a *preliminary report* that had not been formally submitted to the Interior Department for final approval.[29]

But even before the report was available and public hearings completed, Governor Rolvaag and Congressman Blatnik were receiving messages from area citizens, including multimillionaire Jeno Paulucci, vigorously opposing the park. Paulucci, founder and president of Chun King Food Corporation, was a native of northeastern Minnesota's Iron Range and typically followed the regional custom of supporting Democrats. Blatnik and Rolvaag had been the beneficiaries of Paulucci's support in the past. They also knew that he owned an elaborate forest lodge and retreat on the Kabetogama Peninsula. In his personal letters and through his Northeast Minnesota Organization for Economic Education (NEMO), Paulucci attacked in his customary aggressive style the "bureaucrats from Washington, the government land grabbers, and the sleeping bag enthusiasts who already had plenty of territory in the BWCA."[30] Paulucci's letters and public comments intimidated neither Rolvaag nor Blatnik. Both replied that they would study the proposal, and Blatnik indicated in a letter to Paulucci that he thought a properly planned park would be a "boon to the entire region."[31]

On the day of the public meeting in International Falls, the *Daily Journal* admonished its readers to take a long, hard look at the NPS proposal. Having already read the report, the editor said that it was "as vital for what it does not say as for what it does say." The editorial concluded by stating, "If after Saturday's public meeting, there is the least shadow of doubt about Park Service plans and intentions, and if we cannot be assured that this is not a federal land grab or a veiled attempt to extend the so-called wilderness area, then, the Journal sincerely believes we should vigorously oppose the proposed National Park."[32]

The newspaper estimated the crowd at more than eight hundred. George Bagley, Glen Bean, and John Kawamoto from the NPS regional office explained the park proposal. Director of State Parks Hella attended the meeting but did not speak. Wayne Judy and George Esslinger, a Kabetogama resort owner, helped distribute reports before the meeting—the first opportunity most had to read anything official about the proposal for Voyageurs. Kawamoto recalls the meeting as a "tough one." Looking back, he thinks the NPS should have had the report out earlier because many of the speakers were using faulty information generated by those in opposition.[33]

The *Daily Journal* was correct in its observation regarding the limitations of the 1964 report on Voyageurs. It was long on description of the proposed park's association with voyageur history and natural features but either short or lacking entirely on information relating to the fate of private holdings in the park, private land acquisition policies and procedures, loss of tax base when land is federalized, the economic impact on the area, proposed wildlife management policies, and so on. A press release issued by NPS Director Hartzog announcing the report did not help. He said it must be regarded as a preliminary report that had not been formally submitted to the Interior Department for formal approval. With such an introduction one could hardly blame those attending the hearings for wondering when they would get the real facts. The NPS made few friends, if any, at the International Falls hearing.

Most left the International Falls hearing angry and confused. In Minneapolis, owners of summer homes on Kabetogama were not happy either. One resort owner said, "People go to Kabetogama to fish and loaf, they don't give a damn about the rocks."[34] At the hearing in Duluth the chamber of commerce representative repeated what a chamber predecessor had said over seventy years before in the 1890s when the idea of a national park was first advanced. He said the chamber would oppose the park because it would remove land from the tax rolls and hurt the timber industry.[35] At the same meeting, NPS personnel were subjected to the sharp tongue and bad manners of Paulucci. Kawamoto later recalled Paulucci's behavior as aggressive and impolite as "he raked us over the coals." Even Sigurd Olson's mild manner and his reasoned plea for preservation of valuable border resources was no antidote for the Paulucci tirade.[36]

Following the meeting, Paulucci sent a letter to Governor Rolvaag, pleading with him to come out against a national park. "Talk about white heat opposition in northeastern Minnesota Karl, this property that the NPS wants to spend 7 million dollars on so that people can use a tent and canoe is too valuable to our economic behavior and growth to allow it to be taken. It just isn't right for the government to come up here and take this land away from us and turn it into a park for the benefit of the rest of the U.S. as they put it."[37] Two days later, in a more conciliatory letter to Rolvaag, Paulucci suggested a state park for the Kabetogama Peninsula.

The state park alternative surfaced periodically for the next six years, but it never had any significant support in state government. Rolvaag remained supportive of the national park proposal, relying on his conservation commissioner, Wayne Olson, to define and defend his administration's position on Voyageurs. For example, many letters came to the governor claiming a national park would restrict use and enjoyment of the Kabetogama Peninsula. In response, the governor's office would explain that "a national park does not restrict enjoyment of an area, but does restrict destructive uses and makes possible a greater enjoyment of an area."[38]

In spite of the positive, although cautious responses by Blatnik and Rolvaag, the September public hearings and the period immediately after can only be described as the lowest point in the eight-year effort to gain congressional approval for Voyageurs. The *Daily Journal* led off the attack on the proposal with an editorial as soon as the three hearings were completed: "The Park Service should be convinced that its proposal to establish Voyageurs National Park was not welcomed by a majority of northeastern Minnesota citizens and that if the Park Service drops its plans it should be replaced with a plan with 'something of value.'" The editorial then said that at least part of the Kabetogama Peninsula should be designated a state park, and "instead of remaining a roadless area, the peninsula could be developed tremendously by the addition of an access road."[39]

The NPS plan stressed preservation while the *Daily Journal*, ever mindful of the changing attitudes of the M&O and feeling confident that it represented majority thinking among its readers, advocated development on the peninsula. Echoing the sentiments of the *Daily Journal*, although not endorsing a state park, the *Duluth News-Tribune* followed a day later with an editorial opposing a national park on Kabetogama.[40]

CHAPTER FOUR

Progress on Voyageurs Stalled

The new year began with more indications that Voyageurs National Park would be a hard sell, particularly to those residing near the boundaries of the proposed park. In early January 1965, Agriculture Secretary Orville Freeman announced a 150,000-acre expansion of the no-cut zone around the BWCA and designated another 100,000 acres for addition in 1975, a move recommended by his special committee on management policies for the BWCA.[1] The announcement came as a jolt to area loggers and the timber industry in general, who saw this action as reinforcing their firm conviction that the federal government was determined to remove as much land from multiple-use management as possible. In forceful disagreement with Freeman's action, William MacConnachie, the land and timber manager for the Northwest Paper Company in Cloquet, Minnesota, said that "the Secretary's decision subverts professional forestry opinion to that of amateurs and wilderness zealots."[2] The timing of the no-cut announcement could hardly have been worse for those who were trying to promote a national park that would be located just west of the BWCA. The NPS, guided by a preservation management philosophy, would have to insist on no logging at all within the proposed park, and this would not be welcome news in a region where most residents strongly supported the multiple-use philosophy.

At almost the same time as the no-cut policy was released, Boise Cascade shareholders were meeting in Boise, Idaho, where they would approve a board of director's recommendation to acquire the properties of the M&O Paper Company. It would not be long before the NPS learned that the more cooperative stance of the M&O would be replaced by one that reflected industrywide opposition to the expansion of national parks and wilderness areas at the expense of public lands managed under multiple-use policies.

During the first week of January 1965, NPS Midwest Regional Director Lemuel Garrison and Eliot Davis, Superintendent of the Grand Portage National Monument, spent three days in International Falls and the village of Ranier explaining the park proposal and emphasizing the importance of planning for future recreational needs in America. Following his visit, Garrison wrote a letter to NPS Director Hartzog recounting the events of the trip and what he believed was a favorable reception of their message. In the same letter, he identified some of the problems then facing the proposal and concluded his report with a plan for renewed effort to push for acceptance of the Voyageurs proposal. Garrison's plan included the following important components:

- Take steps to generate public support by increasing NPS contact with service clubs and other civic organizations, especially in northeastern Minnesota.
- Continue close contact with Governor Rolvaag's office, staff people in the Minnesota Department of Conservation, and officials in the M&O Paper Company.[3]

Closer contact with Eighth District Congressman John Blatnik's office was not mentioned in Garrison's letter to Hartzog—a sign that the NPS continued to marginalize the individual who would have to introduce and carry the park legislation through the House of Representatives. Assuming there was a strategy for moving the proposal along, it failed to recognize the role of the dean of the Minnesota congressional delegation—a congressman in his eighteenth year in the House.

Blatnik at this date had not yet *formally* announced his support of the NPS proposal, although in public statements he said he was studying the issue. In correspondence with friends and critics in his district he said a national park could be economically beneficial to northeastern Minnesota and deserved careful study.

Regional Director Garrison's blueprint for more aggressive promotion of the park was really tacit admission by the NPS that the proposal was in trouble with many in the International Falls area and that it required concerted action to get it moving. A few days after Garrison outlined the NPS strategy for reviving the proposal, former Governor

Elmer Andersen launched an effort for the same purpose in a speech to the International Falls Rotary Club.

Andersen's speech was remarkable for the systematic manner in which he presented the case for a national park. He would give essentially the same address a number of times across the state over the next five years. Even his opponents were impressed at his ability to present the case for Voyageurs, and none could doubt his sincerity. His Rotary Club speech began by describing the beauty of the Kabetogama Peninsula, calling it an enormous recreational resource that had provided vacation opportunities for many people but now "should be made available for use by more people while preserving its wilderness character for posterity." The best way to guarantee its preservation, he said, was to turn it over to the NPS. At that point he expressed respect and admiration for the professionalism and dedication of NPS personnel, noting that the parks they administered were a great asset to our country. "I cannot imagine anyone seriously suggesting that having National Parks is bad policy for our country, that they should be abandoned and subdivided for sale to private interests. . . ." He reminded his audiences that this peninsula in their backyard had been declared by the NPS as having national significance with natural and cultural assets worthy of national park status. He then asked, "Why settle for a state park, as some have proposed, when it qualifies for a National Park?"

Andersen explained that tax revenue generated from existing private holdings in the park area was very small, and that it would be more than offset by tax dollars resulting from new private investments to accommodate the anticipated increased tourist traffic in the area. Emphasizing a theme frequently advanced by environmentalists in the early 1960s, Andersen advocated meeting the increased recreational needs of a growing population by spending public funds to preserve public recreational facilities for all to enjoy now and in the future. He concluded his talk by stating, "My interest in pursuing this project comes under the heading of 'unfinished business.' I had a hand in starting it, I would like to see it through."[4]

Andersen's address had a positive impact on the business and professional leaders in International Falls. Within two weeks of his appearance, the board of directors of the International Falls Chamber of Commerce and the city's Retail Merchants Association voted in favor of a national park for Kabetogama. This positive local response was tempered, however, by a letter from Mando's (Boise Cascade's name for M&O since the merger) president, Robert Faegre, to Governor Rolvaag on February 18 stating that the company could not support the suggestion that a national park be established in an area where private ownership was predominant—meaning, of course, the Kabetogama Peninsula.[5] Mando's news release on the subject also referred to Agriculture Secretary Freeman's directive to expand the no-cut zone around the BWCA, thereby removing thousands of acres of forest land from production. Unfortunately for the NPS and park supporters, as time would tell, the company also said that it favored a national park but that it should be located on federal lands in the Superior National Forest east and north of Crane Lake including BWCA lands near Lac La Croix.

Mando's public stance on the national park was crafted to place them on both sides of the controversy. They favored a national park for Minnesota, and they advocated a broad multiple-use program for the Kabetogama lands, involving both state and private owners on the peninsula. This alternate site strategy, while extremely useful to the company and the timber industry, proved to be one of the most troublesome issues the NPS had to deal with in advancing the Voyageurs proposal. John Kawamoto said, "I think that was probably as good a public relations diversionary tactic that Boise Cascade ever came up with. It really set us on our heels. . . ."[6] And it contributed to a lengthy, almost four-year delay for the NPS in issuing its second report on Voyageurs, *Master Plan for Voyageurs National Park,* dated 1968.

Supporters of Voyageurs now had to fend off repeated calls by park opponents for studies that would compare the two sites and show why the alternative site in the Superior National Forest was not suitable for national park status. In rebuttal, park advocates acknowledged that the vegetation and geology of Mando's alternative site were similar to the Kabetogama area and both were part of the boundary waters region. However, the lakes of the proposed park (Rainy, Kabetogama, Namakan, and Sand Point) were much larger than those in the designated canoe country to the east and could support heavier recreational use without destroying scenic qualities. Also, in contrast to the isolated alternative site, the Kabetogama area was more accessible by automobile and already had private resort facilities in place to accommodate park visitors. But most importantly, the alternative site in the Lac La Croix area was already designated wilderness canoe country managed by the USFS, and the terms of the agreement between the secretaries of the Agriculture and Interior Departments prevented the NPS from conducting independent studies in the Superior National Forest. Of course, the USFS would resist any effort by the NPS to remove territory in the BWCA for designation as a national park.

About a week after Mando announced its preference for an alternative site, a Duluth planning firm released a report prepared by one of its partners, Charles Aguar, that advocated continued multiple-use management of the Kabetogama Peninsula with an emphasis on recreation. The report said that designation as a national recreation area rather than a national park could best achieve this objective. The planning boards of the two counties in which the proposed park would be located commissioned the study. Both boards had previously adopted resolutions opposing a national park on Kabetogama.[7] The company that conducted the study acknowledged that time limitations had not permitted an exhaustive study of the question and recommended, therefore, more research at several points in their brief report. Nevertheless, this report, combined with Mando's position statement, generated a lot of press coverage and many letters to Congressman Blatnik expressing opposition to the park on Kabetogama and favoring a management approach based on the principles of multiple use.

As these events were occurring in Minnesota, the NPS in Washington, D.C., was reviewing the status of the Voyageurs proposal and several others around the country. Part of that process required a meeting with Interior Secretary Stewart Udall. After hearing the report on Voyageurs, Udall requested that it be completed and that preparations be made for authorizing legislation in 1966.[8] One month later the NPS Midwest Regional Director Garrison submitted to Director Hartzog what his park planning officials called their final recommendations for the Voyageurs National Park proposal.[9] The recommendations dealt with policy issues such as hunting, access roads, minor boundary adjustments to exclude private resorts, and so on. The report also contained recommendations on three issues that, in retrospect, are of special interest.

After recommending that the final boundary be the same as proposed in the preliminary report, that is, only the Kabetogama Peninsula area, the report then recommended that "the matter of a joint study between the NPS and the USFS of the Crane to Namakan Lakes area be pursued until a determination can be made as to whether the area will be studied or whether it will not. If it can be studied, we feel that the final boundaries of the Voyageurs National Park should be outlined above with the provision for addition of the Crane Lake to Namakan Lakes area should this be feasible."[10] The intent of this recommendation was to call attention to the initial report on Voyageurs that envisioned a park from Crane Lake to Rainy Lake as the strongest proposal the NPS could make. Another recommendation stressed that the Mando alternative site be rejected as a substitute for the NPS's proposal and that it not be included as part of the final report. Finally, the report recommended that no legislation be introduced until the final report was prepared and released. The reason stated for this recommendation was that public approval was building and that delay would provide additional time for even greater support. The report pinned its hopes for increased support on an organization just forming—the Voyageurs National Park Association (VNPA).[11]

In retrospect, Andersen's January Rotary Club speech in International Falls marked the beginning of a six-year aggressive campaign to build popular support for congressional action authorizing and establishing Voyageurs National Park. Beginning with his term as governor, Andersen had already devoted almost four years to the cause. However, what momentum the project had in those early years was lost because of the long delay in getting an approved, official proposal from the NPS, emergence of strong local opposition, and the shift in M&O's position from one of cooperation to one of opposition regarding the Kabetogama site for the park. Andersen was convinced that nothing short of a prodigious effort focused on generating statewide public support could rescue the proposal from certain demise.

Andersen's plan for building support was to encourage organizations of all kinds—civic, labor, religious, political—to pass resolutions endorsing Voyageurs National Park. It was a method Andersen had used with remarkable success in 1963–64 to secure statewide support for a proposition to amend the Minnesota state constitution in ways that would encourage new economic development on the Iron Range. Called the Taconite Amendment, its passage in November 1964 assured the emerging taconite mining industry that it would be taxed on the same basis as that of other manufacturing corporations. The amendment passed with over 85 percent of the voters in favor. With the assurance of tax stability, millions of dollars were invested for construction of new iron ore treatment facilities in northeastern Minnesota over the next decade.[12]

Andersen, as a private citizen, led that successful statewide campaign, and he was convinced that a similar plan would result in overwhelming public acceptance of a proposal for a national park in Minnesota. He called on Rita Shemesh, the energetic and capable executive director of the taconite amendment campaign, to head the Voyageurs effort. He also enlisted the aid of a number of prominent Minnesotans to lend their good names, energies, and financial support to the park cause. Finally, an organization was needed to provide the leadership, structure, and continuity required for a lengthy campaign. In February 1965, he informed the NPS that he had taken initial steps leading to the formation of the Voyageurs National Park Association.[13]

Formal incorporation of the VNPA took place in spring 1965. However, the first organizational support for Voyageurs in Minnesota actually came on February 16, 1965, when the United Northern Sportsmen organization in Duluth passed a supporting resolution for the park.[14] And two days later the Greater Minneapolis Chamber of Commerce formally endorsed Voyageurs with a resolution that also emphasized the statewide economic benefits to be derived from national park designation.[15] On March 24, 1965, International Falls businessman Wayne Judy sent Conservation Commissioner Wayne Olson a letter with the names of eleven business and professional men from the International Falls area who were designated by the Chamber of Commerce as the National Park Promotion Committee. Judy said this committee might serve as the nucleus of a statewide Voyageurs National Park committee.[16]

Following up on Andersen's declaration to form a statewide committee, Robert Watson and Archie Chelseth, who worked for Andersen's H. B. Fuller Company, brought together a group of people to plan the formation of the VNPA at a meeting on April 12, 1965, at the North Star Center in Minneapolis. Attending the planning meeting were Wayne Judy and George Esslinger from International Falls, Conservation Commissioner Olson, Glenn Ross of The Nature Conservancy, and Martin Kellogg, Sam Morgan, and Tom Savage from the Twin Cities.[17] Morgan, a St. Paul attorney, drew up the articles of incorporation, which were filed with the secretary of state on May 5, 1965. On May 10 the first meeting of the incorporators and directors was held at the general offices of the H. B. Fuller Company in St. Paul.[18]

Listed as incorporators were Elmer L. Andersen, Thomas Savage, Edwin P. Chapman, Lawrence Vaubel, and Wayne Judy. Listed as directors were Elmer L. Andersen, Lloyd Brandt, Edwin P. Chapman, George Esslinger, Wayne Judy, Martin Kellogg, Sam Morgan, Glenn Ross, and Thomas Savage. Officers elected at this meeting were Edwin P. Chapman, president; Wayne Judy, vice president; Thomas Savage, secretary; and Martin Kellogg, treasurer.

In naming Chapman as the first president of the VNPA, the members were recognizing his longtime advocacy for Minnesota's state parks and his firsthand knowledge of the natural amenities of the border lakes region and its sociopolitical characteristics. Chapman practiced law in Cook County—the far northeastern county in the state—for several years. He was elected Cook County attorney in the early 1940s. He resumed private practice in a Minneapolis law firm in the 1950s, and in 1961 was named judge of the Minneapolis Municipal Court and later Chief Judge of the Hennepin County Municipal Court.

The first organizational meeting was followed a week later by a general membership meeting. Howard Stagner, NPS's acting assistant director for resources studies, and officials from the Midwest regional office, were featured speakers at this meeting. Stagner emphasized that "the name National Park is a mark of distinction, recognized and respected throughout the world. The status that attends the name National Park very quickly generates a very real measure of local pride, a close identity with the community...."[19]

Stagner's remarks were warmly received by the members of the newly formed VNPA, most of whom were residents of the Twin Cities area. However, it is doubtful that residents in the border communities where the park would be located would have been similarly impressed. For example, in casual conversation following the meeting, Stagner learned that the state legislature was considering a moratorium on land exchanges that would prevent exchange of state lands from outside the proposed park for Kabetogama lands owned by Mando. The legislation was being pushed by the lumber and paper industries, including the Mando division of Boise Cascade, and editorially by the major newspaper in northeastern Minnesota, the *Duluth News Tribune*.[20]

At the same meeting, Andersen told Stagner that "he believed the paper company, once favorable to exchange of these lands . . . now realizes that their [Kabetogama] lands have a much higher value to them for recreation when leased, sold, or developed far above the market value of the timber."[21] George Amidon alluded to this a month later at a hearing of the Minnesota Outdoor Recreation Resources Commission when he testified that the Mando company owned about 2,700,000 feet of lake frontage in the proposed national park. He felt this land should be left for private development.[22] Garrison later recalled that when Amidon represented the old M&O, he gave the impression that his company would not oppose the park, but when M&O became a division of Boise Cascade, there was a complete reversal of position. Garrison said, "It was no surprise to me . . . we had met Boise Cascade before and did later and they are anti-parks and recreation. Amidon made this clear."[23]

In spring 1965 a new organization, the Northland Multiple Use Association, joined Boise Cascade in advocating an alternative site for a national park. In a clear reference to controversial park and wilderness expansion underway in the western states at that time, the association sent position statements to Minnesota legislators and President Lyndon B. Johnson declaring that they "opposed a further extension of the 'one use' concept eastward to the remaining Lake and Forest section of Minnesota which is presently enjoyed and utilized by people of all ages under the multiple use concept."[24]

It was evident that by mid-1965, opposition to the park proposal was coalescing around Mando and several borderland organizations that were opposed to any further federalization of the border lakes region—especially if it meant locking up lands under the single-use concept, that is, as wilderness and national parks. It was also evident that the leadership in these organizations looked to Boise for direction. Thus, in summer 1965, with the VNPA in place and a sharper focus on the groups opposing the park, the contest had begun for public support on both sides of the national park issue.

Boise Cascade's position favoring a national park, but only if carved out of existing federal lands, was quickly adopted by other organizations opposing the park on Kabetogama, including segments of the media in northeastern Minnesota. All said that they favored a national park and the national park concept so long as it could be realized on existing federal lands. And the only way the issue could be resolved, they said, was to do a thorough feasibility study of the alternative site initially proposed by Boise, the region east of Crane Lake including lands and waters in the Lac La Croix area. Their commitment to these positions was communicated frequently and energetically to the appropriate government officials, but especially to Congressman Blatnik and the state's two U.S. senators.

The call for a *study* of the alternative site was quickly taken up by a number of individuals and organizations on both sides of the park issue. Even the newly organized VNPA asked for the study, confident that its results would vindicate the NPS's earlier studies and site analysis, thus settling the question so that the proposal could go forward. Given the demand for action on the Boise Cascade proposal, the NPS moved with uncharacteristic speed and vigor to defend its earlier studies and judgment that led to the selection of the Kabetogama site.

Midwest Regional Director Garrison best expressed the NPS position in a detailed letter of explanation to Robert Faegre, vice president of Boise Cascade. He stressed that justification for a truly "Nation's Park" was always subject to "intense and searching scrutiny" by the public and Congress, and he felt confident that the NPS report, which represented a synthesis of much study and thought over many years, would stand the test of such scrutiny. He said the Lac La Croix alternative site proposed by Boise was already "dedicated to the preservation of wilderness canoe country. As such, this area is an entirely separate matter from the VNP proposal. However, these two areas can complement each other to the benefit of Minnesota and the Nation."[25]

Over the next few months many of the points advanced by Garrison would be used by NPS officials in countering the demands for study of the proposed alternative site. Meanwhile, USFS officials and Agriculture Secretary Freeman rejected the Boise proposal, which would require removal of BWCA territory to accommodate the establishment of a national park in the border region.

As noted earlier, the USFS was successful in preventing NPS incursions into USFS lands proposed in the initial report on Voyageurs, and now they were confronted by a highly publicized proposal originating outside the government that would have the same effect. In this instance, Secretary Freeman quickly dismissed the proposal. In letters to the president of the Kabetogama Lake Association and the chairman of the Minnesota Outdoor Recreation Resources Commission, he said that the Lac La Croix site comprised a significant part of the BWCA and that other adjacent lands also included in the Boise Cascade proposal were already appropriately managed by the USFS. "We believe this management is the most desirable and beneficial from the public standpoint, and that establishment of a national park in the Superior National Forest is neither desirable nor necessary."[26] With similar emphasis, Interior Secretary Udall was rejecting the notion of an alternative site in letters to citizens and public officials. In a letter to Minnesota Senator Walter Mondale, Udall's tone expressed impatience with this attempt to divert attention away from the Kabetogama site. Implying that it was time to formalize the Voyageurs National Park proposal, he told the senator that he was asking the NPS to complete its final report and recommendations.[27]

Boise Cascade's alternative site proposal was interpreted by Minnesota's Conservation Commissioner Olson as being in harmony with a nationwide campaign launched by timber producer groups that was designed to prevent further land acquisitions for recreational purposes.[28] Others knowledgeable about Boise's corporate agenda at the time saw it as a way of retaining valuable lakeshore property for eventual development by a newly acquired recreation development subsidiary, the U.S. Land Company. Whatever the motive or motives, Boise's action quickly generated expressions of support for a Voyageurs National Park on the Kabetogama Peninsula from the highest officials of the two affected federal departments—Agriculture and Interior. Within six months both departments had firmly rejected the proposal for studies of alternative sites in the Lac La Croix area or anywhere else. Secretary Udall asked for completion of the Voyageurs proposal in its final form so that the legislative phase could begin. Thus, the two secretaries, in keeping with the spirit and intent of the cooperative agreement signed in January 1963, had kept their bargain.

In the opinion of Regional Director Garrison, all that remained was a joint *public* statement explaining why the Lac La Croix area should remain a part of the BWCA, describing the attributes of the Kabetogama Peninsula site for a national park, and declaring that no further studies were necessary or desirable. Garrison and Sigurd Olson drafted an appropriate statement that was to be a part of a joint press release at the time the final Voyageurs report was distributed by the Interior Department in September 1965.[29]

The NPS hoped that with the release of the report, Congressman Blatnik's office could begin preparing the necessary authorizing legislation, hearings could be scheduled, congressional action taken, and Voyageurs National Park would become a reality. But events did not work out that way. Shortly before the scheduled public release of the report and the joint statement, Congressman Blatnik called the NPS to say he was upset over the timing and the way the report was to be released. He said he would be contacting the two secretaries to tell them that "he and other members of the delegation should have an opportunity to review this more thoroughly before any public announcements are made."[30] The Interior Department withheld the 1965 report as Blatnik requested. It would be over two and one-half years before another formal report on Voyageurs would be published and released to the public by the NPS.

Had the final report on Voyageurs been distributed to members of the Minnesota congressional delegation by the secretary of the interior, it would have been truly embarrassing for Congressman Blatnik. In his phone conversation with the NPS he said he was hearing of strong opposition from local interests, especially the timber products industry. He told them that these local interests remained upset with the Freeman directive expanding the no-cut zone of the BWCA and they also wanted additional studies regarding alternative sites for the proposed park. In light of these circumstances, Blatnik said he had not decided what his position would be on the national park proposal.[31] This combination of bureaucratic mishandling of the final report and at least the perception of strong opposition at home in the Eighth District meant that the Blatnik office would be in no hurry to introduce authorizing legislation on Voyageurs.

Throughout the 1960s when the park issue was being debated around the state, it was clear that the real energy and force behind the proposal came from public officials in several state government agencies, the governor's office, a few influential legislators, and the citizen-based VNPA. It was the VNPA that produced and disseminated the literature and helped organize the educational effort on the park issue, and most of those in leadership positions in the VNPA were from the Twin Cities area. Most of the organized opposition, some of it vehement, came from Blatnik's Eighth District, just as it had on numerous occasions in the past when controversial conservation issues came to the fore. And just as in earlier years, many in northeastern Minnesota harbored resentment that once again the people from the Twin Cities were pushing programs and legislation that they believed would interfere with their freedom to engage in recreational use of the natural resources in their region. Blatnik was expected to resist this Twin Cities–inspired effort to federalize even more borderland territory. Even though Blatnik saw some possible economic benefits from a national park in northeastern Minnesota, he could not ignore the opposition at home. A cautious man, especially when making judgments on political matters, Blatnik chose to go slowly on the park proposal.

Congressman Blatnik's cautious posture on Voyageurs was more complex than just a response to opposition from the wood products industry and a few sportsmen's groups in the border communities. In conversation with the congressman, I gained the feeling that he was not philosophically comfortable with the management concepts of the NPS that stressed preservation over the multiple-use practices of the USFS.[32] His experience with the north woods country came from his work as an education officer with the Civilian Conservation Corps (CCC) during the late 1930s. He spent several years with the CCC in the Ely area of the Superior National Forest, and he expressed great pride in his association with the CCC. Much of his political support came from individuals whose livelihood was closely linked to the timber and wood products industry. And so when some of his friends and constituents would warn against supporting a management proposal that would "lock up" some of the natural resources of his district, Blatnik paid close attention.

Another reason for Blatnik's "go slow" attitude on Voyageurs relates to the strained relationship his office had with the NPS. Also, for some unexplained reason, Blatnik's office had minimal contact with the state administration in St. Paul on the issue of Voyageurs between 1963 and 1966, even though Democrats controlled the governor's office. The NPS worked primarily with state officials in the Andersen and Rolvaag administrations and continued this practice after the change in administration in 1967 and until the authorizing legislation was first introduced in 1968. Governor Rolvaag's conservation commissioner, Wayne Olson, was the public official the NPS relied on most during the period between 1963 and the middle of 1966. The NPS files contain only sporadic references to Blatnik's office. NPS planner John Kawamoto admitted that the seeming avoidance of the congressman was a mistake. And Jim Oberstar, Blatnik's administrative assistant in the 1960s, chided the NPS over its lack of communication with the congressman's Eighth District constituents. He suggested to Harold Jones, Midwest Region Park Planner, that they "send representatives to meet with *individuals* to solicit their support and quiet their fears that park establishment would have some adverse effects."[33] What Blatnik apparently wanted was some effort on the part of the NPS to explain the benefits—especially economic—of a national park in his district, thus countering the arguments of the individuals and organizations fighting establishment of the park.

Finally, Blatnik's reluctance to move aggressively on Voyageurs had something to do with the fact that this was, after all, one of Elmer Andersen's pet projects. Andersen, a Republican, was primarily responsible for launching the national park proposal on Kabetogama while he was governor. He made it a high-priority project during his administration. Later, as a private citizen, he devoted much energy, time, and money to the organized statewide campaign to build support for the park proposal. He regarded it as unfinished business. Andersen and Blatnik were leaders in their respective parties and thus had their philosophical differences. For his part, Andersen harbored some resentment over Blatnik's apparent participation in what Andersen felt were unfair campaign tactics employed by the Democrats in his 1962 reelection campaign against Rolvaag. However, it is significant that in the last few months of the park campaign, these two political leaders set aside their differences and pulled together to see the authorizing legislation through Congress.

Congressman Blatnik's intervention in September 1965 with the Department of the Interior plan to release the Voyageurs report with the secretary's recommendation for congressional authorization contributed significantly to still another lengthy delay in the project's journey to final congressional approval. Meaningful and extensive debate on the issue would not resume until 1967. Individuals and groups on both sides of the question "dug in" for the long battle ahead.

For example, Boise Cascade reaffirmed its alternative site position on a number of occasions throughout 1966, and in one press release criticized the NPS for its proposal to establish a national park in an area where two-thirds of the land was in private, tax-paying ownership. The statement went on to warn that the federal government was apparently prepared to "acquire this land through condemnation, despite the fact that the National Park Service has repeatedly stated at public hearings and otherwise that it uses condemnation procedure only to acquire small parcels of land essential to national park development."[34] The very suggestion that *condemnation* might be used to achieve NPS objectives never played well in the borderland region, where many were convinced that too much land was already under federal control. Using the word *condemnation*—an aggressive term and a procedure that the NPS and other government bodies typically avoided if at all possible—was like waving a red flag.

During 1966, several northeast Minnesota sportsmen's clubs, newspapers, and resort associations joined Boise Cascade in its advocacy of an alternative site for Voyageurs and continued private management of the Kabetogama Peninsula. The most aggressive opposition to the Kabetogama site came from the Northland Multiple Use Association. Organized in May 1965, it sought membership support from residents of northern Minnesota who believed in the principles of multiple-use land management for their region. It claimed a paid membership of more than three hundred by summer 1969 when congressional field hearings were held in International Falls.[35] (About a year after Northland was organized, the NPS considered it the major citizens' group working against the Voyageurs proposal.)[36] The first significant indication that Northland meant to aggressively oppose the park came in the form of full-page ads appearing in the January 9, 1966, issues of the Duluth and International Falls newspapers.[37] The advertisement advocated an alternative site in the BWCA for Voyageurs and continued private ownership of the Kabetogama Peninsula. In an editorial three days later, the *International Falls Daily Journal* took the same position.

Aside from paid organizational pronouncements in the press and position statements by individuals and leaders of groups on both sides of the park issue, the year passed with only modest public involvement in the park question. At the state level the Democrats were engaged in a divisive internal struggle over who should be the party's candidate for governor in the 1966 election—Lieutenant Governor Sandy Keith or Governor Rolvaag. Rolvaag won the nomination, but the party entered the election in a divided, weakened condition and lost to Republican Harold LeVander. Commissioner of Conservation Olson, the most knowledgeable person on the Voyageurs project in the Rolvaag administration, resigned midyear to run for attorney general and lost the election in November to Douglas Head. And so, for the last half of 1966, there was essentially no strong voice for Voyageurs in the state administration. The VNPA had not yet developed a strategy for bringing the message about Voyageurs to the broader statewide public. Indeed, many had never heard of the Voyageurs proposal, and even fewer knew anything about the lead organization working for its establishment.

During 1966 in the offices of the higher officials in the NPS in Washington, D.C., Voyageurs was far from the top of the agenda. The NPS was busy with two park proposals in the West—North Cascades in Washington State and Redwood in California. In the Cascades, the NPS and the USFS had reached an impasse over jurisdiction of some parts of the proposed park, and in California the same kinds of issues were slowing progress on the development of a final proposal for Redwoods. In both cases, opposition to the proposals was strongest at the local level with plenty of support nationally. And these proposals enjoyed the overt support of some of the highest officials in the land—President Johnson, Secretary of the Interior Udall, and Senator Henry Jackson, who was chair of the Interior and Insular Affairs Committee in the U.S. Senate. With boosters like that, the NPS quite naturally devoted major attention to the resolution of issues that would lead to forward progress on both western park projects. In late 1966 when someone asked the NPS about progress on a new Voyageurs plan to replace the 1964 version, the response was, "We continue to work on the revision."

Disturbed by the inactivity and flagging interest, Director of State Parks Hella wrote to the Interior Department asking for a speaker of stature to help restore enthusiasm for the proposed park. In responding, Assistant Secretary Stanley A. Cain at the Interior Department said top people were unavailable at the time and that "after the election would be a much better time."[38]

CHAPTER FIVE

State Administration Leads National Park Cause

When Assistant Secretary of the Interior Stanley Cain told Judge Hella that he should not expect much movement on the Voyageurs proposal until after the elections, he was probably thinking about the outcome of *congressional* races, which could have fiscal and policy implications for the department, its bureaus and agencies, and, by extension, the NPS. What he could not know at the time was that the fall elections at the state level in 1966 would produce a new governor in Minnesota and that the change in administrations would bring new life to the proposal for Voyageurs.

The new governor was Harold LeVander, a new personality in state politics who won a close contest over the incumbent Democrat, Karl Rolvaag. LeVander left a successful law practice of twenty-eight years in the city of South St. Paul to run for governor. His only previous experience as a public official was as assistant district attorney for Dakota County, Minnesota. Given his professional experience and interests, there was little indication that a LeVander administration would bring new energy and enthusiasm to the languishing campaign for Voyageurs. His campaign for governor emphasized such matters as tax policy and a more businesslike approach to the administration of state affairs. But soon after taking office, he surprised and pleased park supporters when he made the proposal a high priority on his activity agenda.

Even though LeVander had not made Voyageurs a top campaign issue, he did voice support for greater attention to conservation matters in keeping with the growing national concern for environmental quality.

The Rolvaag administration, on the other hand, had endorsed Voyageurs on the Kabetogama Peninsula shortly after it was proposed. Commissioner of Conservation Wayne Olson always openly supported the national park proposal and worked closely with NPS officials and planners during his tenure as the state's chief conservation officer. It was Olson who in July 1965 wrote to Senator Walter Mondale stating that the agitation for an alternative site at Lac La Croix was actually a diversionary effort by park opponents, and in the same letter he referred to a nationwide campaign "by timber interests designed to prevent further federal land acquisitions for recreational purposes."[1] Olson also attended the planning session in April 1965 that led to the formation of the VNPA. Unfortunately for the park cause, Olson resigned his position as commissioner in early summer 1966 to run for Minnesota's attorney general, a contest he subsequently lost in the November elections. When Olson left the Conservation Department, the leadership and energy of the Rolvaag administration for the Voyageurs cause went with him. It would be left for the new LeVander administration to pick up the issue, give it further study, and provide a forum for information and discussion at the state level.

Although the new governor had expressed his support for a national park in Minnesota before he took office, he was careful not to endorse the Kabetogama site primarily because Republican leaders in the Eighth District of northeastern Minnesota were not interested in *any* national park proposal and certainly not one in that location. Archie Chelseth, who became Governor LeVander's staff person in charge of coordinating the park effort, said later that "National Park advocacy by Republican candidates in northeastern Minnesota was not viewed as politically advantageous at that time."[2] The governor himself was never particularly excited about the park project—he was more comfortable working on other matters of state business. He did listen to his staff, however, and he sought to understand the positions of organizations and individuals who held strong opinions on both sides of the park issue.[3]

In keeping with that philosophy during his first six weeks in office, LeVander met with groups holding opposing views. Former governor Elmer Andersen and other board members of the VNPA met with LeVander and his conservation commissioner, Jarle Leirfallom, in mid-February 1967. During the meeting they urged the governor to endorse the Kabetogama site for Voyageurs National Park.

A few weeks later LeVander met with timber representatives and others who were just as firm in their opposition to that site. Included in this group were several members of the Minnesota Senate Public Domain Committee and planning consultant Charles Aguar. Aguar had been retained by the St. Louis and Koochiching County Boards to develop an alternative plan that would continue the multiple-use practices of the past while allowing for expanded recreational use of the peninsula. Aguar had already presented his clients with a preliminary report on a multiple-use plan in February 1965, but no formal action was ever taken to carry it forward. He later revised the 1965 report and submitted it again to the county boards in January 1967. The revised document reaffirmed the preference for multiple use and the role of the private sector in developing and expanding recreational facilities in the Kabetogama area. However, the new version included a recommendation that "full consideration be given to designating the Kabetogama Peninsula a national recreation area rather than a Natural Area as proposed in the 1964 National Park Service report."[4]

Aguar saw a national recreation area as a suitable compromise for Kabetogama after observing how firmly committed and fixed to their positions the opposing groups had become. He envisioned a stalemate that could go on for years. Aguar modeled his plan for Kabetogama after one developed for the proposed Apostle Islands National Lakeshore located along the south shore of Lake Superior in northern Wisconsin. Aguar's plan reserved the shoreland and islands of Rainy and Kabetogama Lakes for the national recreation area, "leaving the interior of the peninsula for timber harvesting, hunting and other multiple purposes. A National Recreation Area of more than 126,000 acres would still be a possibility under this proposal."[5]

Aguar's national recreation area plan went nowhere. Wayne Judy, leading park supporter in International Falls, said it was just a diversionary tactic to further confuse the issue.[6] Boise Cascade was not interested since the most valuable part of their peninsula holdings was the shoreline that Aguar was proposing to protect from development, and although it was not public knowledge, they had second-home development plans in mind for this zone.

The Northland Multiple Use Association, following Boise's lead, also announced its opposition to the Aguar proposal and then restated its position that any plans the NPS had for a new national park should be confined to land already under federal control. And the VNPA wanted nothing to do with a national recreation area either.

In late March 1967, when park planner John Kawamoto met with one of Aguar's clients, the St. Louis County Board of Commissioners, he expressed surprise that people were even thinking about a national recreation area. "You can have a national park—why would you want to settle for anything less? Parks are the crown jewels of the American landscape."[7]

Amazingly, in spite of the early opposition and public indifference to the national recreation area concept, it would surface repeatedly during the next three years and was always offered as an appropriate compromise alternative to a national park. This in spite of the fact that the principal players on both sides of the park issue never came close to accepting the national recreation area as a compromise.

As the new governor was hearing from opposing groups on the Voyageurs issue, a dispute arose between the State of Minnesota and the St. Louis County Board over the county's preparation for the sale of tax-forfeited lands in northern St. Louis County, including some lands located in the proposed park. It was a dispute that proved to have a significant, positive impact on the VNPA's efforts to build public support for the park cause. Thousands of acres of land in northern Minnesota became tax delinquent during the 1920s and 1930s as the logging boom came to a close. Seeking to get some of this land on the tax roll again, the county auditor's office made a practice of offering tax-forfeited lands for sale at the request of interested parties. During late February and the first week of March 1967, the county was preparing to conduct an auction sale of 5,000 acres of tax-forfeited land in northern St. Louis County. The sale was scheduled for March 14. Included in the offering were 274 acres of shoreland parcels on the Kabetogama Peninsula that had been appraised at an average price of fifty-two dollars per acre. Boise Cascade, principal private landowner on the peninsula, was interested in 74 acres of the land proposed for auction.

Judge Edwin Chapman, president of the VNPA, learned of the sale one week before the scheduled sale day and immediately requested that the county auditor "defer the sale for a reasonable time to enable us to learn the facts concerning these lands."[8] Chapman noted that delaying the sale would provide interested persons, agencies, and institutions an opportunity to bid on those lands within the proposed park and then donate the lands to the NPS if and when the park was authorized. Chapman was also concerned about the short notice of the sale and the lack of authority from the conservation commissioner to proceed with the sale on the appointed date. Typically, when the county completed its appraisal of all parcels proposed for sale, it would request a waiver of the required thirty-day waiting period before making public notice of the sale. The waiver would arrive, and the county would proceed with its sale. However, in this instance, the Department of Conservation had not granted the waiver request because of questions regarding several appraisals submitted by the county that happened to be located outside the Kabetogama Peninsula area. The county was thus technically not in compliance with the requirements, and the conservation commissioner asked that the sale be delayed until the appraisal matter was resolved. However, the county board challenged the ruling of Commissioner Leirfallom and voted four to three to proceed with the sale as scheduled, insisting that they had acted legally in preparing the parcels for sale.[9]

The sale of tax-forfeited land was held on March 14 as scheduled, over the objection of the conservation commissioner. About 2,800 acres of land, including the 240 acres in the proposed park, were sold. Two days after the sale, Commissioner Leirfallom asked the St. Louis County Board to nullify the sale. If they did not comply with his request, he said the state tax commissioner "may very well ask for the Attorney General's opinion on whether the state should give title to the 2,794 acres purchased in the sale."[10] Placing the blame for the confusion on Leirfallom's office, the board decided not to act on his request. During the discussion, one member stated that the board must stand pat on the sale and that the "next move is up to the state."[11] They did not have to wait long because the state tax commissioner requested an opinion from Attorney General Douglas Head. Head's ruling came on March 27, when he voided the land sale and declared that no state deeds would be issued to the purchasers of land sold at that sale. He also noted that had VNPA President Chapman not called attention to the fact that the county proceeded with the sale without following proper procedures, the sale would have gone through. The county board quickly refunded the purchase money.[12]

The rescheduled sale was held on September 12, and this time there was spirited competitive bidding for the Kabetogama shoreland parcels. Representatives from the VNPA and Izaak Walton League Endowment Fund were on hand to offer bids on the lakeshore plots, with the intention of donating the purchased lands to the NPS when Voyageurs was authorized by Congress. Bidding against the two conservation organizations were Boise Cascade and a northern Minnesota realty firm. Boise's active participation in the bidding sent a signal to observers that the company had more than a passing interest in the recreational potential of the peninsula. The VNPA and Izaak Walton League bids were successful, and the land was later donated to the NPS as planned. Because of the competitive bidding, called "spite bidding" by one county official, the Kabetogama lakeshore lots sold for $28,000—double the appraised value.[13]

As early as February 1967, NPS personnel were hearing comments that Boise Cascade was looking seriously at the potential value of the Kabetogama shorelands if developed for the resort and second-home market. While in Minneapolis, Lemuel Garrison, NPS Northeast Regional Director, visited with members of the VNPA and others interested in the campaign for Voyageurs. In a report to the Midwest regional director summarizing his findings, Garrison noted that the University of Minnesota's Dean of the School of Forestry, Frank Kaufert, believed that "Boise Cascade is not talking at all about pulp timber—they are concerned with their 200 miles of lake front which has a very high sales value."[14] The accuracy of the dean's observation was borne out when in July Boise Cascade acquired the U.S. Land Company, specialists in building artificial lakes and selling the land around them for residential and resort use. With this acquisition "Boise Cascade became the nation's most thoroughly integrated company in the housing field."[15] Shortly after the formal announcement of the merger with Boise, U.S. Land's executive vice president said he saw possible development on Kabetogama either on a conventional subdivision basis or as "sort of a club program where homeowners would share resort facilities."[16]

This observation by a high official at U.S. Land confirmed what VNPA officers and other park advocates had suspected all along, that Boise Cascade was indeed serious about exploring the development potential on the Kabetogama Peninsula, and the possibility of private lakeshore development, financed by one of the largest resort land development companies in the nation, caused some to think it could well doom the movement for a national park.[17]

The VNPA leadership believed that Boise Cascade, a large, diversified corporation, had to be concerned about the damage a protracted dispute with conservationists and public officials would do to its public image and business. Although they could alert the public to Boise's supposed intentions through VNPA newsletters and press releases, what they really hoped for was a pronouncement by a highly placed official that Boise's intended plans were indeed not in the public interest. Up to this point no major officeholder in the state had declared in forceful and unmistakable fashion support for a national park on Kabetogama. Senator Mondale filled that void for park proponents in an address to the fifteenth annual assembly of the Minnesota Conservation Federation in Duluth on September 16, 1967.[18]

Mondale's speech was devoted entirely to the Voyageurs issue and to the need for early positive action to establish a national park in Minnesota. At one point he expressed deep concern over the possibility of private lakeshore development on Kabetogama Peninsula, noting that such development could jeopardize, if not destroy, the opportunity for a national park on the peninsula. He was also troubled by the position held by some that a national park for the area is fine, but it should be located on federal land in the Lac La Croix area to the east of the proposed park. Mondale explained that the Lac La Croix area was an important part of the BWCA and under the jurisdiction of another federal agency, the Department of Agriculture. He then warned that "to urge the Lac La Croix park site and oppose the Kabetogama site is not only to support a proposition that in all likelihood cannot be achieved but to place in serious jeopardy the only site that stands a reasonable chance of acceptance."[19]

Congressman Blatnik spoke to the same audience just moments before Mondale came to the podium to deliver his speech. In what must be regarded as several rhetorical nudges to Blatnik and state legislators in attendance, Mondale emphasized that the state should move soon to get the project in position for consideration at the federal level. The gentle "push" from Mondale was only one of several Blatnik had received from several sources during summer and fall 1967. For example, the *Minneapolis Tribune* ran a story two days after the conference in Duluth citing the pressure building on Blatnik to introduce a park bill.[20] In mid-July, the same newspaper conducted a statewide poll on the proposed park and found that almost two-thirds of those polled felt the state would benefit from establishment of a national park.[21] The same day, the *Minneapolis Tribune* in its lead editorial urged Blatnik to adopt

a clear position favoring the Kabetogama Peninsula as the site for Voyageurs.[22] A few days before the statewide poll, Representative Don Fraser,
a fellow Democrat from the Twin Cities area, said that the Minnesota
congressional delegation should confer on the matter in order to push
toward getting a bill in before the end of the year.[23] During the same
week, Republican Representative Albert Quie wrote to NPS Director
Hartzog, requesting assistance in drafting legislation to establish a park
on Kabetogama.[24]

That was the kind of pressure Blatnik did not like. He was particularly angry over the "goading" from members of the Minnesota congressional delegation, especially when one of them was a member of his
own party. He had an opportunity to express his feelings on the matter
following the dedicatory speech by Interior Secretary Udall at the new
National Water Quality Laboratory in Duluth on August 16. When asked
by a reporter what he thought of the intentions of Representatives Fraser
and Quie to introduce Voyageurs Park bills in Congress, he said local
agreement and full bipartisan support in the Minnesota delegation were
going to be needed before a park bill would be introduced with any
hope of congressional approval. "No congressional committee chairman would spend five minutes trying to adjudicate park differences
within the delegation."[25] This was a clear message to his colleagues and
to the Twin Cities press that he would submit a bill when *he* was ready,
and he had already said that would not occur until early 1968. He simply was not going to let this kind of pressure interfere with his style of
leadership in a district he knew so well. He was a consensus builder. He
wanted to see a proposal that would comply with national park standards, respond to the concerns of constituents living in the area closest
to the proposed park, and still satisfy most of the park advocates. And
he thought he just might have a way to meet these requirements, but he
would not go public with it until he did some checking with the NPS.

In early August, before the Udall visit, Blatnik asked Regional Director
Fred Fagergren and several other NPS officials, including Kawamoto, to
meet with him in his Washington office. He asked them to comment on
the feasibility of a park incorporating the Namakan-Crane Lakes area
under USFS jurisdiction and just the *east half* of the Kabetogama Peninsula. Blatnik believed this plan would satisfy some critics who complained of the huge loss of private land under the proposed park plan,

and the Crane Lake extension would add more federal land to the park, thus appeasing those who saw the NPS plan as just another private land grab by the federal government. Blatnik's scheme would also allow Boise to proceed with its plans for private recreation development on the west half of the peninsula. Kawamoto explained that the NPS could not study the Namakan-Crane Lakes area without the approval of the agriculture secretary, and that the NPS viewed the Kabetogama Peninsula as a discrete "management unit," and that private ownership of the west half would make it impossible to properly manage the park as a natural area.[26]

Alarmed by such a proposal and anticipating more questions regarding schemes for a "split" peninsula, the NPS asked its resource planning office to develop a clear position statement declaring that such an arrangement was unacceptable because the peninsula would then lose its unique character as a natural unit.[27] Blatnik soon realized that his "compromise" proposal could not work, but he continued to think that including the Namakan-Crane Lakes area would add much to the proposal since it would give the visitor a wider range of recreational opportunities.[28] So what was actually an in-house suggestion was never formalized nor publicly discussed and was dropped.

The proposal for a national recreation area instead of a national park, the flap over the botched county land sale, Mondale's speech urging authorization of a national park on Kabetogama, fellow Minnesota congressmen threatening to upstage Blatnik, and continued calls for alternative site studies kept the Voyageurs issue in the public press for the entire spring and summer of 1967. Congressman Blatnik's office was compelled to devote more time to the issue as the pressure mounted.

And pressure from both sides was also exerted on the governor's office to move more aggressively to help resolve the issue. Indeed, leading park supporters were urging LeVander to move quickly and take a formal position supporting the NPS recommendation for a park on the Kabetogama Peninsula. They believed a declaration of support by the governor would cause Blatnik to move more quickly on the legislative front. The LeVander administration did pick up the park issue within weeks after inauguration and continued to study and monitor public discussion and opinion on the issue during spring and early summer. By late July, aides had convinced LeVander that the public interest, as well as his own political position, would be best served if his office developed and carried forward a coordinated plan of *study, research,* and *public discussion* that would focus on all pertinent issues linked with the Voyageurs proposal. By early August a plan to carry out those objectives was well underway.

Governor LeVander's staff included several key individuals who not only possessed the necessary research and organizational skills to carry the Voyageurs project forward but were already friendly to the concept of a national park for northern Minnesota. This was no small matter because two of them had held important positions in the corporate offices of Elmer Andersen's H. B. Fuller Company. One was David Durenberger, an attorney who later became a U.S. senator from Minnesota. Durenberger had been a law partner in LeVander's firm and was serving as the governor's executive secretary/chief of staff. Archie Chelseth, also a former Andersen employee, was a research specialist in LeVander's office and was closely associated with many of the LeVander administration's efforts related to Voyageurs from 1967 to 1969. (Chelseth said he was viewed suspiciously by some staff people as an "Andersen person" in the LeVander administration.)[29] Robert Herbst, who later became assistant interior secretary for fish, wildlife, and parks in the Carter administration's Interior Department, was LeVander's deputy commissioner of conservation.

As part of the effort on the Voyageurs project, LeVander was insistent that an independent report on the national park proposal be prepared for his use and as a public document for those seeking information about the proposal. He wanted an objective report containing no recommendations. The task of producing this report was given to his commissioner of conservation, Jarle Leirfallom. Leirfallom was a graduate of St. Olaf College in Minnesota and continued his studies at Syracuse University, receiving a master's degree in public administration in 1940. He returned to Minnesota to work in state government, serving as head of the state Department of Welfare from 1944 to 1955. He then left state government for ten years to manage his business as owner and operator of several nursing homes in the Twin Cities area. Leirfallom was an avid outdoor sportsman, but on the day the governor named his longtime friend as his commissioner of conservation he emphasized his training and experience as an administrator—a strong, experienced administrator to coordinate the programs in the Conservation Department.[30]

Not long after Leirfallom assumed his new duties, the talk around the capitol was that the new commissioner had some definite misgivings about increases in federal land holdings in the border lakes region at the expense of private and state acreage in that area. He knew, of course, that the Voyageurs proposal for a park at Kabetogama would not only require more federal land but also replace the existing informal use patterns with a plan emphasizing a more passive recreational practice and preservation of the area's natural resources as well. His sentiments on the issue soon became known to park supporters and especially to VNPA board members, who had concerns about the objectivity of a report on the Voyageurs proposal coming out of the commissioner's office. To allay such fears, Leirfallom asked Deputy Commissioner Herbst to make the appointments to the team that would do the research for the project. Herbst chose Roger Williams from the Bureau of Engineering and William West from the Division of Lands and Forestry.

Shortly after the research began, Leirfallom, realizing that park advocates were still concerned about the credibility of a report produced in his department, wrote to VNPA President Ed Chapman stating that he wished to dispel the impression that he was opposed to a national park. He said he wanted an arrangement where all the facts could be placed on the table. "I'm in favor of any park that will be good for Minnesota."[31] But, the concern over objectivity of the final report persisted both within the LeVander administration and among those outside who knew that such a report was being prepared.

On August 17, at the request of Director of State Parks Hella, Kawamoto came to St. Paul to brief Williams and West on the history of the Voyageurs project. In a memorandum to NPS Regional Director Fred Fagergren the following day, Kawamoto said that Hella, a longtime supporter of Voyageurs, was concerned because "Mr. Leirfallom appears to oppose the proposed Voyageurs National Park (principally because of his feeling that there should be less land in public ownership, not because he opposes the park per se)."[32] Hella also told Kawamoto that he and Leirfallom had agreed to remain neutral, that is, to not interfere with the preparation or final content of the report. Kawamoto met with Williams and West a month later just as they were nearing completion of their report. They told Kawamoto that they feared that Commissioner Leirfallom might make changes in the report before it went to the governor, and they were relying on Deputy Commissioner Herbst to convince the commissioner to preserve the objectivity of their report.[33] On October 4, 1967, Leirfallom sent the report on to the governor with a short cover memo devoid of any personal bias concerning the report's content.[34]

The Williams-West report on Voyageurs, modestly identified as an "administrative report," was in fact a balanced, factual source book that presented the history of the park proposal as well as background information on some of the more controversial questions that had emerged since the NPS released its first report in 1963. Arguments for and against the park on the Kabetogama Peninsula were presented in the report. The document also included several proposals for alternate sites for a national park as well as proposals for management of the Kabetogama Peninsula under multiple-use plans administered by local units of government.

Boise Cascade's company policy favoring an alternate site in the Lac La Croix area and its new (1967) plan for expanded recreational use of its Kabetogama lands were appended to the report as was the USFS argument against shifting the park site to the Lac La Croix area because it would require removing that area from the BWCA. Excerpts from the Aguar (1966) plan advocating multiple-use management for the peninsula with a designation as a national recreation area were also included. This plan was rejected by Aguar's clients, the planning commissions of St. Louis and Koochiching Counties, in spring 1967.

The Williams-West report contained two other alternatives to national park status for the Kabetogama Peninsula. One, dated April 1967, recommended revision of county zoning ordinances in order to recognize the scenic and historic values of the Kabetogama area and still preserve the existing multiple-use management practices. The second alternative was a bi-county management scheme that would be administered by a board called the Joint Commission for the Management of the Kabetogama Peninsula. The plan was offered by a St. Louis County commissioner at a county-sponsored land symposium on September 8, 1967. The inspiration for the proposal was Maine's management program for the recently established (1966) Allagash Wilderness Waterway, described at the symposium by the chairman of the Maine Park and Recreation Commission. Maine's plan for the Allagash had been chosen by the state as an alternative to a proposal for a national park in that area.[35]

In the summary of their report, Williams and West reminded readers that states do not determine the location of national parks. The NPS does that after determining the suitability of a site in accordance with a comprehensive set of criteria. Their report concluded with the observation that the NPS chose the Kabetogama Peninsula, and so the state must consider two questions: "(1) Do we want a national park in Minnesota and, if so, (2) How might the problems regarding establishment and management of a park on the Kabetogama peninsula best be solved?"[36]

Shortly after the Conservation Department's report was released, the NPS learned from Representative Blatnik's administrative assistant, Jim Oberstar, that the congressman had finally agreed to the Kabetogama site and that he also wanted to see the Namakan-Crane Lakes area added to the park proposal. Adding this segment was an idea Blatnik had expressed in early August when he met with park officials in his Washington office. In fact, Oberstar said Blatnik had already discussed the matter with Interior Secretary Udall, telling him that he wanted the Namakan-Crane Lakes area added to the proposed park (not to simply move the park eastward—he would leave the entire Kabetogama Peninsula in the park). Blatnik also knew of the prior agreement that prohibited the Agriculture and Interior Departments from initiating *unilaterally* new proposals to change the status of lands under the jurisdiction of the other department. He therefore saw the need to get the two secretaries together to discuss the issue. Oberstar also said that a meeting was being arranged for early November between Blatnik and Governor LeVander to discuss the park issue. Blatnik hoped to get LeVander's commitment to the Kabetogama site and also to extending the eastern boundaries to include the Namakan-Crane Lakes segment.[37]

The Conservation Department's summary report on the Voyageurs proposal was exactly what the governor had requested—an objective formal presentation of the opposing positions that could be useful in future public discussion of the park proposal. It was also accepted by both sides of the controversy as a useful, impartial presentation of the facts. After its release the governor's staff acted quickly to move the debate to another level, an open public forum hosted by the governor. They chose November 28 at Virginia, Minnesota, as the date and place for the meeting, and they devised a format where all sides of the issue could be heard and their positions placed on the record. The Williams-West report would provide detailed background information on the issue, and the forum would afford the opportunity for opposing views to be heard in an orderly, constructive manner. The governor would address the conference, but he would withhold announcement of his position on the park until after the conference.

In the weeks preceding the forum, the press, federal and state agencies, and interested organizations picked up the pace in identifying and explaining the central issues surrounding the Voyageurs proposal. The NPS was busy answering twenty-two questions submitted by Congressman Blatnik and the Northland Multiple Use Association regarding the proposed park and its impact on the state and local levels. The media carried stories and editorials stressing the Kabetogama as the logical site for the national park as well as positions and letters favoring a park at another location in the border lakes region. For example, KDAL, a local radio and television company, announced results of two polls they had taken on the proposal. The first was conducted on September 14, and the other seven weeks later, on November 1. In the September poll 83 percent favored a national park for northern Minnesota. The November poll was more specific as to site since participants were asked "whether a national park should be established on the Kabetogama peninsula in northern Minnesota." To this question, 42.5 percent said, yes; 30.5 percent had no opinion; and 27 percent said, no. In a commentary aired on November 8 interpreting the results of the polls, KDAL, through its news director, Bill Krueger, said, "It seems clear that a large number of people in this area are not really concerned with where a national park is located, just so the state gets one. These same people sit on the sidelines, noting only that they want the national park. They are aware of a national park's economic development assets, and they favor it on that basis." The editorial concluded that "if there is no more public consensus about the park next spring than there is now, congressman John Blatnik should in good conscience be able to recommend the Kabetogama as the location."[38]

Bruce B. Dayton, president of the Dayton Corporation in Minneapolis, was convinced that the Kabetogama Peninsula was well suited as a site for Voyageurs but was deeply troubled by Boise Cascade's resistance to the park at that location. To dramatize his feelings on the matter, he gave his two hundred shares of Boise Cascade stock to the VNPA. In a letter to the association's president, Chapman, Dayton asserted that Boise's stand against the park "reflects great discredit on them and on business in general." He said that as a former director of Minnesota and

Ontario Paper Company (M&O), "I was aware that M&O had more timber resources available to it than it could effectively utilize and therefore I question that its continued growth as an important Minnesota industry is dependent upon this particular timber holding."[39]

An opposite view was expressed by the leadership of the Minnesota Arrowhead Association, an organization with a membership of more than a thousand individuals and business groups whose primary function is the promotion of the tourist industry in northeastern Minnesota. Following the annual meeting of its board of directors, a letter was sent to the editor of the *Daily Journal* at International Falls reaffirming the association's earlier position favoring a national park for the border area "but opposing the establishment of such a park on the Kabetogama Peninsula. We feel that it is not necessary to purchase additional privately-owned lands with the vast government-owned acreage in this area." The letter also praised the governor for planning a special conference dedicated to examining the central issue of the proposal for Voyageurs.[40]

In St. Paul, Governor LeVander was trying to sort out mixed messages on the park issue he was receiving from staff members in his own administration. Several staff people working closely with the Voyageurs project were urging him to publicly support the park. But several weeks before the Virginia conference, Conservation Commissioner Leirfallom sent several memos to the governor reiterating his earlier concerns that establishment of the park would simply place more land in federal ownership. In one memo he said, "One of the acute problems in the border counties today is an excess of publicly owned lands, and to put more land into public ownership does not make sense."[41]

Commissioner Leirfallom's position opposing increased federalization of the border lakes region was shared by many residents in northeastern Minnesota. Their point of view was forcefully presented at the governor's Virginia conference by R. J. Higgins, a state senator from the Duluth area. In his remarks to the several hundred participants, he vigorously defended the principle of states' rights in such matters and proceeded to attack conservation organizations, who he said rode roughshod over those who attempted to oppose their ideas. "These well-heeled preservation groups have managed to sway public opinion by pouring out a veritable flood of carefully conceived, misleading and contrived propaganda which has already severely damaged Minnesota and Minnesotans before the eyes of the nation."[42]

Senator Higgins continued to vigorously oppose the Voyageurs proposal in the state senate and at public meetings until his defeat for reelection in 1970. He was especially aggressive in his opposition at public hearings where NPS personnel were asked to testify. Kawamoto reported that at one public hearing conducted by the Senate Public Domain Committee, of which Higgins was a member, he and a colleague stood for almost two hours responding to questions—many of them repetitious. He became convinced that the real purpose of the meeting was to "attack the National Park Service and including the integrity of the National Park Service representatives."[43]

Senator Higgins was just one of about a dozen presenters participating at the governor's workshop on Voyageurs. In his invitation to the speakers the governor noted that it was not a public hearing. It was an opportunity to take testimony from a select group of participants who had the necessary expertise on the relevant issues surrounding the park proposal on the Kabetogama Peninsula and who could provide answers to the many unresolved questions. One individual in that select group was NPS Director George Hartzog.[44] He pointed out the economic benefits they could expect from establishment of the park and then made two points that he hoped would clarify the NPS position on Voyageurs: the Kabetogama Peninsula qualified on all counts for national park status, and because of the overwhelming support in Minnesota for a national park, the decision on Voyageurs should not be delayed.[45] Senator Mondale echoed Hartzog's admonition for speedy action in a wire sent to the conference through Chapman. Mondale said, "We are not operating in a seller's market and if we don't believe this we should just look at the list of bills before Congress today for projects such as this."[46]

Before the Virginia workshop, Governor LeVander, perhaps as a concession to his conservation commissioner, said he would not commit himself on the Kabetogama Peninsula as the site for a national park until after the Virginia conference. He hoped the information coming out of that meeting would prove helpful to him in making his final decision on the matter. In his remarks to the gathering, LeVander expressed concern that a national park on the peninsula would add more federal land in the border lakes region. He also raised questions concerning land acquisition procedures, hunting policies, and the impact on timber supply for local wood products industries.

NPS Director Hartzog supplied answers to most of the governor's questions. But to the surprise of many, especially to park advocates, the governor introduced another issue that opened up once again the inter-agency dispute over jurisdiction of the Namakan-Crane Lakes area. In his discussion on park boundaries, the governor suggested serious con-sideration be given to revision of the official NPS proposal to include this segment. He cited several reasons for this suggestion, summarized here:

- The Crane Lake addition would enhance the western entrance to the Boundary Waters Canoe Area while also serving as an entrance point on the southeast for Voyageurs National Park.
- A Crane Lake entrance would permit Ely to benefit economically from the new park.
- The smaller lakes (Crane and Sand Point) would add greater variety to the water-based park and would be a safe alternative to the larger lakes in bad weather.
- The addition would make a "better park" from the state's standpoint and would serve the private tourist industry.[47]

The governor did mention the fact that the NPS had studied the Namakan-Crane Lakes area in 1962–63, had concluded that in union with the Kabetogama area, it qualified for designation as a national park, and had therefore included it in their early draft proposals for a national park. Whenever the governor or members of his staff questioned the NPS regarding the inclusion of this segment in a revised proposal, they were told about the early studies that emphasized the historical signifi-cance of the voyageurs route from Crane Lake to Rainy Lake and the physical unity of this portion of the border lakes region. For those rea-sons, the NPS had included the Namakan-Crane Lakes area in their ear-liest draft proposals for Voyageurs.

NPS personnel who did the initial studies on Voyageurs and those familiar with the study reports always insisted it would be a better park if this section were included in the final legislation. Of course, they then had to point out that they were prohibited by the agreement with the USFS, who managed the area, from unilaterally doing any further study. For that reason, the eastern boundary of the park in the official pro-posal ended at the east end of the Kabetogama Peninsula.

It remained for John Borchert, professor of geography at the Univer-sity of Minnesota, to explain to those assembled the importance of recognizing the cultural and scenic values of the entire Minnesota border lakes region. Borchert saw this area as one scenic corridor, one package—a scenic and historic museum that he implied would require careful planning and management if the values of the proposed park were to be protected.[48]

NPS Director Hartzog accompanied the governor on the return flight to Minneapolis, which gave them an opportunity to freely discuss the Voyageurs proposal in light of the information presented at the workshop. From that conversation, Hartzog learned that LeVander truly wanted a national park for Minnesota and that he was now committed to supporting a park on the Kabetogama Peninsula. However, as he had stated in his address to participants, he believed that the proposed park boundaries should be extended eastward to include the Namakan-Crane Lakes area. But somewhere in their conversation, Hartzog got the impression that the governor wanted to see a park proposal that left a portion of the western part of the peninsula in private hands. Upon his return to Washington, D.C., Hartzog shared this information in a memorandum to a staff associate, noting that LeVander did not say so but from his conversation, "I just infer this."[49] Hartzog realized that without the entire peninsula there could be no park, no matter what was done to extend the boundaries on the east.

Congressman Blatnik had a month earlier dropped any reduction in Kabetogama lands as a condition for his support, but it was still alive in the mind of the governor and was apparently put there by his conservation commissioner. Leirfallom had consistently held that too much private land would be required to meet the conditions of the NPS proposal. He and others felt that one way to remedy this situation would be to add more federal land by including the Namakan-Crane Lakes area under USFS jurisdiction and removing some unspecified private acreage on the west half of the Kabetogama Peninsula. In this way, the ratio of federal land to private land would be increased, thus blunting the criticism of those who saw the whole project as yet another federal land grab.

Any fears Director Hartzog may have had that LeVander would actually pursue removal of west Kabetogama lands were quickly set aside when on November 30, just two days after the workshop, the governor called a news conference and announced his support for the park as proposed by the NPS. As he did at the Virginia conference, he recommended that the park boundaries be extended southeasterly to include the "Crane Lake Recreation Area" managed by the USFS, and that authorizing legislation reflect this addition.[50]

On the day LeVander made his announcement, a *Minneapolis Star* reporter quoted Elmer Andersen as saying he was "convinced that Governor LeVander's decision today to give Voyageurs National Park his unqualified endorsement clinched the park for Minnesota. With bipartisan support assured there should be little doubt of early Congressional action."[51] The former governor was correct in his assessment of the bipartisan support for the park, but if he meant early congressional *approval* of the park when he referred to early congressional *action,* he was overly optimistic. Congressional authorization was still three years away on that November day in 1967. To get to that point, he would have to rely even more on his organizational and motivational skills and on some good friends for greater support.

With the governor's public announcement favoring the park on Kabetogama, preceded by a successful conference in Virginia, the campaign for Voyageurs took a significant turn. Park advocates had good reason to claim a giant step forward while opponents remained skeptical that this was the best management policy for the Kabetogama lands. Opposition leaders, as well as most Voyageurs supporters, were unaware of Blatnik's tentative and, at that date, private commitment to the Kabetogama site and his questions directed to the NPS in August about extending the proposed park boundary on the southeast to include the Crane Lake Recreation Area. With the governor's position now clear and public, both political leaders supported the official park proposal, and both saw advantages in the inclusion of the Crane Lake area.

The governor's press conference also included a statement that he would be going to Washington, D.C., on December 6–7 to meet with the Minnesota delegation on the park issue. Press accounts termed the governor's statement as a giant step toward the kind of consensus Congressman Blatnik always said was required before he would introduce legislation in the U.S. House of Representatives. In Washington, Blatnik praised LeVander's stand on the park proposal and said he looked forward to the governor's visit. Publicly, Blatnik's position was for endorsement of a national park in principle, but he remained reluctant to reveal his position on the precise location.[52]

Two Democrats, Senator Mondale and Congressman Don Fraser from the Twin Cities, also congratulated LeVander for backing the Kabetogama site. But the greatest display of political support for the governor's pronouncement came from leaders of his own party. Republican congressmen and the state party chairman saw the issue as now in Blatnik's hands, and they urged him to keep the ball rolling by introducing legislation. This bit of partisan prodding was clear evidence that the Republican Party wanted to make it clear that they were out ahead in supporting the first modern proposal for a national park in Minnesota.

This minor display of partisan pride aside, however, the fact remains that the movement for Voyageurs National Park enjoyed strong bipartisan support during the entire campaign for authorization and establishment. At the state level, the project began with Republican Governor Elmer Andersen's administration in 1962 and continued under Governor Rolvaag, a Democrat, who relied primarily upon his conservation commissioners to work with NPS officials and park advocates. Republican Governor LeVander took up the cause in 1967 and saw it through the legislative stage to congressional approval in December 1970. Governor Wendell Anderson, a Democrat, succeeded LeVander and supported state legislation donating state lands required for final establishment of the park in 1975. While all administrations endorsed and publicly promoted the cause, it was the LeVander administration that provided the greatest energy and leadership toward moving the park proposal into the final legislative phase.

By the time LeVander took office in 1967, a number of conservation and civic organizations, led by the VNPA, had publicly endorsed the park, and public opinion polls showed a majority in favor of a park for Minnesota. It had become a popular issue and was embraced by major Republican Party officials across the state except those in the Eighth Congressional District of northeastern Minnesota. Many Democrats in the same district, especially on the Iron Range, were less than enthusiastic about supporting the park. In spite of growing popularity of the park proposal, much needed to be accomplished. The procedures for establishing a park were not well understood by the general public, and even public officials, who would eventually play a role in the process, were not well informed on the mechanics and sequence of actions required to get park legislation through the legislative process. There also seemed to be a lack of knowledge about national park management policies and the historical traditions and precedents that caused some of these policies to become absolute requirements for national park designation. Matters relating to land tenure and public access to land and water areas in the proposed park were not clear. And of course there was formidable opposition to even the mention of a national park anywhere in the region but particularly in the northeastern part of the state where the park would be located. For some, a national park in this part of the state was unthinkable.

The LeVander administration realized that "gray" areas had to be removed before some could endorse the park and before the larger public could have confidence that a national park was not only in the national interest but in the state's interest as well. LeVander wisely determined that the Voyageurs project was so important that it should be managed by staff people in his own office. His predecessor, Karl Rolvaag, had assigned responsibility for the Voyageurs project to Conservation Commissioner Wayne Olson, who resigned in the middle of 1966. After his resignation, the project received only minimal attention. But early in his administration, LeVander moved swiftly to revive the issue. He moved it to "center stage" to help close the information gap regarding the proposal and its economic and political impact, and to seek answers to the many questions—some very complex—that were being raised by opponents and proponents alike. After the governor's commitment to the park on Kabetogama, it was time to work with pro-park organizations and individuals to help build support for the issue, thus forcing the hand of Congressman Blatnik, who would have to introduce and carry the authorizing legislation in the U.S. House.

The responsibility for organizing the effort on Voyageurs and developing an effective strategy for achieving the project's goals fell to the governor's director of research, Archie Chelseth. Between 1967 and 1969, Chelseth helped keep the Voyageurs proposal high on the administration's action agenda. It was Chelseth who took the lead in structuring the successful Virginia workshop that placed the LeVander administration in a leadership position on Voyageurs. It was Chelseth who defined the national issue for the governor, emphasizing the significance of the proposal to the state and the upper Midwest. It was Chelseth who emphasized the political advantage in being out front on what was becoming a popular issue in the state and what he personally felt was one of the most significant natural resource issues in state history.

A few days after LeVander's press conference announcing his endorsement of the park, Chelseth sent the governor a personal letter of congratulations for his action and followed with three memorandums suggesting how he could maintain momentum on the issue. In his letter Chelseth said, "With your announcement Voyageurs has truly come of age," and that he was "convinced that, as our pre-eminent national resource project, the eventual establishment of the Voyageurs National Park will be a lasting tribute to the wise leadership of your administration. I will do what I can to underscore the wisdom of your decision."[53] In the first of three memos, he recommended that Voyageurs be placed at the top of Minnesota's list for recognition and support by the Upper Great Lakes Regional Commission, which was to meet in January 1968. Chelseth reminded the governor that he had publicly endorsed Michigan Governor Romney's Sleeping Bear Dunes National Lakeshore proposal and Wisconsin Governor Knowles's proposal for an Apostle Islands National Lakeshore, and that he could now call upon the two governors to "endorse the Voyageurs National Park as an integral part of the three-state upper Great Lakes effort."[54]

A second memorandum contained a suggested list of points that the governor should use in his forthcoming meeting with the Minnesota congressional delegation in Washington, D.C. Anticipating a Blatnik park bill early in 1968, LeVander sought to influence the content of the legislation so that the interests of residents and businesses near the park would be protected. Chelseth's suggestions served the governor well. They identified the concerns of those living and doing business closest to the proposed park and those who used the area for seasonal recreational pursuits. The correspondence urged extension of the park to the southeast to include the top half of the Crane Lake area, adjustment of the proposed boundaries of the park so that resorts on Kabetogama Lake's southwest shore would be excluded, no major increase in federal land ownership, and a year-round national park that guaranteed snowmobiling.

Chelseth also suggested exploring the possibility of direct access to the Kabetogama Peninsula by road, and three additional items, which if included in the legislation, would blunt much of the local opposition:

(1) a request that the NPS explore the adoption of selective timber cutting for management purposes (not commercial harvesting); (2) relaxation of hunting restrictions, at least for a few years, to reduce the size of the deer herd; and (3) retention of state sovereignty over fish management. All of these suggestions, except direct road access to the peninsula, would surface repeatedly during the debate over Voyageurs between 1968 and 1970.[55]

In a third memo to LeVander written shortly after the governor's pledge of support for Voyageurs, Chelseth recommended and the governor approved the creation of an "administrative mechanism for coordinating policy-making and administrative activities within the administration."[56] This five-member interdepartmental committee on Voyageurs was comprised of Chelseth; J. Kimball Whitney, commissioner of economic development; Jarle Leirfallom, conservation commissioner; a representative from the State Planning Agency; and one from the attorney general's office. Chelseth recommended and the governor appointed Whitney chairman of the committee. To facilitate the work of the committee and maintain the focus on the Voyageurs project, the governor, at the suggestion of the committee and several close staff members, appointed Roger Williams to serve under the title of coordinator of the Governor's Interdepartmental Committee on Voyageurs National Park.[57] LeVander's advisers closest to the Voyageurs project believed that Williams, co-author of the Conservation Department's comprehensive report on Voyageurs, was the most knowledgeable person in the administration about the park and possessed the communication skills, training, and personality best suited for the assignment.

With the interdepartmental committee and its coordinator in place, the state administration believed it was in excellent position to respond quickly and effectively to matters relating to the Voyageurs project. In one year, the Voyageurs issue had moved to the preeminent position among the natural resource issues in the state, and the LeVander administration was poised to see the project through to final passage in Congress. The success of the Virginia conference, LeVander's announcement of support for the Kabetogama site in early December, and the successful Washington, D.C., meeting with the Minnesota congressional delegation put Representative Blatnik on the defensive. His "go slow" approach had given the Republican administration in St. Paul the opportunity to be viewed as the leading advocate for a popular statewide cause.

Also, the taking advantage of this opportunity to move the Voyageurs issue to the fore was aided, in no small measure, by Elmer Andersen's strong push for the park in public debate and his indefatigable devotion to the cause for a national park in Minnesota. And it did not hurt that some of his former associates and staff people held key positions inside the LeVander administration.

Andersen, a founding member of the VNPA, encouraged a number of his friends, many of them influential business and professional people, to join the VNPA and work with him to help bring a national park to Minnesota. Many of these individuals had considerable experience in the Minnesota state park movement over many years and were no strangers to dealing with challenging conservation issues. Notable among these were Martin Kellogg, a Twin Cities corporate executive; St. Paul attorney Sam Morgan; St. Paul executive Tom Savage; Hennepin County municipal judge Edwin Chapman, who was the former chairman of the State Parks Council and first president of the VNPA; Fergus Falls physician Dr. Norman Baker; and U. W. Hella, director of Minnesota State Parks.

With full knowledge of Blatnik's deliberate style, as exemplified by his determination for consensus on Voyageurs, Andersen moved to build that consensus as quickly as possible by employing the process that had proved so successful in his battle for the taconite amendment in 1964. On November 9, 1967, he announced the formation of a Citizens Committee for Voyageurs National Park, whose purpose would be to mobilize grassroots support for the park.[58] Leaders of the VNPA said that the citizens committee, operating as an extension of the association, would seek to "identify all elements of support for the Voyageurs proposal and to provide a unified voice for individuals and organizations to express their support."[59] As he did with the taconite amendment campaign, Andersen chose leaders across the socioeconomic spectrum who were highly respected within their communities and in many instances throughout the state.

Dr. Charles W. Mayo agreed to serve as honorary chairman, just as he did for the taconite project, and Duluth attorney Arthur Roberts and Dr. Norman Baker of Fergus Falls served as cochairmen. Baker was a longtime leader on the Minnesota State Parks Council and was familiar with a wide range of park and recreation issues in the state. Rita Shemesh, who served so effectively in the effort for the taconite amendment, was named executive secretary of the Citizens Committee. Due principally to the organizational skill and energy of Shemesh, this organization was operational by mid-January of 1968. In June 1970, just two and one-half years later, over fourteen hundred organizations—civic, political, service, religious, and social—had passed resolutions endorsing Voyageurs National Park on the Kabetogama Peninsula.[60] Most were located in Minnesota, but many were regional and national as well. And most passed their resolutions in response to information and encouragement received from individual members and subcommittees of the Citizens Committee.

As the debate over Voyageurs moved to a new and more intense phase, it was clear that growing public support for the park movement notwithstanding, sentiment against the park was still strong in northeastern Minnesota as evidenced by the following:

- An editorial in the *Duluth News-Tribune* in mid-October 1967 praised the advantages of the multiple-use philosophy and advocated its continuance on the Kabetogama Peninsula. It further noted the large amount of land already under federal ownership and then said, "Surely these areas present possibilities for one or more national parks to fill in the pattern and give Minnesota its share in the system."[61] Whether intended or not, this kind of editorial from the largest newspaper in northeastern Minnesota could only add to the confusion over the park proposal. It would lead the reader to conclude that national parks are available to states as a rightful "share" in the park system, and that in Minnesota's case, one could be designated most anywhere in the federal forest and lake lands of northern Minnesota.

- In what must have been a bitter disappointment to Governor LeVander, the Eighth District Republican Party reaffirmed its opposition to a park on the Kabetogama Peninsula in fall 1968. The seven officers of the Koochiching County Republican Committee submitted their resignations (not accepted by the full committee) as their way of protesting the governor's endorsement of the Kabetogama site, and former speaker of the Minnesota House Ed Chilgren, from Littlefork (southwest of International Falls), saw the Virginia conference as an exercise in futility and "just window dressing" for the governor.

- An editorial in the Iron Range newspaper the *Mesabi Daily News* written just before the Virginia workshop raised the issue of conflicting values between metropolitan (Twin Cities) areas and rural Minnesota. "So, it is not strange that metropolitan citizenry—incited by a type of leadership little concerned about little people in the state's forest areas—should, under the guise of conservation and recreation, plump for a national park in the Kabetogama sector, a goal which, if successful, will limit jobs and opportunities in the communities served by the wood product industries." The editorial concluded by stating that "outland Minnesota should be more than a playground and prey for the metropolitan complex."[62] The sentiments expressed in this editorial mirror those made at public forums in Duluth in the 1890s when proposals were made for national parks in the forest and lake country of northern Minnesota.

• Displaying sharp disagreement with the governor's endorsement of Voyageurs and lacking confidence in his assurances that he would seek to protect the interests of nearby residents in authorizing legislation, the International Falls City Council passed a resolution on December 11, 1967, opposing the proposed park on Kabetogama "until and unless private, individual, business and local governmental interests are adequately protected."[63]

• The Boise Cascade Corporation said that because of Governor LeVander's endorsement of the park, "It has been forced to re-examine its entire position with regard to the maintenance or possible expansion of our Minnesota operations."[64]

• Four weeks after Governor LeVander called for a national park that included the Crane Lake Recreation Area, Supervisor John Wernham of the Superior National Forest restated an opinion first expressed at the Virginia conference that the proposed park should not "invade" the Superior by annexing the Crane Lake area. This time he stated his position in a formal press release that enumerated twelve reasons why this action would not be in the public interest and especially not in the interests of those living adjacent to the proposed park. Wernham emphasized the advantages of multiple-use and sustained-yield management of these lands as a way of continuing what had been a successful policy for many years and one well understood and generally supported by the residents of northeastern Minnesota.

The passage of the Multiple-Use Sustained Yield Act of 1960 formally recognized recreation and fish and wildlife along with the traditional concerns of timber, water, and grazing as management responsibilities of the USFS. The Crane Lake Recreation Area was in harmony with the new management philosophy as expressed in this act and therefore provided the staff of Superior National Forest with what they felt was a strong defense of their position on the Crane Lake issue.[65] To lend emphasis and credibility to the staff's argument for retaining control of the Crane Lake Recreation Area, Supervisor Wernham included two points in his list of twelve that bore directly on the agreement both agencies made in 1963 to cease unilateral actions that changed the jurisdiction of lands of the other agency. Point ten read: "On November 28, 1967, Park Service Director George Hartzog said that the proposed Voyageurs National Park boundaries, which exclude the Crane Lake Recreation Area, are satisfactory and sufficient." This comment from Hartzog was made at the LeVander administration's conference on Voyageurs at Virginia one month earlier. Wernham's last point read: "On May 31, 1967, Secretary of Agriculture Orville L. Freeman said that he would not countenance an invasion of the Superior National Forest by a National Park."[66] The battle to retain the Crane Lake area as an integral part of the Superior National Forest was beginning anew.

CHAPTER SIX

The Introduction of
Voyageurs National Park Legislation

The latter half of the 1960s saw the emergence of an "environmental movement" in the United States as a force for change and reform in the way we regarded and used our natural resources. The movement was gaining in public support and influence, and politicians at state and national levels could no longer regard it as a short-lived phenomenon that would fade as the initial energy and interest waned. The new "environmentalism" seemed all encompassing, touching on a host of issues including alternative energy resources, global population growth, energy resources, air and water quality, and the protection and preservation of our land and water resources.

Many Americans, including supporters of the Voyageurs National Park proposal, believed the NPS was the agency best suited by example and tradition to see to the preservation and interpretation of our finest natural landscapes and ecosystems. For national park supporters, the 1960s was the time to move forward with long-sought projects. Public interest in environmental matters was high, and where parks were concerned, there was a receptive political climate in Washington. This was generally true at the executive level and particularly so in the Department of the Interior, the home of the NPS.

Stewart Udall, who served as secretary of the interior during the Kennedy and Johnson administrations, embarked on an expansionist national park policy during his tenure in the 1960s. His program began under NPS Director Conrad Wirth and continued under Wirth's successor George Hartzog in 1964. Udall wanted a superintendent who shared his vision for change and expansion of the NPS, and Hartzog was that person. Measured by the addition of an extraordinary number of units to the National Park System, the Hartzog years of 1964–72 did indeed reveal a common philosophy between the parks director and the secretary.

At the state level, the LeVander administration was moving aggressively with the Voyageurs proposal as if to take advantage of the new interest in parks and recreation in Washington. The governor's conference on Voyageurs, held in Virginia, Minnesota, was labeled by most participants as informative and useful in understanding the issues surrounding the park proposal. Assigning individuals on his staff to specific responsibilities for the park project was another indication of strong support for the park at the state level. And Elmer Andersen's announcement in November of the formation of the statewide Citizens Committee for Voyageurs National Park was another reason for optimism. It was in this relatively friendly environment that the Voyageurs project moved into another significant phase. Crucial to its success was the introduction of a bill in the next Congress by Eighth District Congressman John Blatnik.

As the Ninetieth Congress prepared for its second session, Congressman Blatnik received a letter from Governor LeVander in which he identified eight points he hoped the congressman would consider in drafting legislation for Voyageurs National Park. He had discussed these items generally with Blatnik in December, but now they were spelled out in greater detail:

1. Extend the proposed park boundaries southeasterly to include the Crane Lake Recreation Area.
2. Keep the twenty-five resorts on the southwest shore of Kabetogama Lake out of the park.
3. Guarantee twelve-month staffing of the park, thereby assuring availability of winter recreation opportunities including snowmobiling.
4. Prevent a major increase in federal land ownership through authorizing legislation. Privately held land should be exchanged or acquired at fair market value, and suitable land exchanges made to ensure adequate timber supply replacement for that lost on the Kabetogama Peninsula.
5. Guarantee private vendors an opportunity to operate concessions within the park.

6. Allow selective timber cutting for management purposes. Relax hunting restrictions for the first few years to reduce the deer herd. Retain state sovereignty over fish management.
7. Insure fair treatment for home owners and cabin owners in the park.
8. Permit private operation of commercial houseboats.[1]

LeVander's letter was sent to all members of the Minnesota congressional delegation. Its timely arrival at the beginning of the second session was a not-so-subtle reminder that the state administration wanted to see movement on the necessary legislation early in the new session. Blatnik's reply to LeVander came quickly, but it was a cautious and guarded response. He told the governor what he had said publicly many times, that he wanted to hear all sides of the issue in hope of working out a sound proposal acceptable to a majority of the people. He said he would not only study LeVander's eight points but also consider other issues as well. He made no reference to a target date for submitting the bill to Congress.[2]

Blatnik's office forwarded LeVander's letter to NPS Director Hartzog for comment. In his reply to the congressman, Hartzog said the NPS agreed with six of LeVander's eight points but could not accept the public hunting provision and the inclusion of the 38,000-acre Crane Lake unit in the proposed park. Hartzog said public hunting was banned under a long-standing policy of Congress, and because of an agreement between the secretaries of the Agriculture and Interior Departments, the NPS had "eliminated the Crane Lake area from our final report on Voyageurs which is near completion."[3] Another of LeVander's points referred to a provision for selective logging for timber management purposes—not commercial harvesting. Hartzog told Blatnik that timber harvesting was an incompatible use in a national park, but the organic act of 1916 creating the NPS did permit cutting to control insects or disease.[4] LeVander's proposal for timber cutting was an effort to placate the Minnesota Timber Producers Association and Boise Cascade. Both were vehemently opposed to the park, because they saw in the park proposal a westerly extension of the no-cut policy already in place in the adjacent BWCA.

The governor's people, mindful of the rising anger often expressed publicly by leaders in the wood products industry, sought to demonstrate the LeVander administration's understanding of the needs of the industry by appealing to the NPS to modify its timber-cutting policy in the proposed park area. Fred Fagergren, Midwest Regional Director, became aware of this concern when he was contacted by Roger Williams and Archie Chelseth, the two men on the governor's staff who carried the greatest responsibility for managing his administration's efforts on the park proposal. They suggested that Minnesota work with the NPS on a cooperative effort at timber management on Kabetogama that could make Voyageurs a proving ground for possible new techniques in the management of natural resources. The NPS, of course, would not set aside the no-logging policy, as Hartzog had stated in his letter to Blatnik earlier that month, and when Blatnik introduced his bill later that summer, it contained no provision for commercial timber operations. The logging issue would arise time and again in subsequent public hearings, but the NPS held fast to its long-standing policy forbidding this activity in national parks. It was obvious even in the early stages of the park movement that Voyageurs would be no exception to that rule.

Blatnik said he continued to look for "consensus" on the Voyageurs issue, but he did little to spur movement toward that goal except offer to hear both sides of the controversy. He made no major speeches on the subject and, except for a meeting with Crane Lake residents in mid-1970, held no public hearings devoted solely to the park issue. So the VNPA and its newly formed Citizens Committee for Voyageurs National Park and the park committee working out of the governor's office assumed the task of generating support for the proposed park and, in their view, moving the issue closer to the consensus Blatnik sought.

Rita Shemesh, who led the campaign for the taconite amendment in 1964, was named executive secretary of the VNPA and its Citizens Committee. She devoted the early weeks of the committee's existence to developing a strategy and building an organization whose mission would be to inform the public about the proposal for a national park in Minnesota and what its members could do to help promote the cause. Informed by previous experience in such campaigns, she concentrated her efforts on the members, and especially the leadership, of a whole range of organizations and clubs in Minnesota—social, political, professional, conservation, service, and religious. The basic objective of the Citizens Committee was to secure formal resolutions of support for Voyageurs from as many organizations as possible. Committee members would contact officers and members of an organization requesting an opportunity to present the case for the park, show a film highlighting the scenic beauty of the Kabetogama area, and distribute literature explaining the national park proposal and why it was in the national and state interest to preserve this area. In addition they would provide information about the NPS, bring the membership of clubs and organizations up to date on the status of the campaign, show how their club or organization could help, and then provide them with a sample resolution endorsing the official NPS proposal for Voyageurs. When a group formally adopted a supporting resolution, its name was added to the growing list of clubs and organizations that had taken similar action.

Members of the Citizens Committee were also urged to get local media to make public the endorsing action of a local club, thereby gaining additional positive publicity for the park. Shemesh's office would prepare frequent progress reports on the campaign in the form of press releases for daily and weekly newspapers across the state as well as radio and television outlets in the larger population centers. As the list of endorsements grew longer, awareness of the opportunity to secure a national park for Minnesota expanded across the state. In eight months, the list grew to 330 with representatives from a variety of interest groups in all parts of the state, as illustrated by the following sample: Minnesota AAA, Minnesota Conservation Federation, Republican State Executive Committee, Worthington Gun Club, Fairmont Teamsters Local 487, Little Falls American Legion Post 46, Minnesota Council of Churches, Rainy Lake Boosters Club, St. Paul Rotary Club, and so on.

Conducting an intensive statewide campaign even with a small paid staff and many volunteers was a much more expensive venture than the VNPA had anticipated. Dues for membership in the Citizens Committee were deliberately kept low (two dollars) to encourage broad participation in the program. Therefore, the larger sums required to cover operational costs had to be secured through major fund-raising efforts separate from the membership program. To accomplish this objective, the VNPA turned primarily to the business and professional community in the Twin Cities metropolitan area. Members of this group had already taken the lead in the formation of the VNPA and sustained it with their leadership abilities and commitment to its objectives.

Shemesh, experienced in matters of fund-raising and certainly knowledgeable as to the "giving" potential of this group, proceeded to name a finance committee headed by two prominent Twin Cities businessmen,

Wheelock Whitney and Wallace Dayton. The Whitney-Dayton strategy was to arrange a series of "power lunches" hosted by prominent metro citizens. These hosts would invite prospective donors to a luncheon that was always followed by an informational program explaining the park proposal. The presentation explained why preserving this segment of the border lakes region would be a sound conservation move in the state and national interest, the economic benefits to the state, who the principal opponents were and why they were opposed to the park, and how the funds they were soliciting would be used in the campaign for Voyageurs. The host would also report on the substantial progress the Citizens Committee had already made in generating public support for the park.

This method, which was certainly not unfamiliar to those invited, was successful in raising a substantial amount of money to keep the campaign moving. The finance committee also used letters signed by Whitney and Dayton that made direct appeals for contributions from individuals, corporations, and foundations. In one letter they said, "We are asking you, your organization or foundation, to contribute from $500–$3,000 to help finance this citizen effort during the critical weeks ahead."[5] The response to these fund-raising exercises was sufficient to provide the kind of support that was absolutely essential in sustaining the expanding role of the Citizens Committee in its effort to increase public knowledge about the park. Not all of the funding for the Voyageurs campaign came from the business community in the Twin Cities area. Successful fund-raisers were held in Duluth, and significant financial support came from individuals across the state. But the fact remains that the fiscal support coming out of the Twin Cities area was absolutely crucial to the success of the Citizens Committee campaign, especially in northeastern Minnesota.

One section of the state that the VNPA and its Citizens Committee focused on in their campaign to win support for the park was Blatnik's Eighth Congressional District. Their strategy was to develop a strong Citizens Committee chapter in the Duluth area, the largest population center in the district. In early March, Edwin Chapman, president of the VNPA, went to Duluth to meet with the newly organized chapter and to review plans for promoting the park in northeastern Minnesota. Chapman noted the strong support for the park in the Twin Cities area, where the committee was successful in getting numerous endorsements for the park in just the first two months of its existence. Also, the extensive media coverage of the park controversy, including numerous supporting editorials in the *Minneapolis Tribune*, helped sway public opinion in favor of the park. Public opinion polls consistently showed the park to be popular in the metro area. Chapman said what was needed was a similar aggressive effort in the Duluth area, dedicated to winning converts to the park cause. That, he said, could be accomplished by following the methods and procedures worked out by Shemesh and the VNPA executive committee for the newly organized Citizens Committee.

In contrast to the Twin Cities area, experience showed that the Duluth chapter would get no assistance from the Duluth media or the local chamber of commerce. Quite the opposite was true for the Minneapolis–St. Paul area where the press was generally supportive of the park. In the case of Minneapolis, the chamber had taken the lead in organizing the VNPA several years before and was openly aggressive in its support of the park proposal.[6] It was a "consensus building" campaign that helped convince Congressman Blatnik that Voyageurs was indeed a popular cause even in his own district.[7]

The Duluth chapter of the Citizens Committee was the largest of those formed in outstate Minnesota. It lobbied state, local, and county elected officials, made numerous public presentations explaining the park proposal, secured new supporting members, wrote and encouraged others to write letters to Blatnik urging legislative action, and most important of all, secured resolutions of support from a wide range of organizations across the Eighth District.

To measure the impact of the campaign in northeastern Minnesota, the VNPA engaged a professional polling organization to conduct an opinion poll in the Eighth District in late May 1968. The results showed that only 21 percent opposed the park on the Kabetogama Peninsula. Sixty-one percent favored it, and 17 percent were undecided.[8] This remarkable show of support for the park was due to the work of the Duluth and International Falls chapters of the Citizens Committee and, in no small measure, to the tireless efforts of Shemesh, who coordinated the statewide effort. Those who worked closely with her on this campaign marveled at her energy and enthusiasm for the task. In addition to the newsletters, press releases, and more formal communications originating in her office, she would often send the volunteers personal handwritten notes thanking them for their devotion to the campaign and stressing the importance of their individual effort in moving the campaign toward its goal—a national park for Minnesota. Also, many editors and politicians received letters exhorting them to actively support the proposed park, and she never forgot to thank them—if they responded favorably to her request.

In early spring 1968, Bill Krueger, the most influential radio and television commentator in the Duluth area, acknowledged in two editorials the success the Citizens Committee was having statewide in obtaining a greater consensus for the national park. He also added that despite the opposition from Boise Cascade and some resorts, "we will have the park on the peninsula. We cannot hope to have unanimity on this matter." In his April editorial he said it was time for Congressman Blatnik to proceed with authorizing legislation.[9] This was as close to a media endorsement of Voyageurs the public in the Duluth area would ever see or hear during all of the years of debate over the park issue. This, despite the wide-ranging support shown by many citizens and organizations including one of the region's most influential sportsmen's organizations—the United Northern Sportsmen.

The sportsmen club's study committee headed by E. C. Pearson and Anton Sterle prepared a position paper on the proposed park, which the club approved on February 13, 1968.[10] The report was a thoroughly documented thirty-page review of the NPS proposal. The report's particular value lay in its analysis of issues related to establishment and management of the park. Topics such as land acquisition, wildlife management, timber resources, water levels on the four large lakes, and use of aircraft in the park were presented along with identification of opposing opinions and suggestions for the most effective ways to meet the challenges posed by each. In retrospect, one of the most valuable parts of the report dealt with the subject of land acquisition. The complexities of existing land ownership were identified along with a review of proposals already advanced for bringing the land under federal ownership should the park be authorized. One method cited in the report was outright purchase at fair market value along with the observation that with congressional passage of the Land and Water Conservation Fund (LWCF) in 1964, this method quickly became an effective way to acquire new park lands.[11] The LWCF legislation provided funds to states for the planning, acquisition, and development of recreation resources as well as monies to finance new federal recreation lands. The fund's popularity increased in ensuing years when amendments to the legislation brought more direct assistance to local units of government.

In recalling some of the timely and valuable contributions in the quest for authorization of Voyageurs, Elmer Andersen said that the United Northern Sportsmen's report was a remarkable and timely piece of research. It was completed just a few months before the first Voyageurs bill was introduced, and it came from a highly respected sportsmen's group in Congressman Blatnik's own district.[12]

In early 1968, the United Northern Sportsmen Club's report, a growing number of organizational endorsements for the park, and fresh opinion polls with positive support for the park all pointed toward greater public awareness and backing for a national park on the Kabetogama Peninsula. But whatever encouragement park supporters could take with these gains in public approval, it was soon tempered by the unexpected, spirited opposition to Governor LeVander's call for inclusion of the Namakan-Crane Lakes area in the proposed park.

Commonly referred to as the "Crane Lake Addition," it included most of Namakan and Sand Point Lakes along with lands adjacent to those lakes. It was what the USFS called their Crane Lake Recreation Area—a property they had successfully kept out of the official NPS proposal after a bitter interagency dispute in 1963–64. There was almost no public knowledge of that argument. This time, however, the USFS would have to "go public" with their case, and they were determined to make a convincing argument for keeping it under multiple-use management. They realized that Congress would determine the fate of their recreation area if Blatnik included the Crane Lake Recreation Area in his legislation. They saw little hope of stopping the transfer at that level. Their best hope was to build such strong local opposition to the loss of the property that the congressman would change his mind. For too many years the USFS had watched many of its prime scenic areas disappear into adjacent national parks. Therefore, to secure these areas they gave them special recreation or preservation status, hoping thereby to preclude their transfer to the NPS. Such was the case with the Crane Lake Recreation Area, which was formally established in 1966.[13]

The Superior National Forest staff, through its supervisor, John Wernham, argued vigorously for retention of the Crane Lake Recreation Area. In an address before service clubs in Ely, Minnesota, in the fall of 1968, Wernham defended the ability of the USFS to manage prime forest recreation lands and offered a challenge to the NPS. He said retention of the Crane Lake area under USFS management would afford the "opportunity to compare areas with similar terrain, vegetation, and wildlife when managed by practices applied to National Parks, Wilderness Areas (BWCA), Recreation Areas (Crane Lake) and forest lands in other ownerships. We would have an opportunity here to determine for future generations what should be the management practices for forest recreation lands."[14] This proposal, credited to Frank Kaufert, dean of the School of Forestry at the University of Minnesota, was a response to a long-standing insult, felt by some foresters who contended that the NPS arrogantly assumed "they alone recognized and appreciated higher social and spiritual values inherent in natural things."[15] Throughout the ensuing debate, the USFS continued to defend their management standards for the Crane Lake Recreation Area and urged that it be kept out of the proposed national park. The highest officials of the USFS forcefully made their case at all of the congressional hearings on the park. For example, in testimony at the hearings before the House Committee on Interior and Insular Affairs in July 1970, USFS Deputy Chief John McGuire said that under USFS management the Crane Lake Recreation Area "will create an opportunity for the Forest Service to blend the management of the Superior National Forest with the new park in a way that will maximize the public benefits that can be realized from the boundary water region. We are anxious to share our long experience in dealing with protection and public use of the resources that characterize this area."[16]

LeVander's call for inclusion of the Crane Lake Recreation Area was just as unpopular with the resorts and business community of Crane Lake as it was with the USFS. The vehemence of the Crane Lake community's opposition as expressed through its commercial club was a surprise to the LeVander people. Anticipating some opposition, LeVander proposed a boundary that would be drawn along the north shore of Crane Lake, thereby excluding the resorts and business activity along the south and west shores. But when the governor's coordinator for Voyageurs, Roger Williams, met with Crane Lake residents to discuss the park proposal, he found that they did not want *any* of the Crane Lake area included in the park proposal. They were satisfied with USFS management of the recreation area and were opposed to a park policy that would eliminate hunting and timber harvesting. They also feared that a national park would bring in too many people, thus discouraging their traditional clientele, who liked the uncrowded aspects of the area. And they were concerned that the park would encourage greater private and commercial development on the Canadian side of the boundary lakes.

Williams said that Crane Lake residents thought it "ridiculous to build a quality park facility on one side of the border, while allowing private take-over on the other side."[17] When Robert Congdon, president of the Crane Lake Commercial Club, testified at the Washington hearings in July 1970, he spoke again of the same concerns about Canadian development that Williams had reported in 1968. No mention was ever made by the Crane Lake representatives that the Midwest Regional Office of the NPS had been given assurances by the Ontario government that they would cooperate with the United States through appropriate land management regulations on the Canadian side should the park be authorized.[18]

The park movement now had two more adversaries, the USFS and the Crane Lake community. Both were openly courting public opinion with their opposition to the Crane Lake addition and in an indirect manner threatening to slow up the movement for the park. Only a few of the active proponents at that time were aware of the original and unpublished 1963 NPS proposal calling for a park extending from Crane Lake to near International Falls on Rainy Lake, and they were not aware of the protracted dispute between the USFS and the NPS over the inclusion of the Crane Lake area in that proposal. Most supporters came into the park movement in 1966, and by far the greatest number joined the effort after the formation of the Citizens Committee in December 1967. They were committed to supporting the official NPS proposal on the Kabetogama Peninsula. All of the campaign literature referred to the park on that site. When it became apparent that the controversy over the proposed inclusion of the Crane Lake Recreation Area could interfere with the primary goal, leaders in the VNPA and Citizens Committee were instructed to stay out of the Crane Lake dispute altogether. The official position of the VNPA was to support the NPS proposal, which described a park on the Kabetogama Peninsula. If the Crane Lake addition came up while promoting the park at a public meeting, the correct response was to simply say, "If Crane Lake is to be included in Voyageurs Park, Congress will have to add it."

When Blatnik was approached by a *Minneapolis Tribune* reporter in mid-February 1968, he was asked when he expected to introduce legislation on Voyageurs. He replied, "around Easter." He acknowledged support for the park in his district was growing, but he was still concerned about what he called the major remaining issue, "negotiations on an agreement for land exchanges to compensate timber interests, principally Boise Cascade Corporation, for loss of major holdings on the peninsula."[19] He said that the state was responsible for these negotiations. The same article said that Blatnik favored incorporation of Crane Lake into the park, and that he had suggested this to Governor LeVander before the governor convened the Virginia conference in November. He saw Crane Lake as an issue but one that could be resolved by Congress. He knew that Secretary of Agriculture Freeman would have to oppose transfer of U.S. forest land to the Interior Department to accomplish the addition of Crane Lake. Secretary Freeman would "have to bow to that determination."[20] What he apparently did not realize at the time was that the Crane Lake community was adamantly opposed to the inclusion and that they were gearing up for a battle to keep it from happening. It was the kind of confrontation Blatnik disliked most—constituents openly and aggressively opposing him on a local issue.

As spring came to the northland in 1968, opposition to the park was most evident at the geographic extremities of the proposed park: Rainy Lake and Kabetogama on the northwest, and Crane Lake on the southeast. In the northwest, stiffening opposition came from local residents and second-home owners regarding the proposed federal control of the Kabetogama Peninsula to satisfy the wishes of "outsiders." And the gnawing land exchange question with Boise Cascade remained to be resolved. In the southeast the resistance to the Crane Lake addition advocated by Governor LeVander and Blatnik triggered angry responses from the USFS and the community at Crane Lake. The latter, a proud and independent resort community, could see no economic advantages to a national park at their back door. The USFS, through its supervisory staff at the Superior, served notice that it would aggressively resist efforts to transfer the Crane Lake Recreation Area to the NPS.

The Crane Lake area was not the only place where the USFS had to oppose potential loss of a chunk of its acreage to satisfy the objectives of an NPS project. In 1968 territorial losses threatened national forests in two western states where new national park proposals were nearing the final stages of congressional review: Redwood in California, and North Cascades in Washington. Congress authorized both parks in fall 1968. In testimony at the Redwood hearing, Secretary Freeman strenuously opposed using USFS lands in the Redwood Purchase Unit "as trading stock to acquire private timberlands within Redwood National Park." At the same hearing he testified that some of those who proposed a Voyageurs National Park in Minnesota were suggesting a raid on the Superior National Forests—in aid of the project. "We will continue to resist all efforts, large or small, to put National Forest lands on the trading block to bargain away the resistance of private timberland owners whose lands are needed for important public programs."[21] When Roger Williams read this testimony, he immediately sent out a memo to members of his committee, saying, "We have been discussing exchange of Boise lands for Forest Service lands within the Kabetogama Purchase Unit. It becomes obvious that the Forest Service will object vigorously to any proposal involving their lands whether they are located inside or outside a Forest Boundary."[22] In the same memorandum, Williams emphasized Blatnik's reluctance to introduce park legislation until the state "negotiates" the land exchange issue with Boise Cascade. Williams said that moves were under way to resolve the land exchange question and that to facilitate discussions with Boise, the state Division of Lands and Forestry had prepared three alternative exchange proposals that would soon be ready for presentation to Boise officials.

Working out a land exchange agreement whereby forest lands outside the proposed park would be exchanged for Boise lands on the Kabetogama Peninsula had been on the state's agenda beginning with the Rolvaag administration in 1965. The M&O Company owned almost 46 percent of the land proposed for the new park, and there was always hope that an acceptable plan could be worked out when the paper industry was still under the control of the M&O Company. However, some time before Boise officially assumed control of its M&O subsidiary and certainly after the merger, the company's position hardened on the subject of land exchange. There had been no movement on this issue in three years. The task of developing workable exchange proposals by the Division of Lands and Forestry was not made easier by Freeman's opposition to the use of USFS lands as "trading stock," and as Conservation

Commissioner Leirfallom discovered in the first week of June 1968, Boise officials were not interested in looking at *any* proposals from the LeVander administration.

Boise Cascade's firm policy against reviewing any land exchange proposals coming from the LeVander administration was explained with great candor in a June 4 meeting that Commissioner Leirfallom held with Boise's Woodlands Manager, George Amidon. Leirfallom had requested the meeting in hopes of opening the lines of communication with Boise and getting them to study the state's new exchange proposals. When he returned to his office in St. Paul, Leirfallom dictated a memorandum summarizing his conversation with Amidon.[23] The memo reveals just how far apart the governor's office and Boise Cascade were on the Voyageurs issue at that time.

The documentation of this question shows that from early 1965 onward there never was a time when land exchanges between Boise and the state or federal governments were possible. Some of the points made by Amidon during this meeting support this observation:

- Boise Cascade was not happy with the LeVander administration's performance on matters relating to the timber industry.
- Former Governor Elmer Andersen was unreasonably antagonistic and unfair (to the company), and they were concerned about the extent to which he represented the administration's ideas.
- From 1962–65 the M&O had been cooperative and participated in possible exchange discussions. However, after the Freeman directive expanding the no-cut zone around the BWCA, the company backed off from further discussions, feeling that they had been misled. (Boise Cascade took over the M&O in 1965.)
- Freeman's action was an indication that wilderness groups were running hog wild. Therefore, Boise Cascade refused to discuss with Wayne Olson, congressional representatives, and other politicians any exchanges that tended to put Boise into agreement with wilderness devotees and preservationists with whom they did not agree. They would have to take the same attitude with the proposed exchange proposals coming from the LeVander administration.

During the course of the meeting, Leirfallom sought to assure Amidon that the governor was vitally interested in the property of the timber industry and suggested that Boise's interests would be better served by "maintaining a constructive dialogue" with the state administration and other parties concerned. Perhaps as a way of revealing to Amidon that not everyone in the LeVander administration thought the same way on Voyageurs, he told Amidon that he himself had to acknowledge that "a lot of these park experts are short on practical knowledge of the area." He was referring to some of the not-so-pleasant weather, the swamps, mosquitoes, wood ticks, and so on that park visitors would encounter. In this memorandum and other documents and in discussions with LeVander staff people working on the Voyageurs project, the commissioner left some doubt about his own enthusiasm for the Voyageurs project.[24]

Boise Cascade's reluctance to even discuss land exchange proposals with public officials was well known among the leading advocates of the park. Some supporters eventually came to see this as part of Boise's strategy to defer introduction of enabling legislation. Boise also noticed that Blatnik, who had made the exchange agreement a precondition before submitting his park legislation, always placed the blame for the lack of a land exchange agreement squarely on the LeVander administration, and this was contributing to increased tension between Blatnik and the governor. Andersen and other VNPA leaders thought Blatnik's insistence on a resolution of the exchange question before submitting his park bill was unrealistic. Andersen expressed this concern in a letter to NPS Director Hartzog in mid-April 1968: "I believe there is a time when you agree on the policy of a matter and a later time when you work out all the details. I do not believe Boise Cascade is ever going to agree on any program but will seek to feed questions to Blatnik that could keep this in study and report form for a long time. I believe Representative Blatnik is sincere, but I also believe he is exceedingly conscious of any opposition and sensitive to it, where what is needed at this point is some courageous leadership. That is why I get a little impatient, but do my best to restrain it."[25]

Representative Blatnik hoped to introduce his Voyageurs legislation at about the same time the NPS released its new park plan, a revision of the 1964 draft plan. Blatnik told a reporter in February that he might be submitting his bill around Easter time, and in a telephone conversation sometime in March, Hartzog told Andersen that the NPS would be ready with its plan by May 15. However, when Andersen picked up his April 5 *Minneapolis Tribune* and saw that the release date had been set back to sometime in June, he was astounded. He began making telephone calls to Washington, D.C., and Omaha, trying to reach Director

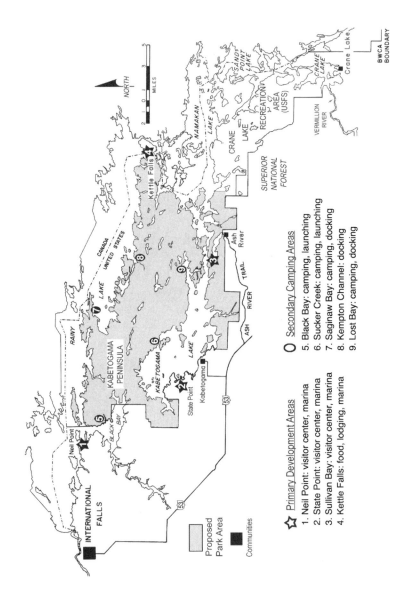

Primary Development Areas

☆ Primary Development Areas

1. Neil Point: visitor center, marina
2. State Point: visitor center, marina
3. Sullivan Bay: visitor center, marina
4. Kettle Falls: food, lodging, marina

○ Secondary Camping Areas

5. Black Bay: camping, launching
6. Sucker Creek: camping, launching
7. Saginaw Bay: camping, docking
8. Kempton Channel: docking
9. Lost Bay: camping, docking

Proposed Park Area

Communities

Master plan for proposed Voyageurs National Park, 1968. Most of the elements in this plan were included in a draft plan in 1965, which was then withdrawn by Interior Secretary Udall at the request of Congressman John Blatnik, who wanted a plan that featured public recreation use. This 1968 master plan emphasized, in considerable detail, public access and recreational opportunities in all seasons.

Hartzog and Regional Director Fagergren, but with no success. He finally reached John Kawamoto, the park planner who had been closest to the Voyageurs project since it was launched. Kawamoto explained that the delay was related to the director's decision to present the final report in a master plan format, and this would require more time.[26] Hartzog's shift to a master plan format was actually caused by Blatnik's dissatisfaction with the NPS's already prepared draft plan—the plan Udall had to pull back at Blatnik's request in 1965. The congressman thought it too general and superficial. He wanted the text and illustrations in the plan to emphasize public use. He was determined to reassure the opposition at home that once the park was established, it was not going to be "locked up." This was a not-so-subtle reference to the opinion held by many local residents concerning the management restrictions of the adjacent BWCA. Kawamoto, assigned to help put the 1968 plan together in its final form, said that the NPS had never intended to adopt the management policy of the canoe country wilderness. Nevertheless, as a way of guaranteeing that the plan would meet his conditions, Blatnik requested that the NPS planners work out revisions and details of the plan in his office.[27]

The 1968 plan was a revision of the NPS's 1965 draft plan with alterations to meet the congressman's conditions. It was designated a master plan and was completed in a two-week period by park planners working in daily sessions with Jim Oberstar, Blatnik's administrative assistant. Reflecting on this assignment ten years later, Kawamoto said in a tactful manner that it was not a career highlight for him, and it was "kind of a strange way of writing a master plan."[28] The plan, through its text, large-scale maps, and photographs, described and emphasized a park with year-round activities for the visitor. The use of motorized watercraft, deemed essential on the three large lakes in the park, would be encouraged, and the plan mentioned the use in winter of "over-snow equipment as appropriate when used on existing roads, designated trails and frozen lakes."[29] Kawamoto would say later that in the end when the plan was released, it had the concurrence of Blatnik, who had no objections to any part of the plan.[30]

Long experience as a legislator taught Congressman Blatnik that timing was extremely important when introducing legislation. In this instance, he wanted the NPS to release its master plan recommending a Voyageurs National Park, minus the Crane Lake area, of course. He would follow a little later with a meeting at Crane Lake to explain to the community the reasoning behind his intent to add the area to the proposed park. Blatnik's office alerted the rest of the Minnesota delegation of his intentions.

The date for the master plan release was to be July 2, and the legislation would follow on July 9. However, both events had to be rescheduled when Blatnik learned that his plan had been leaked and reported in press accounts in Minnesota. Those opposed to the park, including the Crane Lake Commercial Club, went into action to generate even more opposition, especially to Blatnik's intention to include most of the Crane Lake Recreation Area in his park bill. His carefully drawn timetable had to be revised, providing even more time for opposition forces to organize against the park.[31]

Public knowledge of his legislative intent and particularly the angry response at Crane Lake drew a charge from Blatnik that placed the blame on Governor LeVander for the Crane Lake uprising by "failing to do his homework with property owners at Crane Lake."[32] He either did not know or would not acknowledge the fact that Williams, LeVander's point man on Voyageurs, had met with Crane Lake residents several times since the first of the year regarding the proposed Crane Lake addition. Nor did he acknowledge that including the Crane Lake area was a suggestion he himself had made to the governor in late fall 1967. However, he acknowledged, to his staff if not publicly, that to get his park legislation on track again he would have to meet with the Crane Lake community as soon as possible. He said he wanted to pay the Crane Lake people the courtesy of talking to them before he submitted his bill. To that end he asked his staff to schedule a meeting at Crane Lake for July 13, when he could make the case for his position and cool things down before submitting his bill on the new date, July 19.

To keep the LeVander administration and Congressman Blatnik's office together on the Crane Lake issue, Williams sent a letter on July 11 to Jim Oberstar, reaffirming the state's position on Crane Lake and urging him to review the matter with Blatnik "to ensure a consensus between your office and the state administration prior to our discussion with Crane Lake residents this weekend."[33]

Representative Blatnik's meeting with the Crane Lake Commercial Club took place on Sunday, July 14. The congressman, in defending his plan to include the Namakan-Crane Lakes area, said it would provide a much greater range of activities for park visitors, help preserve more of the voyageurs route in the border lakes region between Canada and the United States, provide access to the park from the east, and help business by bringing more visitors to the Crane Lake community. He also stressed that the park boundaries he and the governor were proposing would exclude all but four of the twenty-nine resorts in the community. Before leaving the meeting, Blatnik said he would try to reduce the total acreage planned for inclusion from 38,233 acres to about 34,000. However, he remained firm in his resolve to include this area in his legislation. When the commercial club took a vote on the question the next day, 165 were opposed and only 14 were in support of the park with the Namakan-Crane Lakes addition. When the same group was asked about the NPS proposal for a park on Kabetogama *without* the Crane Lake addition, the results were essentially the same.[34]

Representative Blatnik did not fare any better when he met the same day with members from the Northland Multiple Use Association and the Minnesota Arrowhead Association in International Falls. Both groups consistently opposed the park on Kabetogama, and at this meeting they urged Blatnik to delay submission of his bill until the state legislature had an opportunity to examine alternative management schemes involving St. Louis and Koochiching Counties. But Blatnik held his ground and told the group that he would introduce his bill when he returned to Washington, and that if he delayed much longer someone or maybe all other members of the Minnesota delegation would introduce park legislation anyway.[35]

In making this observation of the inevitability of Voyageurs legislation, Blatnik was tacitly recognizing the growing popular support for Voyageurs across the state. He knew that his colleagues were hearing from constituents who wanted explanations for the delay. One can also be certain that other members of the Minnesota delegation knew full well that Blatnik was not going to be upstaged on this issue and that he would act in the face of growing local opposition. Even the *International Falls Daily Journal,* certainly not an advocate for the park, recognized in an editorial Blatnik's courage in facing such strong opposition to the park: "Excluding declarations of war, perhaps no issue has ever exerted more pressures on a congressman than those on Eighth District Congressman Blatnik during the past four years of the Voyageurs National Park controversy. It must be said, to Blatnik's credit, that he held off introduction of the bill as long as he possibly could to allow study and a consensus within his district."[36] True to his promise, Blatnik introduced his first Voyageurs bill on July 19, 1968. The *Minneapolis Tribune* noted the occasion with the headline, "Voyageurs Park Proposal Ends Turbulent Ride to the Potomac."[37]

Blatnik's 1968 Voyageurs bill entered the legislative stream less than four months before the fall elections. He realized that there would be no opportunity for hearings in the closing weeks of the Ninetieth Congress and therefore noted in his preliminary remarks that his bill would expire at the end of the year and would have to be reintroduced in the new Congress. "This will give people an opportunity to suggest further modifications, and of course there can be changes within reason." He also said that for the first time the public would have a "definite proposal describing the features of the park, and setting forth terms and conditions under which the park would be established by law."[38]

Among the provisions in the bill were a number of what Blatnik called "safeguards." These were intended to minimize "any adverse effects" caused by the new park for local residents. They included all of LeVander's eight points. Among other things, the safeguards provided for hunting and trapping, boundary placement to exclude almost all of the private resorts bordering the park, and reimbursement to the two affected counties for any loss of tax revenue due to federal land acquisition. LeVander and Blatnik were deeply concerned over the bitter feelings emerging from the controversy over Voyageurs and sought to mollify the local opposition by including provisions in the legislation that they surely knew were not permitted in national parks. These conditions continued to appear in the text of the legislation used at the field hearings in 1969 and the Washington, D.C., hearings in 1970. Most disappeared in the conference committee report of the final bill sent to President Richard M. Nixon in January 1971.

Local residents who read about the safeguards in their local newspapers and heard them mentioned and discussed at public hearings were no doubt reassured when Blatnik included them in his legislation. Later, when the final version of the authorizing legislation dropped the hunting, trapping, and payments in lieu of taxes provisions and the NPS began to administer the park on the basis of the authorizing legislation, some accused the federal government of misleading them.

Much was made of LeVander's eight points and Blatnik's safeguards by the originators of the measures themselves. Blatnik and LeVander frequently made references to "protecting the interests" of local residents by their carefully drawn legislation. However, the NPS could never accept public hunting, commercial logging, or payments to local districts in lieu of taxes in legislation for Voyageurs or any other national park. Of course, the call for inclusion of the Crane Lake Recreation Area was off-limits (even though many in the NPS knew it would be a better park with that area included) because of the interdepartmental agreement. Even in the face of Director Hartzog's declaration that hunting, logging, and the tax provision could never be accepted by the NPS, they continued to appear in succeeding revisions of the legislation. It is not surprising that many residents in northeastern Minnesota, especially those nearest the park, would come to the conclusion that they had been deceived. More than twenty years after the park was established one can still hear this claim in communities near the park.

Adding the Crane Lake Recreation Area seriously complicated efforts to move the park proposal forward. Local residents now had another reason to oppose the park, and for many, it confirmed their suspicions that this was simply a land grab by the federal government. Actually most of the added land and water area was already under the control of a federal agency, the USFS. For many residents, a greater concern centered on the policies and procedures the park would employ in the acquisition of private property if the park became a reality. These were stated for the first time in official form in Blatnik's initial Voyageurs legislation on July 19, five days after his meeting with residents at Crane Lake. In conversation with several residents of communities bordering the park long after the park was formally established, I learned that questions about private property acquisition arose early and continued long after the park was established when acquisition began. The events surrounding the land acquisition process remain bad memories for some in these communities. For example, local businesses that depended on seasonal purchases of supplies from cabin owners and resort owners saw revenue decline as the buyouts began.[39]

The VNPA board did not take an official position on the Crane Lake addition, but they were surprised by the intensity of the opposition expressed by the Crane Lake community. Some thought the addition was a bad idea and agreed with the editorial board of the *Minneapolis Star,* who said that taken together with positions held by other opponents, the entire project was in danger. "It seems to us that the big question is whether or not the inclusion of the Crane Lake tract jeopardizes the chances for passage of a Voyageurs bill. Crane Lake people seem strongly opposed to the enlargement. If they and other opponents are potent enough to defeat a bill in Congress then the NPS proposal would seem the wiser course."[40]

CHAPTER SEVEN

The Reintroduction of Park Legislation

When Congressman Blatnik submitted his Voyageurs National Park bill in July 1968, he told the House that no hearings would be held on the bill in that session, but they could expect the legislation to be reintroduced when the new Congress convened in January 1969. In the interim he anticipated public discussion on the merits of the legislation, and he fully expected interested parties to make comments and even suggestions for modifications in the bill. Also, he was not surprised to see opponents and proponents use the time to muster public support for their respective positions.

VNPA Executive Secretary Rita Shemesh wasted no time in bringing her leadership groups together to map a strategy for what she hoped would be the "final push" to get congressional approval for a park on the Kabetogama Peninsula. She began by reserving facilities on Rainy Lake for her September "workshop." Leaders from the VNPA and Citizens Committee were invited along with key members of Governor LeVander's staff, including Archie Chelseth and Roger Williams, the governor's two main advisors on the park project. Shemesh saw the meeting as an opportunity to develop a coordinated plan for the campaign ahead, and she was not disappointed. Buoyed by beautiful fall weather and a boat trip to the historic Kettle Falls Hotel at the eastern end of the peninsula, participants were eager to exchange ideas and specifics on ways to generate more popular support for the park. They left the session with certain knowledge of the support and cooperation of the governor's office and confidence in the organization's leadership. This meeting was the only time during the entire Voyageurs campaign that so many VNPA board members and Citizens Committee people came together for planning and motivational sessions.

Several times during the Rainy Lake meeting the point was made that with park legislation before Congress, the VNPA should consider expanding its effort from one that concentrated its energy at the state level to one that also recognized the need to build support nationally. This matter was given rather serious consideration at the November meeting of the VNPA board. The VNPA newsletter reported in its December 1968 issue that "the Executive Committee was asked by Board resolution to explore the possibilities of expanding the present Voyageurs National Park Association to a Voyageurs National Park Association of America."[1]

When Elmer Andersen learned that a national organization was under study, he cautioned against such a move. In a letter to board member Lloyd Brandt, he said, "the VNPA as now constituted is excellent from a corporate standpoint," to carry out its most important assignment.[2] Andersen reasoned that the association was properly positioned to carry out its *primary mission*, which was to build solid support for the park in Minnesota, especially in Congressman Blatnik's Eighth District. In deference to Andersen's experience in these matters, and because of the heavy monetary cost required to mount a national effort, the VNPA board dropped the matter. It decided instead to seek the endorsement of nationally recognized conservationists, environmental organizations with national memberships, and prominent business, professional, and political leaders.

By mid-1969, the park proposal had received the endorsement of a number of prominent citizens including former Interior Secretary Stewart Udall, Charles Lindbergh, and radio and television personality Arthur Godfrey. Formal endorsements also came from the Sierra Club and the Izaak Walton League. These endorsements were welcome because they brought national attention to the park proposal. But it was critical to the success of the campaign to increase support in the Eighth District. This need was confirmed when Blatnik challenged the VNPA to work harder in Iron Range towns like Hibbing, Virginia, and Chisholm as well as in communities farther north that were closest to the proposed park. He wanted to see more support for the park in these areas to blunt the criticism he was getting for his efforts on behalf of the park. He was convinced that his relatively poor showing in some Iron Range communities in the 1968 elections was directly linked to the controversy over the park.

Archie Chelseth, the governor's closest advisor on Voyageurs, anticipating the coming 1969 session of the state legislature, became concerned that the final thrust for congressional action could be hampered by resolutions and legislation coming from that body. He advised LeVander and his park coordinating committee to discourage both friendly and unfriendly moves on the part of legislators regarding what the state's position should be on the park.[3] For example, when the legislature's most ardent park supporter, Representative Willard Munger, from Duluth, indicated his intent to introduce a resolution memorializing Congress to support Voyageurs, he was quickly discouraged from following through with his intentions. And shortly after Andersen was elected president of the VNPA in February, he instructed the VNPA board in much the same way.

In a letter to Shemesh, Andersen said that the general consensus had been to do nothing to stir up the legislature at the session and give opponents something to talk about.[4] And so the strategy followed by the state administration and the VNPA was to watch for bills deemed harmful to the park cause and with the help of legislators friendly to the initiative, to stop the progress of such legislation. As it turned out, the first serious challenge to the park proposal by state legislators did not come in the form of a piece of legislation but from the activities of one of the state senate's standing committees.

The Senate Public Domain Committee, charged with oversight responsibilities in the management and disposition of state lands (most of them located in the northeastern part of the state) first appeared as a standing committee in the 1963 session. The committee's chair from 1965 until its demise in 1971 was O. A. Sundet, a veteran legislator who represented several agricultural counties south of the Twin Cities. Typically, the chair of a committee plays the dominant role in setting the committee's agenda, the pace of its proceedings, and the general political philosophy of its majority. However, when Voyageurs was the subject of a hearing, it was readily apparent that this was not the case with Sundet's committee. At these sessions another committee member, Senator Ray Higgins, of Duluth, played the dominant role. Higgins left no doubt as to his opposition to the conversion of private lands into public lands, especially if these lands became federal lands managed by an agency whose philosophy and mission were preservation. His testimony at the governor's Virginia workshop sent a clear signal that he would fight the park proposal at every opportunity. For Senator Higgins, the perfect forum for making his case was a public hearing sponsored by the Public Domain Committee.

Senator Higgins firmly believed that persistent inquiry into the ramifications of a national park for northeastern Minnesota was legitimate business for the Public Domain Committee. He maintained that the purpose of the numerous hearings on Voyageurs was to investigate the *state* government's responsibilities in regard to the establishment of the park.[5] For the officers of the VNPA and for NPS personnel, these hearings were often painful sessions. Leaders in the movement for the park often insisted that the hearings were simply "set up to provide a forum for the opponents of the park."[6] Some Public Domain Committee members would take exception to this assertion. But however structured, the hearings actually *did* provide a good opportunity for those opposed to the park to express their views and then see some record of their testimony in the public press, especially in the newspapers in northeastern Minnesota.

The USFS, Timber Producer's Association, Minnesota Arrowhead Association, Northland Multiple Use Association, and Boise Cascade Corporation all took advantage of these opportunities to spell out their positions in a friendly environment. And for Higgins and other legislators opposed to the park and convinced that the Minnesota legislature was being deliberately bypassed on this issue, public hearings in the committee rooms of the legislature as well as at outstate locations provided a forum for an alternative view of the park proposal.

Congressman Blatnik submitted to Congress a revised version of his Voyageurs legislation on April 23, 1969, thus fulfilling a promise made a year earlier when the first bill was introduced. Blatnik's legislation was endorsed by the other seven House members in the Minnesota delegation. In his statement accompanying the reintroduction Blatnik took care to emphasize that "the bill includes a number of important safeguards guaranteed by law to minimize as much as possible any adverse effects upon the people living and working in the area."[7] Among the more controversial safeguards were provisions for trapping and deer and waterfowl hunting until the establishment of the park by the secretary of the interior, an action that often takes two to three years after a park is authorized.

Blatnik declared that federal land ownership in the state would hardly be increased: "The bill opens the door for a three-way private-State-Federal land exchange that would offer Boise Cascade state held timber-land comparable to their present holding within an economical distance from the mill."[8] In stressing the hoped-for three-way land exchange, he was apparently unaware of Boise Cascade's adamant opposition to any land exchange, a position expressed to Commissioner Leirfallom. Or perhaps Blatnik was aware of the paper company's position but wished to stimulate action on the process by including it in his congressional legislation.

In late April 1969, just a few days after Blatnik reintroduced his bill and with little more than a month remaining in the Minnesota Legislature's session for 1969, Senator Higgins and like-minded colleagues in both houses of the legislature submitted two bills that had they passed, would have certainly stalled or perhaps even killed the chances for park approval in the Ninety-first Congress. It was precisely what Chelseth and Andersen had warned about earlier in the year. One bill would have established a seven-member planning commission. A part of the bill, Section 1 of S.F. 2530, in referring to the natural resources of the area, said that the purpose of the legislation was "to develop and coordinate the best utilization of these resources, to avoid irrevocable commitment thereof to any single use and to establish an appropriate policy of multiple resource use." That phrase alone ruled out a national park for the area. A majority of the members (three) of the proposed commission (five) were to be appointed by the two county boards, leaving the governor and the Eighth District congressman with one position each. The legislation also would have required that the Land Exchange Commission, a constitutionally based commission, "could not approve any lease, sale or exchange of public lands without prior review and approval of the boundary commission."[9] This provision targeted land exchanges between the federal government, the state, and private owners. At that time, such exchanges were believed to be essential if the state were to secure a national park.

The second bill called for establishment of an interim commission "to consider the state's responsibilities relating to the possible establishment of a national park."[10] This bill was quickly labeled a harassment measure by park supporters, who remembered that the legislature already had a study group—the Minnesota Resources Commission—and it had studied the Voyageurs proposal and endorsed it twice. Shortly after the two bills were introduced, VNPA president Andersen urged members to contact legislators and encourage them to oppose both bills. Andersen told a group of park supporters at a meeting in Hinckley, Minnesota, that the bills were hastily drafted counter moves to Blatnik's reintroduced legislation and that Governor LeVander had assured both Chelseth and Anderson that if the bills passed, he would veto them.

Leaders in the state legislature judged the two bills as weak, and their introduction near the end of the session did not provide sufficient time for proper study and evaluation. Even Chair Sundet of the Public Domain Committee assured Andersen that the two bills would not go anywhere in the legislature. Shortly before the 1969 session ended, an effort was made by park opponents in the legislature to have the Senate Rules Committee set up an interim study group, a Natural Resources Commission, to study the problems related to establishing Voyageurs and report back to the legislature at its next session. This proposal also failed.

Even though anti-park legislators were unsuccessful in their efforts to move their legislation through the 1969 session, they did succeed in creating a time-consuming diversion for the VNPA. Every meeting of the VNPA board had to assess the progress of the anti-park legislation and make certain that their allies in the legislature were properly informed as to the serious consequences if such legislation passed. The last thing they wanted was the emergence of a hostile state legislature armed with legislation unfriendly to the park just as they were actively promoting park legislation with the new national administration.

Richard Nixon took advantage of a divided Democratic Party in the 1968 fall elections to easily defeat Vice President Hubert Humphrey for the presidency. When Blatnik first introduced his Voyageurs bill in 1968, it was in a Washington political environment that had regularly demonstrated its support for environmental reform and innovation through the legislative process. In the first eight years of the 1960s, the Kennedy and Johnson administrations and Congress supported a number of additions to the national park system. The new areas included Canyonlands, Redwood, and North Cascade National Parks in the West, Indiana Dunes and Pictured Rocks National Lakeshores in the Midwest, and Cape Cod and Cape Lookout National Seashores in the East. Voyageurs supporters had hoped to add their park to that list before the end of the decade. But the results of the fall elections in 1968 raised fears in the ranks of many conservationists across the country that the Nixon administration would be less friendly to new environmental and park legislation.

Apprehensions turned to alarm when they learned that the president would be appointing Walter Hickel, the former governor of Alaska, to be the next secretary of the interior. Legislation for new parks had little chance of congressional passage unless endorsed by the Interior Department. Hickel brought to Washington a record that according to some conservationists, repeatedly favored economic development over conservation and preservation. They cited as an example his request in 1967 that the Interior Department grant an application allowing exploratory drilling for oil in the Arctic Wildlife Range of Alaska.[11] Hickel was nominated to succeed Stewart Udall, who in administering the Interior Department made environmental quality a major concern in matters of resource development. In contrasting the two men, *Time* magazine said that conservationists saw Hickel as "so depressingly different that some reacted as if Satan had been promoted to guard St. Peter's gates."[12] By the time Hickel came to the Senate for confirmation hearings, it was apparent that the concern over his nomination went far beyond the leaders and members of environmental organizations. One eastern senator received over thirty-five hundred letters and telegrams on the Hickel controversy, and most opposed his appointment.[13]

The Senate Interior Committee took four days to question Hickel before sending his nomination to the floor for confirmation. During the hearings Hickel defended his record as governor and gave assurances that he would manage the Interior Department in a manner that was sensitive to environmental quality. At the White House, the president, if he was not prior to the hearings, became acutely aware that the quality of the nation's environment was a major concern across the country, and that failure to recognize this fact could have serious political implications for his new administration. As evidence of this awareness and to blunt criticism of his appointment of Hickel, Nixon let it be known that he would name Russell Train, then president of the Conservation Foundation, to be undersecretary of the interior.[14]

Setting aside all the talk and maneuvering in Washington, the VNPA was determined to move the Voyageurs cause forward both in Congress and inside the new Republican administration. In a press release in February on the day he was elected VNPA president, Andersen cited the enormous support for the park in Minnesota. He also stressed the strong bipartisan support as evidenced by the park's endorsement by the entire Minnesota congressional delegation. He firmly believed that the opportunity to finally secure a national park for the state had arrived: "We have our foot in the door and this is the do or die year."[15]

During the annual meeting of the VNPA, he announced a ten-point plan to advance the park proposal. Included among the points was a Washington kick-off, which meant a VNPA delegation going to Washington to meet with Minnesota congressmen and national conservation leaders to acquaint them with the park proposal. This effort, scheduled for the second week of March, also included separate meetings between Andersen and individuals who could make the difference for Voyageurs: Blatnik, Hickel, Wayne Aspinall (chairman of the House Interior Committee), and NPS Director Hartzog. Andersen's primary reason for scheduling the Washington kick-off was to prod Blatnik into reintroducing his park bill so that the legislative process could begin in earnest.

The day Andersen was to begin his talks with Blatnik and others on his list, the St. Paul, Duluth, International Falls, and Iron Range newspapers carried a story by Albert Eisele of the Knight-Ridder newspapers' Washington bureau that revealed that all was not sweetness and light in the Voyageurs camp. The two principals in the park movement, Andersen and Congressman John Blatnik, were often at odds as to the proper course of action and the tempo of the effort. The story also showed that Blatnik had a thin skin when it came to any semblance of interference with his management of legislative matters for which he was responsible. According to Eisele, Blatnik's reaction to the Andersen visit was, "We need this like we need a hole in the head. His coming here isn't going to accomplish anything except stir up a lot of trouble. If he wants to help us get a park he should stay back there and build up some support for it. All he is going to do now is wake up a sleeping tiger and stir up more opposition to the park." Blatnik still harbored some resentment over a newspaper article in late February in which Andersen was quoted as predicting that Blatnik would be introducing a new park bill in a "few days." Blatnik told Eisele, "Andersen doesn't have any business announcing for us when we'll have it ready. If there's any announcing to be done, I'll do it."[16] Blatnik also criticized Governor LeVander for not working out an agreement with Boise Cascade over land exchanges on the Kabetogama Peninsula.

Blatnik, completely embarrassed by the Eisele article, left an urgent message for Andersen to call him as soon as he arrived in Washington so that he could explain the situation surrounding the Eisele story. He later explained to Andersen that Eisele had betrayed his confidence by printing the content of his conversation with him. In reporting on his Washington meeting at the VNPA board meeting later in the week, Andersen said, regarding the Blatnik episode, "He didn't make an issue about it and I could only accept John's apology and sincerity."[17] Andersen also told the committee that Blatnik was concerned that his political opponents on the Iron Range were using the park as a campaign issue against him. He also told Andersen that "the young Turks are out to unseat him in his district."[18] Blatnik again urged the VNPA to be more aggressive on the Iron Range in getting groups and clubs to issue statements on behalf of the park.

In retrospect, Andersen's Washington visit, although beginning on an unpleasant note, may have achieved its objective, which was to get some assurances that the park proposal would begin to move forward again. (Congressman Blatnik, after adding a hunting provision primarily at the request of Governor LeVander, reintroduced the bill the next month following his meeting with Andersen.)[19]

Andersen wrote to Blatnik a few weeks later after explanatory articles regarding the episode were published. In his letter Andersen said, "The subsequent publicity removed the ill effects of that first unfortunate story and I think we needn't be further concerned about it."[20] In a biographical sketch commemorating Andersen's eightieth birthday in 1989, the author Richard Broderick said, "One of the abiding characteristics of Andersen's life is his tendency to look toward the future rather than dwell upon the past."[21] In 1969 Andersen saw as a part of the future for the people of Minnesota a national park in the border lakes region, and he was not going to allow a few offending remarks to interfere with achieving that goal.

In northern Minnesota, the reintroduction of the Voyageurs bill generated statements critical of the congressman's action as well as those that were highly supportive. Opposition views from the Minnesota Timber Producers Association, Boise Cascade, the Crane Lake Commercial Club, and some segments of the resort communities on Rainy and Kabetogama Lakes appeared in the press. The public also heard from some state legislators who had opposed the park from the beginning and were especially frustrated because of their inability to get a proper review of the park proposal in the state legislature. The proponents, as expected, were delighted with Blatnik's action and were expansive in their praise of his dedication and loyalty not only to the people of his district but to the state as well.[22] In a letter sent to all VNPA board and committee members, Shemesh urged them to send letters to Blatnik commending him for his leadership and pledging continued backing and support for his action. She closed her letter with a special call-to-action message: "Your own personal efforts can make the VNP dream come true! Let's all make this the final push!"[23] Shemesh hoped that the "final push" would result in a park by the close of the first session of the Ninety-first Congress in late 1969. But she, like most others on either side of the controversy, could not imagine in April 1969 the many twists and turns the legislative process would take before final passage in December 1970.

The Hickel appointment was the first overt evidence that on conservation issues at least, a philosophical shift was under way in the executive branch of the national administration. Directly and indirectly, this shift had its impact on Voyageurs, and it produced interminable delays in the legislative process.

The first indication that the Nixon administration would move more slowly on new parks came in March 1969, when it declined to support legislation on Apostle Islands National Lakeshore because of the uncertainty of funding for land purchases. After that decision, the administration asked that Congress reduce the appropriations from the Land and Water Conservation Fund for federal land purchases from the $154 million requested by the outgoing Johnson administration to $124 million.[24] Blatnik's office said the administration's action would not affect the Voyageurs bill because it was legislation requesting authorization— the funding could come later. But Colorado Democrat Wayne Aspinall, chairman of the House Interior and Insular Affairs Committee, which had to approve the legislation for final floor action, saw the cuts as "maybe ruling out serious consideration of any new parks in 1969."[25]

It appeared in early summer that Aspinall would not even schedule field hearings on Voyageurs because of a feud between him and the administration for cutting back on acquisition funds. However, after appeals by Blatnik and many letters requesting a hearing on the park in Minnesota, Aspinall cleared the way for a field hearing on August 21 in International Falls, conducted by the Subcommittee on Parks and Recreation Chair Roy Taylor. Almost four months had passed since the Voyageurs bill was reintroduced. In the absence of formal clearance on Voyageurs by the Department of the Interior, the uncertainty of fiscal support for new parks, the painfully slow response by Representative Aspinall to move on the bill, and the limited time available in the first session of the Ninety-first Congress to see the bill through to conclusion, Shemesh's dream of a "final push" ending in victory in 1969 was shattered.

Before the House field hearings in late August, Andersen met with the St. Louis County Board to try to win their support for the park. He reasoned that endorsement by the governing body in the county where the park would be located would demonstrate the kind of local support Aspinall always looked for when his committee considered a new park proposal. However, consistent with its position throughout the campaign for Voyageurs, the county board chose to take no action after politely listening to Andersen. The county board's inaction, in light of earlier behavior, was really an expression of opposition and was in harmony with opposition also expressed by the Duluth Chamber of Commerce, the Minnesota Arrowhead Association, and several area newspapers including the *Duluth News-Tribune* and the *Mesabi Daily News.* All of this revealed that opposition to the park remained strong with government officials, the media, and some commercial enterprises in the region.

Public hearings like the one on Voyageurs in August 1969 have been standard congressional procedure for new park proposals because all national parks are created by an act of Congress. This procedure was followed even for the earliest parks, established in the late nineteenth and early twentieth centuries. However, units like Yellowstone, Crater Lake, Sequoia, and Glacier were created out of public lands in the sparsely settled western half of the United States, thus making for a less complicated process in preparing and approving legislation for new park units. Park creation became more complicated, particularly after World War II when more and more new proposals came from the eastern half of the United States, where population densities were much higher and settlement patterns more firmly established. Local resistance from property owners within the boundaries of proposed parks and from residents on the periphery made new park formation and approval far more difficult. The NPS now holds hearings in Washington *and* in the area closest to the proposed park. The latter, called field hearings, are usually well attended and sometimes contentious. They give members of the opposing sides their first opportunity to explain their positions and concerns before congressional representatives who must ultimately make the final decision on a new park proposal.[26]

At the August 1969 field hearing for Voyageurs, Chair Roy Taylor and two other congressmen, all members of the Subcommittee on Parks and Recreation, were greeted by approximately two hundred people. A local newspaper estimated that about two-thirds were year-round residents in International Falls and neighboring communities or summer residents who owned property in the proposed park area or nearby. The balance was made up of individuals who favored the park and were active in the campaign for its authorization. Most in the latter group were from the Twin Cities region, Duluth, and the Iron Range. Those appearing as participants spoke to their concerns, often in a spirited fashion. These concerns were familiar to the committee members who had attended field hearings in the past where a new park was being proposed.

Before Voyageurs finally won approval in Congress, three hearings were held: the International Falls field hearing, a House subcommittee hearing in Washington in July 1970, and a Senate hearing in Washington in December 1970. Of the three, the International Falls hearing was the only one that really reflected the local and grassroots feelings regarding expansion and management of public lands. At the field hearing the most frequently mentioned concern by those opposed to the park centered on opposition to enlarging *federal* holdings in the border lakes region. After the hearing, my evaluation of comments made during the hearing by those opposed to the park showed that the two most frequently mentioned issues were outright opposition to anything federal and recommendations that the proposed park be shifted from the largely private lands on the Kabetogama Peninsula to existing federal lands in the Lac La Croix area of the BWCA. Only one person mentioned a national recreation area, with its less rigid management requirements, as an alternative to the proposed national park.

The third most commonly voiced concern was "people pressure." The field hearings were held at a time when media reports were describing startling increases in national park visitation with attendant negative impacts on park resources. Fears of losing the quiet and solitude of the sparsely populated Crane to Rainy Lake area were genuine and expressed with sincerity by a number of those who testified or sent letters for the hearing record.

Concerns that national park status would place restrictions on traditional use patterns, particularly hunting, were also expressed.[27] Others were fearful that boating accidents would become a problem as visitors with limited boating experience showed up to enjoy the "wonders" that were best seen from the water. A few thought the Kabetogama Peninsula and surrounding lakes lacked the scenic qualities required for national park status. Referring to the committee's "tour" of the park made from an airplane, one witness said, "This may have given our airborne visitors an impressive view of 'lovely shimmering lakes,' but a closer, low-flying mission would have uncovered stagnant, murky-green waters, bogs and marshes."[28]

Also mentioned, but with surprisingly less frequency, were concerns about future timber supply for the area's wood products industry, loss of property tax revenue as lands were shifted to park status, and the Crane Lake addition. On the subject of timber supply, Boise's representative, George Amidon, was asked what percentage of the company's timber supply over the next twenty-five years would actually come from their lands in the proposed park. His response was an estimated 4 percent. But he quickly added that his company's *real* concern and that of the industry nationally was the thousands of acres of woodlands being taken out of timber production across the country just to satisfy the growing appetite for wilderness for people who did not understand the supply situation in his industry.[29] Boise Cascade realized that a more narrow claim, that a park on the Kabetogama Peninsula would result in damaging timber shortages for their nearby mills, would be challenged with data from an economic study completed by the University of Minnesota-Duluth in 1964. This study, *The Economics of the Proposed Voyageurs National Park,* demonstrated conclusively that timber supplies for the local wood products industries were then in surplus and that the annual property tax losses from proposed park lands would be less than $25,000. The Sielaff study, considered thorough and conservative by many, effectively eliminated timber and tax losses as compelling reasons for opposing the establishment of the park.[30]

The Crane Lake Commercial Club opposed the Crane Lake addition in emphatic fashion. Though not mentioned frequently at the International Falls hearing, the issue would generate considerable interest at the Washington hearings when the USFS made its case.[31]

Pre-hearing efforts by the VNPA to coordinate testimony given by supporters showed up in the post-hearing assessment. From the beginning of the organized campaign for Voyageurs in 1965, emphasis was always on two objectives: to preserve and protect the natural and cultural resources of the Kabetogama area, and to promote the tax and economic benefits of national park status to the state and especially to the economy of northeastern Minnesota. Witnesses were encouraged by the VNPA leadership to prepare statements that emphasized these objectives. Protecting and preserving the natural amenities of the peninsula lakeshore and interior lakes was a popular goal for many park supporters. In their statements to the subcommittee, writers expressed alarm at the poorly regulated lakeshore development already under way on many lakes around the state. One witness summed up his growing concern this way: "Voyageur [sic] National Park should be established as soon as possible, before critical land and shoreline on the Kabetogama Peninsula is lost to commercial development."

The tax and other economic benefits that would result from establishment of a national park were given even greater emphasis. Repeated references were made to the increased tourism to be expected with national park designation. Edwin Chapman, VNPA's first president, after noting the scenic and historic values of the park area, summed up the economic advantages by saying, "the communities surrounding the park would enjoy not only increased valuation of their properties but the influx of new investment money to provide the facilities for the traveling public and the travel dollars which tourists bring into the region. This combination of both economic and recreational opportunities is hard to beat."[32] Chapman's statement was representative of many others made at all of the hearings and in VNPA promotional literature. These claims of economic benefit to the region were predicated on the firm and sincere belief that the beauty of Voyageurs, like some of the great western parks, would attract substantial numbers of visitors each year. Indeed, economic benefits for northeastern Minnesota and the state generally were principal reasons motivating the Minneapolis Chamber of Commerce to take a leading role in promoting the establishment of the park.[33]

Not everyone testifying on behalf of the proposed park mentioned economic factors. Some rather eloquent statements extolled the natural and cultural values of the park area as well. The aesthetic and spiritual values to be discovered in this region were proclaimed in eloquent fashion by several speakers, including Dr. Arnold Bolz, a physician practicing in northern Minnesota and a widely acclaimed nature photographer. He spoke of the inborn need for human "contact and immersion in the natural scene" and our need to experience the "spiritual benefit from this encounter." He saw the rocks, water, and trees of the area worthy of protection for those who wish to have this experience.[34]

Sigurd Olson, nationally recognized nature writer and crusader for the wilderness status of the BWCA, saw Voyageurs as the last step in providing protection of the entire voyageurs highway between Lake Superior and International Falls: "This last section must be given the same protection for it is as beautiful and significant as the rest. Failure to accomplish this would mean the ancient highway of exploration and trade would be incomplete."[35]

The executive committee of the VNPA met the week after the International Falls hearing to review the events of the daylong session. The consensus was that the hearing went well for park proponents.[36] In their opinion, the case for a national park on Kabetogama was well stated and was now a part of the official record with the Congress. The committee also concluded that although a number of individuals representing organizations opposing the park testified, none represented groups that had statewide memberships. However, closer examination of the official hearing record and some of the press accounts show at least three issues would prove troublesome for park advocates in the months to come. These included public hunting, land acquisition, and the Crane Lake addition.

Blatnik's 1969 legislation included a provision permitting hunting and trapping that was absent in the original bill in 1968. This hunting section was written into the new legislation primarily at the request of Governor LeVander, who hoped to satisfy some staff people in his Conservation Department and to dampen criticism from some Eighth District Republicans who never endorsed the proposal for a national park on Kabetogama. The governor included the hunting provision in his official position statement that was sent to the subcommittee before the hearings. In that statement, he also advocated continued waterfowl

hunting in the Black Bay area of the proposed park.[37] (Congress removed Black Bay from the park in 1983.)

Commenting on the inclusion of hunting in the Blatnik bill, Representative Taylor said that hunting was not allowed in any other national
park, and he doubted that the precedent should be set with Voyageurs.
"If it's going to be a national park, you give up hunting."[38] Taylor said
that hunting may be OK in a recreation area, but national park status
means giving up timber harvesting, mining, hunting, and other multiple-
use activities. The emphasis is on recreation and conservation. Taylor's
committee had encountered the same issue just a year earlier during
the hearings on the proposed North Cascades National Park. On that
occasion, NPS Director Hartzog said in his testimony that a special committee addressed the whole issue of wildlife management in parks in
1962. They found the long-standing congressional policy prohibiting
hunting to be solid and that it should be continued. He said that the
NPS was not prepared to recommend any change in that policy.[39]

When it was the National Audubon Society's turn to testify, its representative said that the society adhered to the hunting prohibition enun-
ciated repeatedly by the NPS. He said the Audubon Society was troubled
by the Voyageurs proposal because it permitted houseboats, seaplanes,
and cabin cruisers. He suggested a change in title from national park to
"Voyageurs National Recreation Area."[40]

The prohibition of public hunting in national parks was well known
to Congressman Blatnik and Governor LeVander and certainly to their
staff assigned to the project. More than a year before Representative
Taylor's field hearing in International Falls, and six months before Congressman Blatnik entered his Voyageurs bill in the House, Governor
LeVander sent a letter to Blatnik, on January 8, 1968, stating "eight points"
he believed should be included in his forthcoming legislation on the
park. On the hunting point LeVander wanted the bill to say, "A relaxation of hunting restrictions, at least for the first few years, to reduce
the deer herd should be guaranteed." LeVander's letter was copied to the
entire Minnesota congressional delegation and soon found its way to
the Interior Department. Secretary Udall asked Director Hartzog to send
a detailed response to questions raised in the LeVander letter to Blatnik.

Hartzog's response, dated February 19, 1968, noted general agreement
on six points. The point on adding the Crane Lake area could not be
dealt with because their hands were tied by the interagency agreement

between Agriculture and Interior. Disagreement came on the hunting issue. Hartzog wrote, "pursuant to the long-standing policies of the Congress, public hunting is not permitted in national parks." The director went on to say that NPS policies provide for control through natural predation, public hunting outside the park, live trapping, taking research specimens, and direct reduction by park personnel. In a letter to Director Hartzog on March 9, 1968, in which he commented on Hartzog's response to Blatnik, LeVander said, "It is my recommendation that Congress establish a policy which would permit qualified licensed hunters to be selected from the public for the purpose of shooting one deer and removing the carcass for their own use. This program should be jointly sponsored by the state and Park Service in conformity with a specific reduction plan." LeVander concluded by saying, "I realize Park Service policy does not regard recreational hunting as a compatible use and the participants in this program would derive a recreational benefit. In this instance, however, recreation and management can be combined in achieving a desired goal with resulting benefits to both parties."[41]

Despite repeated statements of policy regarding public hunting in the national parks, some members of the hunting community put pressure on the governor and Blatnik to oppose such a ban in the proposed park. Their strongest ally within the LeVander administration was Conservation Commissioner Leirfallom and his Deputy Commissioner Clarence Buckman. Their support for hunting was made evident when just two weeks after the field hearings in International Falls, Buckman appeared before a Minnesota Senate Public Domain Committee hearing and on September 5, 1969, testified that it was absolutely essential from a wildlife management standpoint that hunting be allowed in the proposed park. He maintained that with few predators in the park area, public hunting became an essential tool in a wildlife management plan. Governor LeVander may or may not have agreed with Buckman on the scientific merits of his wildlife management argument, but he was acutely aware of the pressures of the pro-hunting groups. Blatnik and LeVander, therefore, decided to include the hunting provision in the bill and let Congress take it out. In this way they would protect their standing with the sport hunters in the region around the park.

On land acquisition, the Blatnik legislation generally followed NPS boilerplate language and policy by identifying the several methods whereby the NPS could acquire property for the proposed park. However,

Governor LeVander's position on state land transfer was at odds with the policy of the federal government. The governor did not appear at the International Falls hearing, but he filed his official position statement on Voyageurs with the committee several days prior to the hearing. In his statement he noted that of the 28,400 acres of state lands within the proposed park, approximately 25,000 acres were trust fund lands. Because of the special status of these lands and the legal requirements of the trust, LeVander recommended a procedure that would meet these conditions. He said that the most direct method for acquiring state-owned lands would be condemnation and, with the state's consent, purchase by the NPS. Condemnation would satisfy the strict legal requirements for sale of trust fund lands, and the money received by the state would be used to reimburse the permanent trust fund.[42] This procedure may have been satisfactory to the state but was not to the NPS. The subject did not come up during the hearing, but Representative Taylor told reporters after the hearing that LeVander's procedure had never been used before. He doubted whether the federal government had such power to condemn. States have always been expected to donate lands for national parks. Taylor declared that if Minnesota "is not willing to cooperate in establishing the park then we are on the wrong basis."[43]

Again, as in the case of public hunting, it is hard to believe that the LeVander administration was not aware of the precedent-shattering proposal they were making with respect to federal acquisition of state lands. It appears that LeVander was now listening more to his top officials in the Conservation Department for direction on Voyageurs policy than to his own administrative staff and the interdepartmental coordinating committee for the proposed park. This drift apparently began after Chelseth left his position in the governor's office in January 1969 to work in the private sector. While on the governor's staff, Chelseth made the Voyageurs project one of the LeVander administration's top priorities, keeping the governor well informed on the subject and maintaining close communication with the NPS. There were few ambiguities in the state's position on Voyageurs as long as Chelseth held his administrative position. As with hunting, the state's position on land acquisition was at variance with federal practice and would have to be resolved during the last few months of the legislative process on Voyageurs.

The challenge from the USFS over Crane Lake, the third troublesome issue, would continue, and the Crane Lake Commercial Club intensified its campaign against the park. The VNPA had already decided to remain neutral on the Crane Lake issue since it involved an interagency dispute beyond the association's capacity to influence. But the Crane Lake Commercial Club had decided not only to oppose the addition but to oppose the park proposal on Kabetogama as well. The VNPA regarded this as serious, and its hope was to continue a dialogue with the people at Crane Lake and keep the issue "localized." What park advocates had not anticipated, however, were bureaucratic roadblocks originating with the new Nixon administration and a stubborn Interior and Insular Affairs Committee chair, Representative Aspinall.

The VNPA emerged from the International Falls hearings with its organizational structure and membership loyalties fully tested. This was its first formal encounter in the national legislative arena, and its executive committee labeled it a success and began planning for the next set of hearings in Washington, sometime in 1970. The frustrations of the previous three-plus years would be equaled—some say exceeded—by those encountered during the final fourteen months leading to passage of the Voyageurs legislation. Some of the battles would carry forward as before.

Udall, secretary of the interior in the Kennedy and Johnson administrations, gave the department's blessing to Voyageurs early in the movement for the park. He continued to support it as an honorary advisor to the VNPA after he left office in 1969. The apprehensions expressed by environmentalists when Nixon appointed Hickel to replace Udall have already been noted. Now park supporters would have to convince the Interior Department's new chief and top administrators that Voyageurs was worthy of their endorsement as well. Shortly after Hickel was confirmed by the Senate, Governor LeVander and VNPA president Andersen invited the new secretary to visit Voyageurs. Hickel accepted the invitation and visited in mid-September 1969, a month after the congressional field hearings.

The Hickel visit hosted by Governor LeVander turned out to be more pleasing to park opponents than to proponents. The secretary felt compelled on several occasions during his visit to suggest that perhaps a national recreation area would be a more appropriate designation for the Kabetogama area than a national park. He said that his comments were not based on the lack of scenic quality of the area but rather on the insistence of Blatnik and LeVander that hunting be a permitted activity in the park. He told reporters that powerful congressmen have vowed that "we will never allow hunting in a national park."[44] This comment was a clear and unmistakable signal that he would never recommend a Voyageurs park proposal that included hunting and trapping. After thinking about Hickel's firm declaration, LeVander was caught in a "no-win" situation. No matter how he moved, he would offend one group or another. Park supporters continued to be upset with LeVander's persistence on public hunting. Many wrote to the governor, and a few counseled him in person, stressing the fact that a park with no hunting had been endorsed by hundreds of organizations across the state. Every poll taken showed overwhelming support for a park that met the standards of the NPS. And his persistence in this matter always played out in the public press as a major "controversy" just when advocates were trying to emphasize the positive qualities of the park proposal. But LeVander remained loyal to his Conservation Department staff, Commissioner Leirfallom, and his own convictions in this matter. His political instincts told him to seek a compromise, and after he heard Hickel's repeated reference to a national recreation area as an alternative, he began to think that this could be a way out of his predicament.

When approached by reporters regarding Hickel's alternative, LeVander told them that he would continue to work for a national park, but that "elasticity" in Minnesota's approach might further ideas about multiple use. Later in the day of Hickel's visit, he said designation of Voyageurs as a national recreation area would most likely arise as a compromise proposal before a congressional hearing, and "a rose would smell as sweet by any other name."[45] That and other comments by LeVander set park advocates back on their heels. They regarded his remarks as a serious blow to the movement. They had hoped to use the Hickel visit as an opportunity to demonstrate the unanimity of the national park supporters. They and their leaders were committed to securing a national park for Minnesota—not a national recreation area, a state park, or anything else.

One proponent was moved to fire off an angry letter to the governor as soon as she learned about his remarks. She said, "A park by any other name would smell as sweet? Well I think it stinks. It smells strongly sulfuric, as if the paper mills had been working."[46] Others, who were familiar with the Minnesota political scene, saw LeVander's comments as inspired by a desire to placate the Eighth District Republican leadership, which had *never* been supportive of the national park proposal.

Before Secretary Hickel returned to Washington, he met with about 150 residents at a Crane Lake resort. The meeting was arranged so that he could hear from opponents, a request he had made before he left Washington. What he got was more than an earful—it was an anti-park, anti–federal government, anti–Twin Cities display. Several speakers said the federal government should do nothing to change the present arrangement, that is, keep the Crane Lake Recreation Area managed by the USFS. It was a plea for the status quo. And one speaker brought up the decades-old claim of "outside" interference in the lives and livelihood of border lakes residents when he took a verbal swipe at the Twin Cities park advocates: "It's time for people to stop jumping to the tune played by the pied pipers of Minneapolis."[47] This energetic, high-decibel session was probably nothing new to Hickel, who had heard the claim of outsider influence many times in his years as governor of Alaska. He may even have voiced some of the same concerns at that time in his public career. As for park advocates, the Interior Department reported to the VNPA leadership that the secretary's schedule did not include a meeting with park proponents.

Park supporters always realized that to advance authorizing legislation through the legislative process would require the Interior Department's blessing. Great hopes had been placed on the Hickel visit as an important step in moving closer to the department's endorsement of the park. But the reality was much different than the dream. Opponents won the day. The credit for the win actually went to the two political leaders who were supposed to provide the muscle for the crucial effort to gain timely acceptance for a *national park* from the executive branch and move the proposal on to final congressional hearings and passage. These key people were Representative Blatnik and Governor LeVander. Blatnik's addition of hunting and trapping to his reintroduced bill for Voyageurs and LeVander's seeming acceptance of the national recreation area as an alternative to a national park caused the Hickel visit to lose its hoped-for focus. The intended objective was to show off the wonderful natural resources of the park area and the strong public sentiment for its inclusion as a national park.

Park campaign leaders were dismayed and discouraged at the turn of events. They were especially upset with LeVander, who had completely misread the wishes of the opposition. Not once during Hickel's meeting with opponents at Crane Lake was a national recreation area mentioned as an alternative or compromise solution to the controversy. They did not want federal control via the National Park System for any of the lands and water from Crane Lake to International Falls. This was an anti–federal government demonstration. As Hickel made his way back to Washington, park proponents realized that they would have to move quickly to regain the momentum and put the campaign back on the path to congressional acceptance.

The managers of the park campaign realized that the hunting provision in the Blatnik bill served to divert attention away from the cultural and natural values of the park. They also learned that a national recreation area as an alternative was unpopular and wholly unacceptable to opponents and supporters alike. On the hunting issue, they felt they could deal with this matter by simply persuading Blatnik and LeVander to remove the objectionable section of the bill. But to the surprise of many in the VNPA, this proved impossible until the final hours of the legislative process in December 1970. Another set of problems, however, was emerging in Washington at this time that served to retard progress on the park bill for many months.

One problem, completely unforeseen earlier in 1969, was President Nixon's Bureau of the Budget.[48] This unit, which was reorganized and given a new name in 1970—the Office of Management and Budget (OMB)—was given greater authority to screen departmental and agency budgets with the express purpose of reducing federal expenditures. Its director, Robert Mayo, said his aim was "prudent budget restraint." President Nixon had great confidence in his director and told his cabinet officers on one occasion, "When Bob Mayo speaks, I mean it."[49] Only months after assuming his new role, Mayo "spoke" in a manner that proved to have a direct bearing on the progress of Voyageurs legislation in Congress.

During the same week that Hickel was making his visit to Minnesota, Aspinall, chair of the House Committee on Interior and Insular Affairs, received a letter from Mayo saying that because of a severe shortage of funds for land acquisition, Congress should not expect full funding for land acquisition in parks and recreation areas probably for some time to come. The Bureau of the Budget reduced the amount of money available to $124 million.[50] Without even discussing the matter with his committee, an angry Aspinall decided that his committee would consider no further park authorizations.[51] Some called his action transparently political. It was calculated to embarrass the Nixon administration, but it also embarrassed and angered other members of Congress who had projects in line for approval and now saw them stalled by Aspinall's unilateral action.

Aspinall, like many of his colleagues, was upset by the administration's decision to ignore 1968 congressional legislation that authorized $200 million annually for land acquisition. These monies were to come from the Land and Water Conservation Fund and were to be available through 1973 for new proposals like Voyageurs. Blatnik saw Aspinall's moratorium on authorization hearings as unnecessary since funding for land acquisition is typically delayed several years after authorization of a new park.

Voyageurs was not the only park proposal affected by Aspinall's decision. In Wisconsin, Apostle Islands National Lakeshore also faced delays, which prompted Senator Gaylord Nelson, its chief sponsor and one of the leaders of the environmental movement in Congress, to ask the president's Environmental Council for an immediate review of the budget office's ruling. The Bureau of the Budget's pronouncement was also challenged by Senator Henry Jackson, chairman of the Senate Interior and Insular Affairs Committee. He saw this policy as hampering land acquisition for North Cascades National Park in his state of Washington. Voyageurs was one of the earliest park proposals to be caught up in the growing power of the Bureau of the Budget but certainly not the last. In fact, the office's influence over NPS proposals became so pervasive that one analyst was prompted to observe that the budget office could be as threatening to new area programs of the NPS as its regular adversaries, the USFS and strong private economic interests.[52]

"Voyageurs Backers Begin Rescue Drive" was the headline of a front-page story in the *Duluth News-Tribune* one week after the Hickel visit to Minnesota. A quick assessment of the situation made it very clear to Andersen that the best way to get Voyageurs back on the path to congressional authorization was for him to pay a personal visit to key officials in Washington. The visit would be used to emphasize the commitment of Minnesotans and conservationists around the country to Voyageurs. And it would be necessary to contact park proponents in Minnesota and continue efforts at building support for the park.

Working through Minnesota Congressman Clark MacGregor's office, Andersen scheduled a set of meetings with top Nixon aides, the secretary of the Commerce Department, budget office officials, NPS project

coordinators, and all members of the Minnesota congressional delegation. In contrast to his Washington visit earlier in the year, Blatnik welcomed Andersen, and the two met to discuss ways of breaking the stand-
off. Blatnik said that the first objective should be to gain a favorable
report from the Department of the Interior and a similar affirmation
from the budget office. Then and only then could they expect hearing
action from Aspinall. Andersen hoped for hearings before the year was
out, but that hope quickly faded with continued inaction by both agencies.

At home, Shemesh encouraged a vigorous letter-writing campaign to
appropriate public officials, namely Nixon, Mayo, Hickel, and Aspinall.
Several writers, including Sigurd Olson, downplayed the hunting provision, implying that it could be removed in the final version of the bill.[53]

By late October, in the absence of a report from the Interior Department, it became obvious that hearings by the House Subcommittee on
Parks and Recreation would not be held in 1969. Blatnik made it official
on November 7 when he told reporters that the Interior Department
had not completed its report on Voyageurs, and the budget office would
not review the legislation until they received the report. Putting the best
face on the dilemma, Blatnik said he was not discouraged, because the
park proposal that his people had worked out was a good one and had
the support of the entire Minnesota delegation. He saw the bill passing
the House before the end of the Ninety-first Congress. He also reminded
the press that the Voyageurs proposal had been in limbo since the Nixon
administration came to office. He remained optimistic because the proposal had floundered before but then moved ahead.[54]

For the opposition, the leaders of the two largest wood products companies in northeastern Minnesota reaffirmed their disapproval of the
park on Kabetogama in letters written during the last few months of 1969.
Both Boise Cascade and Northwest Paper Company expressed concerns
about the wisdom of expanding federal control over border lakes lands
to an agency that would replace multiple-use management with one
focusing on preservation and recreation. In a letter to President Nixon,
R. V. Hansberger, president of the Boise Cascade Corporation, repeated
his company's position that they favored a national park in Minnesota
but not on Kabetogama. He appended a statement dated July 17, 1967,
outlining Boise's position on the Voyageurs legislation that emphasized
the shift of more private lands to federal control.[55]

William MacConnachie Jr., a vice president of the Northwest Paper Company at Cloquet, Minnesota, sent letters to Governor LeVander and Congressman Aspinall, explaining his opposition to the park proposal. In his letter to LeVander he urged state control of the proposed park lands: "Citizens in Minnesota have done, and can do a better job in forest and park management than federal agencies."[56] In his letter to Aspinall, MacConnachie decried the "shameful pressure tactics of park proponents to circumvent the will of locally affected citizens through a well-financed 'mass propaganda' campaign." He felt that the hearings held by Taylor, Hickel, and LeVander went against the proponents and hoped Aspinall and his committee would not be swayed by their campaign.[57] And the state Senate Public Domain Committee scheduled yet another hearing on Voyageurs. NPS personnel attended this meeting and were bluntly told by Senator Higgins that he and others on the committee did not believe the NPS was capable of managing either wildlife or forests.[58]

As Congress prepared for the Christmas recess, all hopes for any movement at the legislative level in 1969 vanished. Aspinall continued to insist on reports from the Interior Department and the budget office before he would hold hearings on any new proposals for parks or recreation areas. When asked about the status of the report from the Interior Department, Alan Kirk, an aide to Hickel, said some strong conflicts needed to be addressed and resolved before sending a favorable report to the Bureau of the Budget and Congress. Given the determination by LeVander and Blatnik to keep the hunting clause in the bill, one can assume that at least one of the "unresolved conflicts" was tied directly to the intransigence on the part of the governor and the congressman to compromise on this issue.

Another problem for the Interior Department at this time was LeVander's proposal requesting in effect that the federal government pay the state for the trust fund lands as a condition for state transfer of the lands in the proposed park to the NPS. This proposal came to light in LeVander's position statement to the Taylor subcommittee at the field hearings in International Falls. It had not received much public notice at that time, but it would hang heavy over the park project during the Washington hearings in 1970. Both issues became serious impediments to legislative progress on Voyageurs in the next Congress. Had they been removed from the Blatnik bill in a timely fashion following the International Falls hearings, it is conceivable that progress on park legislation would have been faster and smoother.

Kirk offered an additional reason for the lengthy delay at the Interior Department when he cited the many demands on the department that went well beyond the funds available to meet them. He said the Interior Department was in favor of more parks, but the question was when and where. When told of these comments and observations by Kirk, Blatnik said he was "puzzled" by the conflicting reports coming out of the Interior Department. "Hickel should call the Minnesota delegation together and explain to them just what the problems are."[59]

If Blatnik was puzzled, Andersen was frustrated to see the Voyageurs project bogged down in the two Washington offices. In a letter to LeVander he said the reluctance of federal agencies and departments to move on these matters was having an eroding effect on the Republican position. "Can you suggest anything we might do? I am not one for waiting around."[60] Later that month he wrote to Roger B. Morton, chair of the Republican National Committee, asking him to find out just what the "hang-up" was in the Interior Department that was holding up the Voyageurs proposal. He told Morton that continued inaction on Voyageurs could be harmful to Republican chances in the 1970 political campaign.[61]

CHAPTER EIGHT
Deadlocks and Bottlenecks

The decade of the 1970s, often called the environmental decade, was characterized by aggressive congressional and executive action to halt the continued deterioration of the nation's natural environment. *Newsweek* magazine devoted most of its January 23, 1970, edition to what it called "The Ravaged Environment." The articles in this special edition described serious cases of air, water, and soil pollution, shameful waste of natural resources, and growing public concern over what many were calling our national environmental crisis. Environmentalists, armed with a whole "new" vocabulary, emerged as the leaders in a crusade dedicated to restoring the nation's natural systems to a healthier state. The popular press and scientific journals were filled with articles using terms such as *ecology, ecosystem, biosphere, preservation, environmental quality, land ethic,* and so on.

In response to public demand for strong measures to halt the excesses of industrial polluters and stimulate enforcement action on the part of state and local governments, in late 1969 the Congress passed the most comprehensive and far-reaching environmental legislation in history, the National Environmental Policy Act. But public interest in environmental matters went well beyond pollution abatement measures. It also included concern for the quality of the nation's natural resources, including threats to vanishing scenic landscapes. According to historian Samuel Hays, "The environmental movement actually began to take shape in the late 1950s and early 1960s, largely around objectives associated with public land management."[1] There were also demands for expansion and

better care of existing public outdoor recreation facilities and establishment of new ones, including new national parks and national recreation areas.

Many Minnesotans and growing numbers from across the country
viewed the Voyageurs proposal as wholly consistent with the national
mood for protection of our natural resources. Many who testified at
the International Falls hearings used terms like *protection* and *preservation* in making their case for a national park on Kabetogama. Such sentiments were no doubt on the minds of many members of the more
than one thousand organizations that had endorsed Voyageurs by early
January 1970. However, the Voyageurs proposal, widely acclaimed at home
in Minnesota and among the leading conservation organizations in the
nation, was hopelessly mired in bureaucratic wrangling, indifference,
and inertia in Washington.

The bottlenecks were well known to proponents of the proposal for
Voyageurs: the Bureau of the Budget, the Department of the Interior,
and Chairman Aspinall of the House Interior and Insular Affairs Committee. Governor LeVander made some contacts in Washington in early
January to see what might be done. In a letter to Elmer Andersen he
simply repeated what was general knowledge, that the budget office would
not act until the Interior Department sent them their report on Voyageurs.
And Aspinall would not move until the budget office released funds for
land acquisition.[2] LeVander believed that Nixon was going along with
the budget office's new policy that no park authorizations would be
made without appropriations. To make the situation even more discouraging, Wayne Judy, VNPA board member from International Falls,
reported that park opponents believed they had the Voyageurs project
blocked and that the park was seldom mentioned around town.[3]

The Washington stalemate and how it might be broken became the
central topic of discussion during VNPA executive committee meetings.
It was during one of these meetings that Rita Shemesh reported a suggestion made to her by Robert Herbst of the national Izaak Walton
League office. Herbst's advice was to make direct contact with Nixon
aides and advisors at the highest level. He specifically mentioned Charles
Colson (later of Watergate fame), who was Nixon's special counsel on
environmental affairs. She also received a letter from Charles Stoddard,
former Interior Department regional official, who told her that personal

contacts with those close to Nixon were very important: "Grave decisions are made largely by personal relationships."[4]

On the strength of those suggestions and those of VNPA board members, the association opened a campaign directed at the White House. Members were urged to write to the president as well as to Budget Director Mayo and Secretary Hickel. Shemesh, leading by example, began writing twice weekly to the president, each time announcing the total number of endorsing organizations. In her April 6 letter she was able to say that over twelve hundred organizations nationwide had endorsed the proposal for a national park on the Kabetogama Peninsula. She also wrote a three-page letter to Colson explaining the merits and the broad national appeal of the Voyageurs proposal and then commended the president for acknowledging in his state of the Union message the need to set aside funds for more parks and recreational areas.[5]

Shemesh saved her most urgent plea for assistance in her "contact President Nixon" campaign for U.S. Representative Clark MacGregor, a longtime acquaintance and senior Republican from the Twin Cities. Many other VNPA members from the Twin Cities area were acquainted with MacGregor and shared his political philosophy. They hoped that with the new Republican administration, MacGregor's influence at the White House would be substantial and that he could be counted on to keep the park project on track. However, after one year of the Nixon administration, the Voyageurs project was bound up in a three-way tussle between two executive department offices and a House committee chairman. And MacGregor's office, according to VNPA leaders, had been anything but aggressive in its efforts to remove bureaucratic roadblocks and get the proposal to the legislative phase. Noting this, Shemesh sent a letter to MacGregor, pleading with him to get moving on Voyageurs. "*You* and *only you* are the *only man* in Washington—indeed, the entire country—who can get us this very important approval from President Nixon. Since you are planning to run for the Senate I can't image a finer political feat on your part than to be able to come back and tell the people of Minnesota that you personally were instrumental in getting VNP approval from President Nixon."[6]

Two months later, with still no official action by either the Interior Department or the budget office, Shemesh sent Representative MacGregor another letter, this time minus the "niceties" of earlier correspondence.

"Clark, will you please tell me when you plan to start doing something in behalf of Voyageurs National Park. We have counted on you, as an identified Nixon Republican, to move things along with the Department of Interior and get approval from the administration."[7] She repeated how important positive action on the park would be in his senate campaign. Then, perhaps to shame him into action, recounted how Sigurd Olson, faced with a similar bureaucratic delay on an Olympic National Park bill, went directly to the offending department and explained the urgency of the situation, and within twelve hours, the bill was cleared for congressional hearings.

Shemesh's impatience and frustration with the deadlock may have focused on only one member of the Minnesota delegation, but in a television editorial, George Rice of WCCO-TV in Minneapolis blamed the entire delegation for lack of enthusiasm for "pushing the park through political channels."[8] Rice suggested that they were trying to play the park issue both ways by talking encouragingly with park advocates while trying not to offend the timber and pulp interests who did not want a park. He thought some of the congressmen wanted the report stuck just where it was.

The day before the WCCO-TV editorial, Andersen addressed a group of University of Minnesota students who were participating in events surrounding the first Earth Day observance. His remarks may have motivated the writers at WCCO to editorialize on the dilemma facing park supporters at that time. In his speech Andersen characterized the stalemate in Washington as illustrative of just one more frustration in a "decade of indecision" for park advocates. He said it was hard to believe that the Interior Department and Congress would continue to delay action on a proposal that had the overwhelming support of the public. In the spirit of the day, Andersen challenged students to take up the cause for Voyageurs as a practical environmental achievement.[9]

The level of frustration over the delays in Washington was perhaps greatest with the leaders of the park movement, the executive committee of the VNPA. Most were business and professional people unaccustomed to the foot-dragging maneuvers, interdepartmental squabbling, and lethargic behavior on the part of some members of Congress, all combining to hold back action on the Voyageurs legislation. They feared it would be difficult to hold on to the high level of enthusiasm for the cause among the general membership if the stalemate dragged on much longer. It was particularly upsetting when plausible explanations for the delay were not forthcoming. Rumors were abundant, but explanations were unconvincing.

VNPA members familiar with the timber and wood products industry were especially wary of the role Boise might be playing in softening the support of some business people and public officials toward the park and in reinforcing local opposition to the proposal. Even though Boise was issuing few public statements detailing its opposition, it was suspected by some VNPA leaders of working behind the scenes to achieve its aims. Boise was careful to explain and clarify its position on Voyageurs to the state administration and the NPS. For example, Boise sent a letter to the NPS director's office on January 28, 1970.[10] In this letter and in all Boise communications on the park, no mention is made of their long-range plans for private second-home development on Rainy Lake by their newly acquired land development subsidiary. Andersen, when speaking for the park proposal, had on a number of occasions alerted his audiences to what he believed to be Boise's real intentions on Kabetogama—lakeshore residential development. He summed up his feelings on this subject in a letter to a park critic in southern Minnesota. Although not mentioning Boise or any other developer by name, he said, "We have the opportunity for the compound value of preserving a beautiful area for all time while also keeping it available for public use rather than having it ultimately divided up and put into a few private hands."[11]

Private lakeshore development, often poorly planned and unregulated, was what had already compromised the scenic values of hundreds of lakes in the state. The fear that this pattern of shoreline development and loss of public access would be repeated on the shores of the Kabetogama Peninsula brought many into the movement for a national park. With these concerns in mind and the certain knowledge that the general public was unaware of the potential for full-scale shoreline development by a major corporation, the VNPA executive committee began discussions on a recommendation by one member that "a stronger, more militant approach be adopted regarding Boise Cascade's policy on Voyageurs."[12] Several members had already been gathering information, most of it published, about questionable land speculation activities by Boise. There was some discussion about hiring legal assistance to check on some allegations and prepare a report on the topic. But Andersen counseled against plans to push the case publicly, thinking it ill advised at that time in their campaign for the park. There was consensus, however, to continue collecting data on the subject of lakeshore development but to use the material only if necessary during the congressional hearings or with the Minnesota legislature.[13] Martin Kellogg, a member of the committee and later president of the VNPA, best expressed the course the association would take on the Boise matter when he said, "It wasn't necessary to attack Boise Cascade directly but to point out the environmental damage done at other land development projects and what would undoubtedly be the fate of Kabetogama unless it is preserved as a national park."[14]

Shemesh's urgent plea for letters to Washington officials to break the stalemate on Voyageurs began to bear fruit in early May 1970. In a letter from Congressman MacGregor on May 4 she learned that the Interior Department had submitted a favorable report on Voyageurs to the budget office. She also learned that he was angry at her repeated claims that he had not moved aggressively on Voyageurs legislation. In his letter MacGregor stated, "Interior has submitted a favorable report to the Bureau of Budget for clearance. On the basis of my recent conversations, I am convinced that the Budget Bureau is dealing expeditiously with the Voyageurs proposal. The proposal is not stalled. It is moving." He concluded on a somewhat acerbic note that "any efforts on your part to spread poison concerning my role in this matter will seriously damage the prospects for continued progress."[15] Representative Albert Quie also sent a letter to Shemesh, noting the Interior Department's action in sending a favorable report to the budget office.[16] Quie's letter further explained that the budget office would now be in a position to develop an administrative policy on Voyageurs.

The MacGregor and Quie letters shed some light on the reasons for the long delay in gaining administrative approval for Voyageurs. In the previous administration, Secretary Udall had openly favored the park proposal, and so Interior's approval was never in question, and the Bureau of the Budget played no major policy role in such matters. Looked at in the light of the Nixon administration's more complicated policy formulation procedures, Representative MacGregor's "assignment" was not an easy one to accomplish. President Nixon took office with a commitment to tighten the budget, and an expanded role for the Bureau of the Budget was viewed as a means of accomplishing that objective. The new process required that all affected agencies provide reports relevant to the Voyageurs proposal and that these reports be reviewed and studied before the budget office made its recommendation.

Representative Quie in a letter to Shemesh dated May 11 reveals what might have been the most important reason for the lengthy delay in securing budget office approval for the park proposal. He wrote that the budget office had just received comments on the proposal from the Department of Agriculture and that it was the *last* agency to respond to the budget office's requirement that all such proposals pass through its office for cost approval.

Additional comment on the Agriculture Department's delay came a week earlier in a story by Albert Eisele, Washington bureau reporter for the Duluth newspapers. Representative MacGregor told him that the USFS sharply disagreed with the Interior Department's report on Voyageurs because of the inclusion of the Crane Lake addition and that there was a problem in "harmonizing" the Agriculture and Interior Departments reports.[17] This would indicate that the Agriculture Department had more to do with the "stalemate" than was known at the time. An overlong delay in submitting its report can be seen as working to its advantage since the delay could have forced the Voyageurs issue into the next Congress, where its chances of survival would have been slim. Later events in moving the park bill through Congress showed that the timing was crucial, especially in the last weeks of the session. Further delay by the Agriculture Department in the spring could well have doomed the Voyageurs bill for that session. But the VNPA's aggressive letter writing and telephone campaign to elected officials in Washington urging them to pry the proposal from a bureaucratic stranglehold put it back on the legislative path. The record shows that MacGregor played a key role in prying the Voyageurs project out of the interdepartmental deadlock and on to the congressional path.

The Voyageurs proposal cleared the budget office in mid-May, and Secretary Hickel announced the Interior Department's favorable report on Voyageurs on May 27. As soon as Blatnik received word that the favorable report from the Interior had arrived in congressional offices, he wrote to Shemesh: "The ball is back in our hands again. Congress has the initiative and hopefully we can more expeditiously move toward enactment during this session."[18]

The leadership of the VNPA hailed the recommendation on Voyageurs from the Interior Department as the most important achievement to date in the campaign for legislative authorization. After taking pleasure in the congratulatory messages from federal agencies, members of Congress, and conservation leaders, they began making preparations for the Washington, D.C., hearings, which Congressman Aspinall had called for mid-July. Association leaders began working through a list of potential speakers who would present the case for Voyageurs at the hearings. VNPA president Andersen again urged those chosen to testify to avoid the two major controversial issues: public hunting and the Crane Lake addition.[19]

Some VNPA members who were well acquainted with Governor LeVander encouraged him to drop the hunting and trapping issue before the scheduled hearings. This would avoid an embarrassing confrontation with members of the congressional committee who were committed to upholding the long-standing NPS policy that prohibited these activities. VNPA leaders also asked members at large to write letters to the governor, opposing his stance on hunting. Archival records show that he received numerous letters during June 1970. When responding to these letters, the governor would defend his position by stating, "I have advocated public hunting as a management tool to control game populations in accordance with the management program which would be designed by, and mutually acceptable to, federal and state agencies."[20]

LeVander's response was essentially the position of Conservation Commissioner Leirfallom, who had consistently expressed the concern over federal control of the resources of the boundary region. When Laurence Koll, the governor's environmental affairs advisor, met with the VNPA executive committee on June 4, he told them that the governor felt he did not have to defend the position he took in 1967. He said, "At this time it would be unnecessary and unwise to revise in any way his previous position."[21]

During the briefing on the Washington hearings, Shemesh reported a telephone conversation with NPS legal counsel Mike Griswold, who said they could expect opposition at the hearings from three groups: the timber industry, which would support the Boise Cascade position; anti–big government people; and the USFS, which was working quietly but effectively in opposition to the Crane Lake addition.[22] In the same conversation, Griswold commended the VNPA for its splendid effort in mobilizing support for the Voyageurs proposal. He said it was an effort second only to the historic California redwoods crusade, which brought about the establishment of Redwood National Park in 1968.

As the VNPA was lining up its Minnesota speakers to fill the slots allotted by the subcommittee, the Minnesota Senate's Public Domain Committee issued a position paper on the Voyageurs bill. The committee insisted that it had a responsibility to study the Voyageurs proposal on behalf of the legislature and that action on the Blatnik bill should be postponed until a cost-benefit analysis was ordered and completed. The committee's position was that only then would the state have sufficient data and information to make a proper decision on Voyageurs. The paper also said that the historical and scenic values of the proposed park site had been overstated. The Public Domain Committee believed that the study it was recommending would reveal deficiencies in those values. The very attributes were at the heart of the NPS's and Voyageurs supporters' arguments for national park status.[23]

To counter the claims of the Public Domain Committee, Representative Thomas Newcome, a conservative and chair of the Minnesota Resources Commission (MRC), was authorized by the MRC to testify at the Washington hearings and to present the MRC's findings on Voyageurs. Andersen and LeVander had always held that the MRC, which had endorsed the park several times during the previous five years, was properly constituted and authorized to act on behalf of the Minnesota Legislature in this matter. LeVander downplayed the Public Domain Committee's position, noting that the committee really spoke for a few people in the senate who were opposed to the park. However, LeVander had "dissenters" within his own cabinet when it came to supporting his publicly proclaimed position on Voyageurs.

Less than a month before the Washington hearings, Commissioner Leirfallom sent a memorandum to Larry Koll, LeVander's chief advisor on environmental affairs, suggesting that the state should reassess its position with respect to the inclusion of the Crane Lake area in the proposed park. Leirfallom admitted that these were second thoughts on Crane Lake. His original reasons for including the Crane Lake area were tied to an assumption that the NPS might amend some of their policies to conform more closely to multiple-use management and public hunting to control animal populations in the proposed park area. He said he now realized that the NPS was not going to relax their "old line rules," and he thought that the state should not put more fishing areas into their "deep freeze" and add 38,000 more acres to no-hunting status. His memorandum also included praise for USFS management policies for the Crane Lake Recreation Area. Leirfallom closed with a question that revealed his antipathy toward the NPS: "Should it [Crane Lake] be swallowed up by a system that many believe to be outmoded?"[24]

In a second memorandum to Koll, five days later, Leirfallom referred again to the contrasting management practices of the NPS and the USFS. He also said the governor could change his position on Crane Lake and thereby expedite park establishment immediately. On this point, Leirfallom had company among park advocates inside the VNPA, albeit for different reasons. They saw it as an encumbrance that could lead to no park legislation at all. Leirfallom, however, saw it as a philosophical issue: multiple-use management versus resource management that focused on preservation.[25] But in spite of differences of opinion between the governor and some officials in his Conservation Department, LeVander held firm to his position that the Crane Lake Recreation Area remain in the Blatnik bill.

The staff of the House Subcommittee on Parks and Recreation moved quickly to make arrangements for the Washington hearings, which were scheduled for July 17–18. Both sides were well acquainted with each other's positions and could anticipate hearing many of the same arguments that had been presented at earlier hearings and public meetings and in the media in Minnesota.

Voyageurs continued to attract open support from the leadership of both political parties, thus retaining its reputation as a proposal that always enjoyed strong bipartisan support. There was little open discussion or opposition to the park on the part of state legislators, primarily because they had no specific park-related legislation to consider. Those who did express opinions generally voiced familiar doubts and concerns. State Representative Alfred E. France of Duluth did not think that Voyageurs would be a high-quality national park; State Senator Rudy Perpich, an Iron Range liberal who became governor in 1976, said it was just another "land grab"; and a Duluth conservative said the concept of a national park for Kabetogama was too restrictive. Senators Ray Higgins from Duluth and O. A. Sundet from rural southern Minnesota best exemplified exceptions to this pattern of limited opposition. Both held strong opinions in opposition to the park and effectively used their membership on the Public Domain Committee to promote their views.

To counter the opposition voiced by Senator Higgins and other conservatives, two Duluth liberals, Representatives Earl Gustafson and Willard Munger, made their support of the park proposal an important part of their campaigns. A third candidate, Ralph Doty, was Higgins's opponent for his Minnesota senate seat. He also made support for Voyageurs a central part of his campaign and was successful in defeating Higgins in the fall election. But the examples just cited were exceptions rather than the rule, as most candidates in northeastern Minnesota avoided taking strong stands for or against the park.[26]

The congressional hearings held in Washington on July 17–18 presented another opportunity for both sides of the controversy to present their arguments. For opponents, it was a chance to present their position before a panel that could better understand how the Voyageurs proposal related to the broader issue of natural resource management and the kinds of pressure the timber industry was exposed to nationally. For park proponents it was an opportunity to show the strength of their case for Voyageurs as evidenced by the widespread public support generated during three years of intensive campaigning.

Over thirteen hundred organizations had endorsed the park by the time of the 1970 Washington hearings. Park supporters arriving in Washington for the hearings could count among their number prominent public figures and leading conservationists. They were well rehearsed and eager to lay before the subcommittee the logic and significance of their cause. But their carefully prepared case for Voyageurs was severely compromised by an unfortunate turn of events set in motion by the testimony of one of their chief supporters—Governor LeVander.

CHAPTER NINE

Congressional Hearings

It is unlikely that anyone was prepared for what occurred during the two-day House Subcommittee hearings on the proposal for Voyageurs National Park. Toward the close of the second day, it appeared to some that the campaign for Voyageurs could be lost primarily because of the unyielding position taken by Governor LeVander on two issues: donation of state lands for inclusion in the park, and public hunting. Even though the subcommittee heard from more than forty witnesses, seven emerged as key figures during the procedure. Governor LeVander; Congressman Blatnik; Elmer Andersen; Sigurd Olson; Stanley Holmquist, state senate majority leader; Thomas Newcome, state representative and chair of the Minnesota Resources Commission; George Amidon, Regional Manager for Boise Cascade; Dr. Alvin Hall, St. Louis County Commissioner; Jarle Leirfallom, state commissioner of conservation; Dr. A. T. Banen of International Falls; and NPS Director George Hartzog were principal witnesses. For the subcommittee, Chairman Taylor of North Carolina, James McClure of Idaho, John Kyl of Iowa, Wayne Aspinall of Colorado, and Morris Udall from Arizona played active roles.

Congressman Blatnik, first to testify, identified three areas in his bill where he believed there was "quite a difference of opinion." First, Blatnik and Governor LeVander strongly supported the inclusion of the Crane Lake Recreation Area, even though the official NPS proposal did not. Public hunting and commercial fishing in the proposed park represented a second area of disagreement. Blatnik cited federal payments to local units of government in lieu of taxes on property acquired for the park as the third issue where opinions were far apart.

To these three disputed points identified by Blatnik should be added two more that the congressman had not anticipated as problems before the hearings. LeVander insisted that the federal government acquire the state's school trust fund lands within the proposed park by eminent domain (condemnation), determine a reasonable market value, and then reimburse the trust fund account. In short, he felt the federal government should simply buy the trust fund lands.[1] The second point of disagreement Blatnik had not anticipated was repeated reference by committee members to a national recreation area as an alternative to national park designation for Voyageurs.[2]

It became clear in the early stages of the hearings that the subcommittee was determined to hear witnesses state their positions on the set of issues just cited. Members would frequently remind witnesses of the standards required for national park designation and where provisions in the Blatnik bill were at variance with these standards.

Following Blatnik's opening statement, the first four individuals to testify were members of the Minnesota congressional delegation, Joseph E. Karth, John Zwach, Donald M. Fraser, and Albert H. Quie. Each was eager to voice support for the Blatnik bill and to reinforce Blatnik's oft-repeated claim of strong bipartisan support for the park in Minnesota. However, the committee was more interested in learning how they stood on certain provisions of the Blatnik bill that ran counter to the criteria for national park status.

When Representative Karth voiced support for Blatnik's provision for hunting and trapping, Representative Kyl said, "I think it only fair to inform my colleagues at this point that we are not going to permit hunting or commercial fishing or trapping and some of these other things in a national park." Emphasizing that the committee was not likely to break precedent on these matters, he asked Karth *and Blatnik* if they would still favor establishment of a national park if, one, hunting and trapping were prohibited and, two, if payments in lieu of taxes were not provided for in the legislation. Blatnik quickly responded by saying, "If this is the decision and the judgement of the majority of the committee, of course we shall abide by the decision."[3] Blatnik's response to Kyl on both issues can be interpreted as a quick retreat from or outright abandonment of the position on both matters in his park bill.

On the same subject, Representative Aspinall asked Quie if he wanted a national recreation area or a national park. Quie responded in much the same manner as Blatnik: a national park. By agreeing to abide by the decision of the committee on hunting and trapping, Blatnik was no doubt attempting to set the matter aside and get on with other less controversial topics. Nevertheless, the hunting issue would surface repeatedly during the hearings. The most ardent supporters of the public hunting provision were Governor LeVander and Conservation Commissioner Leirfallom. Both, at least in the eyes of the friends of Voyageurs attending the hearings, contributed mightily to bringing the park cause to its lowest point during the second day of hearings when they vehemently defended it as the proper wildlife management tool for the proposed park. For park supporters, the first hours of the hearings were not promising, and the situation did not get much better as the proceedings continued.

NPS Director Hartzog, accompanied by Midwest Regional Director Fagergren, was the next witness. When Hartzog finished with a brief description of the proposed park area, he moved on to what he called "substantive amendments" of the Blatnik bill that he said would remove inconsistencies with NPS policy for national parks. Hartzog identified these inconsistencies as public hunting, uncontrolled commercial fishing, or control of fishing by the state rather than the secretary of the Interior Department.[4] At this point, Aspinall broke in with a comment to the effect that the NPS might have given some advice and aid to the backers of the bill early on, the implication being that if they had, the inconsistencies might have been removed before the bill came to the committee for review.[5] He was also upset by the fact that the NPS had taken so long to formally state their position on the park.

The tone of the hearings did not improve, at least in the minds of those in support of the park, when Representative McClure took his turn with Hartzog. McClure pursued a line of questioning that at times proved embarrassing for the director. Reflecting on this part of the hearing, John Kawamoto said it was an awkward time for him as well as Hartzog. By almost any measure, Kawamoto was the most knowledgeable person in the NPS on Voyageurs. But instead of being seated next to the director where he could have been of direct assistance to Hartzog with specific information on Voyageurs, he was in a row behind.[6]

McClure, a skillful interrogator, began a line of questioning that frequently placed the director on the defensive. It did not help that Hartzog, presumably because of the demands of other park business, was not able to get into the details of the Voyageurs project until late in the planning process. The late 1960s, when the campaign for the park was in full swing, were demanding years for the administration of the NPS. Redwood and North Cascades National Parks came into the system in 1968 after difficult and protracted struggles. In addition, three national lakeshore units on the Great Lakes were added between 1966 and 1970: Pictured Rocks, Sleeping Bear Dunes, and Apostle Islands.

Hartzog's initial attitude toward the Voyageurs project was also a factor. Kawamoto related that during the time when NPS personnel were developing the official position on Voyageurs, some had doubts as to whether Hartzog would even go along with national park status because the water levels of the proposed park's major lakes were manipulated by dams. Two dams were constructed at either end of Rainy Lake early in the century to accommodate electric power generation for the wood products industry at International Falls, Minnesota, and Fort Frances, Ontario. Traditionalists in the NPS, and there were many at this time, were concerned that in the rush for new parks, long-standing standards for entry into the system could be compromised.[7]

Hartzog eventually approved the national park designation for Voyageurs, but not before staff professionals argued that these were natural lakes with minor fluctuations in levels and not in the same category as reservoirs formed by simply damming up rivers. Also, even though the Kabetogama Peninsula had been logged and some parts burned over and was not therefore in a "pristine" condition, the landform had not changed and was still basic to the area. Kawamoto said that all of these factors were laid out, and that the primary argument made for a national park was that "we needed to look beyond today, perhaps, say, a hundred years from now or beyond and [look at] what condition this area would be [in] if set aside as a national park. The condition being that it would be rather unique by that time. The natural vegetation would be reestablished, and there wouldn't be any more cutting. Sustained yield would be gone, and then the appearance would be a natural appearance."[8]

NPS professionals and many supporters frequently emphasized the importance of preservation and restoration of natural resources as a long-term goal at Voyageurs. They also emphasized the cultural significance of the voyageurs during the fur trade period and the importance of Rainy Lake, which was the focus of several canoe routes used by the voyageurs on their way to the interior of the North American continent.

Status as a national park would bring the last remaining stretch of the border lakes region on the American side under federal protection. No doubt Kawamoto would have been able to bring these attributes to the attention of Hartzog had he been at the witness table with the director.

McClure continued to ask for reasons why this area was unique when the geology and vegetation was not that dissimilar from that in the BWCA to the east. This was the argument frequently made by the timber people and anti-federal opponents who said they were for a national park but on existing federal land at an alternative site in the federal corridor. At one point McClure asked, "Why should we go out and buy up the only substantial private property, at a cost of $20 million, if all we are seeking to do is change present use from multiple use into a narrower use?"[9] At another point he said, "I submit that the real reason you are looking to this is that it is easier to fight private owners than it is to fight the Forest Service."[10]

Near the close of his lengthy question period, Representative McClure said to Hartzog and to a colleague who had asked him if he would yield that he wanted to pursue just one step further: "I just want to get on record what I think some of the real issues are." In a display of wry humor, Hartzog replied with the overstatement of the day: "It is always a great delight to respond to the gentleman's questions."[11]

Several subcommittee members tried to get Hartzog to elaborate on the Crane Lake inclusion, which was part of Blatnik's legislation. When Representative Taylor asked if the NPS supported the Department of Agriculture's recommendation that the Crane Lake Recreation Area be removed from the park bill, Hartzog simply replied, "Those are my directions, yes sir."[12] At a later point in the hearing, Representative Kyl asked Hartzog the same question, and he answered without elaboration that the NPS deferred to the Department of Agriculture on the issue. His abrupt responses to these questions seemed to signal a reluctance to discuss the matter at all. Even though NPS planners had originally recommended that the Crane Lake Recreation Area be a part of the proposed park and had justified that position in the draft proposal (1963 draft plan), he was now required to express the Interior Department's 1970 position that it be removed from the Blatnik bill, thus acceding to his department's desire not to offend the USFS.

The VNPA continued to follow its policy of staying away from the Crane Lake issue for fear of losing the entire project. They offered no formal support for its inclusion. Making the argument for its retention in the legislation would, therefore, be the sole responsibility of its author, Congressman Blatnik.

Blatnik got that opportunity when he asked for and received permission for time to address the committee solely on the issue of the Crane Lake addition. He began by tracing the route of the voyageurs on a map through Crane, Sand Point, Namakan, and Rainy Lakes and noting the physical characteristics of the entire proposed park area: "It is an integrated, interrelated part of the same geographic and historic area—all the more reason why pure logic would dictate that it be as one entity. All aspects of the Crane Lake area—historical, geographic, physical, topographic and location—urge that this area and Kabetogama be an organic entity under one administration." He assured the committee that it was never his intent to bring the two agencies in dispute over his proposal. "Our sole objective was to make a relatively small piece of an area into a park. In every sense of the word it would be a better park with Crane Lake added to it."[13] He concluded by saying that it would be impossible to manage the park economically or efficiently with two federal agencies.

When Blatnik finished his defense of the Crane Lake inclusion, Representative Taylor asked him if he would still support the bill if the committee saw fit to follow the recommendation of the USFS and the NPS and delete the Crane Lake Recreation Area. Blatnik said he would, but "in all earnestness, knowing that area as I have for forty years, also having a little experience with legislative and executive reorganization, of which I am chairman, I hope the Congress with its good judgement, and particularly this committee with its wide range over many years of experience in very controversial and emotionally supercharged matters, will include the Crane Lake area...."[14]

This was the kind of statement that his House colleagues well understood. This congressman, in whose district the park would be located, *wanted* the park boundaries as described in his bill. He might be willing to compromise on some points in the legislation, and he might say in a public hearing that he would accept a park without the Crane Lake addition, but the tone of his voice and the logic of his arguments, no doubt made in private conversation before the hearings, said otherwise. The House and Senate committees bought Blatnik's arguments, which emphasized the physical unity of the area, inclusion of the Crane Lake addition, and the efficiency of single-agency administration. They also desired to accommodate a highly respected colleague. In this way they observed the time-honored practice in the Congress of deferring to the local congressman on matters involving his constituents. The Crane Lake Recreation Area became part of the final authorizing legislation.

Some individuals who were close to the park issue during the 1960s have been curious as to why Blatnik, a cautious politician, would seemingly jeopardize the chances for Voyageurs by arguing so persuasively for inclusion of the Crane Lake addition. One can speculate that there were several reasons and that they were compelling in Blatnik's view. He was reaffirming what had been implied in the first unpublished report by the NPS study team in 1963—that the border lakes region west of the BWCA should be managed by a single agency and that preservation of the historic voyageurs' route and the scenic and physical character of the region should be of primary concern. He believed that the NPS was best suited to carry out that objective.

Blatnik had heard this argument often from his close friend and respected advisor Sigurd Olson. Olson had always hoped for a "seamless" management policy for this entire area. Blatnik, the practical politician, saw the value of efficiency and uniformity through public ownership and single-agency management.

In retrospect, the decision to include the Crane Lake addition in the final legislative version for Voyageurs was a wise one. Apart from the environmental advantage of keeping natural systems intact and under one agency, its inclusion provided definite political advantages as well. As the public debate over the entire park issue dragged on, Representative Blatnik must have realized that to leave the Crane Lake area out of the park for possible addition at a later date, a common suggestion at the time, would only result in another period of protracted and divisive debate. Old wounds would be opened, and angry confrontations would be the lot of yet another generation in the border communities.[15]

Near the close of discussion on the Crane Lake issue, Blatnik asked Chairman Taylor for time to present an argument in favor of the hunting and fishing provision in his bill. By this time Blatnik surely realized that this committee would never allow public hunting in Voyageurs if it were to be a national park. But Blatnik apparently felt strongly about this issue. He placed his argument in historical context by arguing, "Hunting was basic to the voyageur, for survival and for trade. It was part of the commerce of those days. . . . Commercial fishing was basic. The hook and the seine and the net were all introduced by the voyageurs to the Indians."[16] He asked that the committee give hunting and commercial fishing a trial run—give it a five-or-so-year period to help make Voyageurs a year-round park.

Congressman Kyl's response to Blatnik's appeal was brief and to the point: "I just want to say once more it is just not possible and it is not going to happen." Kyl and Taylor again mentioned a national recreation area as an alternative to a national park if hunting and trapping were so important to the area. Blatnik responded by reaffirming his commitment to national park designation. He thanked the committee for allowing him to present his case for hunting and said, "I hope we let it rest at that."[17]

The committee came away from the hearings with a very clear message from Congressman Blatnik. He had moved away from public hunting as a requirement for his support. He would look to the state instead of the federal government for help with the in lieu of taxes issue. And he wanted a national park, not a national recreation area.

The first day of subcommittee hearings also included testimony from three state legislators who held key leadership positions in the legislature. They would also play important roles in 1971 when that body debated the state land donation legislation, a requirement Congress attached to the authorizing legislation. Senator O. A. Sundet, chair of the Senate Public Domain Committee, testified for his committee, which urged that Congress postpone the park legislation until the state legislature met in early 1971. He contended that there was insufficient information on which the legislature could base its decision on matters related to Voyageurs.

Senator Sundet was followed by Representative Thomas Newcome, chair of the Minnesota Resources Commission, a research and advisory agency created by statute. Newcome said the MRC was working on a report to advise the legislature on what the state must do to implement a national park in Minnesota should the Congress pass authorizing legislation for Voyageurs. The MRC had on two previous occasions endorsed the concept of the park, and he personally favored its establishment. On the question of donating state land to the NPS to meet the conditions of the authorizing legislation, Newcome felt the legislature would comply. When Senate Rules Committee Chairman Stanley Holmquist testified, he said that in his judgment, "The state of Minnesota, either through private funds or through legislative action, would be glad to accommodate the Voyageurs National Park, so that the property would be contributed on that basis."[18]

It was about 6 P.M. when Chairman Taylor adjourned the first day of hearings. He and his colleagues could take some satisfaction in knowing that all of the "sticky" issues (public hunting, Crane Lake addition, payment in lieu of taxes, and state land donation) had been considered. In every case, key people like Hartzog, Blatnik, and the two state legislators, Newcome and Holmquist, had provided assurances that they were willing to work out solutions so that Voyageurs could become the state's first national park.

Park supporters in the hearing room took some comfort in this display of cooperation and resolve for the park. But they were evidently surprised at the close questioning of several congressmen who represented districts where the timber industry was a major factor in the district economy. They left the hearing room with some misgivings about the way things had gone and hoped for a better experience on the second day. But it did not happen. Some were stunned and disconsolate by the events of the following day.

The hearings resumed on Friday, July 17, to hear testimony from the St. Louis County Board of Commissioners, Governor LeVander, representatives from the wood products industry, and others stating positions for and against the park.

Commissioners Alvin Hall and Fred Barrett presented the St. Louis County Board's position opposing the park. Hall echoed the state senate Public Domain Committee opinion that Congress should "hold up establishment of the park and give the state of Minnesota an opportunity to act responsibly and protect these lands for future generations."[19] Commissioner Hall advocated the establishment of a commission, authorized by the state, to manage these lands. Later that day, George Amidon said that Boise Cascade, along with other private owners and local governments, would give consideration to cooperating with a commission-type body to regulate the lands in lieu of a national park.

Governor LeVander was introduced to the committee by Blatnik, who praised the governor for using his office so effectively to advance the cause for Voyageurs. The governor began his testimony by introducing Commissioner Leirfallom and three other officials from the Conservation

Department, Dick Wettersten of the game and fish division, U. W. Hella, state parks director, and Clarence Buckman, deputy director of conservation. LeVander's environmental affairs advisor Larry Koll and Assistant Attorney General Philip Olfelt were also introduced as resource people for this hearing. Only LeVander and Leirfallom actually participated in the hearing process. After the introductions and assurances by the chairman that the governor's lengthy statement would be placed in the record, Representative Taylor gently reminded the governor to "hit the high spots."

The governor chose to open his testimony by reviewing the past history of national park studies and proposals for Voyageurs beginning with the 1891 recommendation. He then moved on to the position he outlined in August 1969, which requested that the Blatnik bill include eight provisions that he maintained would best protect the interests of the people of Minnesota. Representative Blatnik accepted, indeed he agreed with LeVander's provisions and had included them in his legislation.

The NPS, as discussed earlier, had no problem with six of the points presented by LeVander, since several were essentially NPS policy for additions to the system. However, they could not accept the inclusion of the Crane Lake Recreation Area and certainly not the positions on hunting and logging, which essentially challenged the authority of the NPS. To some extent, inclusion of what were really the Blatnik-LeVander "eight points" was an effort to cover their "political backsides" in northeastern Minnesota. The principal difference between Blatnik and LeVander on these provisions was the vehemence with which LeVander argued for their retention—especially the timber and wildlife management provisions.

It was obvious from the beginning that the governor meant to explain his case with details and conviction. Early in LeVander's testimony Chairman Taylor had made a plea for brevity in view of the many witnesses yet to be heard. Shemesh said later that this apparently confused and angered the governor and may have had something to do with the negative impression he left with the committee.[20]

In the face of time constraints, LeVander still persisted. At one point he lectured the committee members on their need to "recognize the unique needs of this first water-based park. Consequently, we must expect that the traditional policies of the NPS that apply to all parks will have to be tailored to provide for the best use of this park and the greatest protection of this environment. Such modifications made on behalf of this unusual water-based park could not be construed as establishing a precedent for all parks." The governor tried to make this case by asking the committee to "accept the concept that public hunting should be authorized and utilized as a management tool in accordance with the laws of Minnesota."[21]

This comment brought an icy response from Chairman Aspinall of the House Interior and Insular Affairs Committee. He acknowledged the sincerity of the governor in promoting his case, but this committee, he said, must see that areas coming into the National Park System come in with the proper credentials. He then continued, "I want you to know that I cannot agree to a bill which provides for hunting in a national park. I just can't do it."[22] Aspinall then admonished the people who were sponsoring the legislation to make up their minds pretty soon whether or not they wanted a national park.

To make matters worse for the park cause, when Leirfallom was given several minutes to testify before the committee, he chose to ignore Aspinall's advice and Taylor's plea for brevity. Leirfallom began with a defense of the Conservation Department's reputation for wildlife management and why their position on public hunting as a management tool should become part of the wildlife program in the new park. Chairman Taylor interrupted Leirfallom: "It is out. It is just that simple. I mean hunting and commercial fishing are out."[23]

As the hearing continued, committee members made frequent references to a national recreation area as the way to accommodate the apparent demand for public hunting. Representative Morris Udall of Arizona later capped the discussion by saying, "You can have a national park without hunting like every other national park, or we can pass a bill making this a national recreation area."[24]

The mood of park supporters in the hearing room dropped even lower when the governor resumed his testimony and turned to his proposal for federal acquisition of approximately 25,000 acres of school trust fund lands within the proposed park. The governor, concerned about the constitutional requirements involved with transfer of trust fund lands, recommended a procedure that required the federal government to purchase the lands and deposit the proceeds in the state's permanent trust fund account. In his prepared statement, LeVander said, "The most direct method for acquiring State-owned lands would be condemnation and, with the State's consent, purchase by the NPS. Condemnation would satisfy the strict legal requirements for the sale of trust fund lands and the money received by the State would be used to reimburse the permanent trust fund."[25]

Under LeVander's plan, the trust fund lands would be appraised, and the government would pay the fair market value, just as it would for acquisition of private lands. Chairman Taylor questioned the governor at length about the definition, location, and status of the trust fund lands. After the questioning, Taylor told the governor, "I personally will oppose purchasing this land, whether it is through negotiations or condemnation. Our policy has been to accept such land by donation."[26]

To reinforce his point regarding NPS policy, Taylor cited several recent examples in which states donated lands for inclusion in new or expanded existing national park properties, including Cape Hatteras National Seashore and Great Smoky Mountains National Park. After listening to this exchange between Taylor and the governor, it is no small wonder that many in the room wondered why this variance with congressional policy on land donations was not noticed beforehand. They questioned why the governor and his staff did not work out an acceptable plan to resolve the issue before the hearing.

The mood of the advocates for Voyageurs who had made the trip to Washington was somber to say the least. Some, who had worked for almost eight years on the park project and had strong emotional ties to the park cause, were shocked at the turn of events. This was simply not the kind of hearing they had envisioned. In less than two hours, the governor had presented a position statement on Voyageurs that included two conditions in direct opposition to long-standing NPS policy regarding land acquisition and wildlife management. In the process, the governor had angered the two congressmen—Taylor and Aspinall—whose support was absolutely essential if Voyageurs was to receive congressional approval.

Park opponents were probably just as surprised at the course of the hearings. The focus was on the troublesome testimony of park supporters and on issues that had not been emphasized in public debate in Minnesota. Governor LeVander was seen as a champion for Voyageurs, first, for hosting the Virginia conference in fall 1967, and, second, for then a few days after that meeting, announcing his support for Voyageurs and placing his administration in the forefront of the park movement. Now he was viewed as a negative factor just when the advocates were finally able to go before the one legislative group that could make or break the whole enterprise. Even some of Chairman Taylor's committee colleagues seemed stunned by the testimony they had just heard. Shemesh wrote to Olson a few weeks later about LeVander's testimony: "He had such a great opportunity to go out of office in a blaze of glory and he completely muffed the ball."[27]

Park proponents did not have to wait long for the gloom to give way to a spirit of optimism. When Governor LeVander had finally completed his testimony, Chairman Taylor announced that all government witnesses had been heard from and the committee would begin hearing from the remaining witnesses on the list. He then called Andersen, president of the VNPA, as the first witness in the final group.

Andersen began his testimony by noting that over thirteen hundred organizations from across the state had endorsed the Voyageurs proposal. Without mentioning a national recreation area, he stressed that this broad support was for a *national park* in Minnesota. He said, "I believe there are more interpretive services, there is a greater emphasis on history, there is a greater emphasis on science, there is a greater emphasis on interpretation in a national park than in some of the other designated areas, and we believe that would be a very important value, not only for the people of our own state, but for the people at large."[28]

Regarding the problems associated with land donation, Andersen suggested if the requirement of reimbursing the trust fund could not be resolved legislatively, "It can be accommodated by public subscription to reimburse the trust fund and make the land available."[29]

In the brief time allotted to him, Andersen essentially pledged his personal dedication to the resolution of the few remaining issues preventing congressional authorization. He said this with such conviction that Chairman Taylor and several committee members were moved to congratulate him on his effort. Taylor said, "Governor, you have a way of pouring oil on troubled waters. You make us think it can be done and a few minutes ago I was beginning to be very doubtful."[30] Representative Udall, well known in congressional circles and in Arizona for his "down home" humor in situations like this, told Andersen, "With your enthusiasm and diplomacy, you should have gone into politics." Andersen replied, "I did, but I was not fully appreciated." Udall returned with,

"Is that like the politician who retired on account of illness—the voters got sick of him?"[31] Needless to say, the laughter that followed this exchange completely changed the mood of the hearing.

A few minutes later Sigurd Olson testified that the proposed park's spiritual and intangible values were its greatest resources. He also noted that with the inclusion of the Crane Lake area, the final gap in the protected section of the border lakes voyageur route would be closed. The dream and objective of the Quetico-Superior Council to "weave a protective screen" along the famous voyageurs highway from Lake Superior to Rainy Lake would be realized.[32]

The testimonies of Andersen and Olson bolstered the hopes of park advocates, but far from resolving the thorny issues, the hearing actually highlighted them and revealed some gaping holes in the unified front the VNPA had hoped to present. Those in attendance who opposed the park could take some comfort in the knowledge that the proponents were now clearly on the defensive. Answers to the difficult questions raised in the hearing were almost entirely the responsibility of the pro-park people.

A quick assessment of the situation by park supporters showed that before the park legislation could make any further progress, Governor LeVander would have to assure the House Subcommittee on Parks and Recreation that state-owned lands would be made available without payment for inclusion in Voyageurs. Shemesh contacted Lee McElvain, legal counsel to the Committee on Interior and Insular Affairs, for guidance on the proper course for the VNPA in light of the events that occurred at the Washington hearings. He replied that the single most critical issue for Voyageurs right then was some assurance from LeVander that the state would endeavor to work out a satisfactory resolution of the land acquisition and public hunting issues. Blatnik told her exactly the same. In letters to Andersen and Olson, she told of her conversations with McElvain and Blatnik, saying it was imperative that LeVander write a letter to Representative Taylor providing unequivocal assurance especially on the matter of land donation. In her letter to Andersen, Shemesh asked, "Could you hold his hand or a club over his head while he writes the letter?"[33]

Lloyd Brandt, a member of the VNPA executive committee and manager of the legislative department of the Minneapolis Chamber of Commerce, wasted no time in writing to Aspinall concerning the LeVander testimony. He placed the blame for the hunting issue on Commissioner Leirfallom, who "has long been critical of the National Park Service method of treating over population of certain animals in national parks. Hunting is not a real issue—an annual kill of 300 deer in the park area loses all significance when compared with the 100,000 plus deer harvested in the state each season."[34]

On the land donation issue, Brandt said there was no question in his mind that the legislature would make the land available without cost. Brandt's letter succinctly expressed the issues and the path to resolution of the two remaining substantive roadblocks to authorizing legislation. The committee would follow the wishes of Congressman Blatnik on the inclusion of the Crane Lake addition, and Blatnik could give assurance that hunting was not a major problem. But the governor would have to provide the assurance of state cooperation on land donation. The land donation problem had to be regarded as the principal remaining issue. Following considerable pressure by VNPA members, Governor LeVander, in a letter to Representative Taylor, gave what he believed was the necessary assurance.

LeVander's letter began by defending his earlier position that federal purchase of the trust lands at fair market value and deposit of the sale-generated funds into the state's trust fund were the most expeditious ways of acquiring the lands. He then acknowledged that Taylor's committee on parks and recreation would not consent to this procedure as a matter of policy. Therefore he told Taylor that either legislative or private funds would be used to reimburse the trust fund, thus eliminating the need for any federal money.[35]

At its September 10 meeting, the VNPA executive committee, apparently seeing no ambiguity in his letter, praised LeVander for communicating his assurances to Representative Taylor that the state would indeed donate its trust lands for park purposes. The VNPA and the governor hoped this action would meet the subcommittee's requirement for final authorization of Voyageurs National Park. It remained now for the VNPA to maintain the pressure in Washington to ensure the movement of the bill through the legislative process. Andersen reminded the VNPA executive committee that the bill must win approval from the Interior and Insular Affairs Committee by September 30. This was necessary to meet the deadline for legislation to be reported out of committees if it was to be approved by the House in that session.

Three steps in the process remained: the executive session on Voyageurs by Taylor's Subcommittee on Parks and Recreation, presentation of the bill to Aspinall's full Committee on Interior and Insular Affairs, and the reporting of the bill out of the Interior and Insular Affairs Committee by September 30 in order to be considered by the House in the Ninety-first Congress.

CHAPTER TEN

Final Passage

At the September 10 meeting the VNPA executive committee was told by its executive secretary, Rita Shemesh, that it was absolutely imperative that action be taken on the Voyageurs legislation in the current session of the Congress. She said that although the operating funds for the association were dwindling, they were sufficient to see the bill through the remainder of the year. If, however, the legislation failed passage in this Congress, a major fund drive would be necessary, and the VNPA would have a difficult time regenerating public support for another run. Others voiced concern about what the 1971 state legislature might do to create public doubt about the merits of the Voyageurs project.

Given the gravity of the situation, Shemesh appealed to members to accept responsibility for calling key people in Washington who could assist in keeping the legislation moving.[1] The wisdom of Shemesh's urgent call for direct action by the VNPA committee members was confirmed on the next day, September 11. She received a telephone call from Lee McElvain, a consultant working for the House Subcommittee on National Parks and Recreation. McElvain told Shemesh that the Voyageurs bill was not scheduled for markup that month, and he did not hold out much hope for action by the subcommittee or the full committee for that session.[2] With this alarming report from a person working closely with the subcommittee, she decided to use even more aggressive tactics to get the bill moving again.

Shemesh realized that Voyageurs' only chance was to persuade Taylor and Aspinall to move the authorizing legislation to the top of the agenda for action during the final session of the Ninety-first Congress. In turn, the one person who had the best chance of persuading these congressmen was the author of the legislation and one of the key members of Congress—John Blatnik. She dispatched a letter to him on September 15, just two weeks before the deadline for the bill to clear the Interior and Insular Affairs Committee. Her letter said, "You John, are the only person that can motivate Taylor and Aspinall to see it through. I believe we have done everything needed; the next move is now yours. I know we can count on you, John."[3]

About the same time Shemesh's letter reached Blatnik's Washington office, the news wires were carrying stories about the results of the September 14 primary elections held around the country. A story published in the *New York Times* on September 17 reported the defeat of Representative George Fallon, a Democrat from Maryland and chair of the House Public Works Committee, who was seeking his fourteenth term in the House. For those close to the campaign for Voyageurs, Fallon's defeat was quickly interpreted as a major boost for the park cause. Blatnik, who was second in seniority to Fallon on the Public Works Committee and held a "safe" seat as Eighth District Congressman in Minnesota, was immediately seen by his colleagues in the House as the chair designate of this powerful committee. Requests for roads, bridges, water pollution control facilities, and so on in the congressional districts always moved through the chair's office. Blatnik would not have to wait long to find out just what Fallon's defeat would mean to the chances for passage of the Voyageurs legislation.

On Friday, September 18, Blatnik's administrative assistant Jim Oberstar, who remained in Washington while Blatnik campaigned back in Minnesota, learned of Aspinall's doubts about the usefulness of LeVander's recent letter. LeVander had proposed federal condemnation of state-owned lands to establish the value of those lands and then proposed payment to the educational trust fund by legislative appropriation or private subscription. Aspinall held that this proposal gave no assurance that the federal government would not be required to pay for the land after condemnation.

Apparently after much wrangling during the July hearings over the land donation issue and LeVander's subsequent submission of a "clarifying" letter to Representative Taylor, the question was still not resolved to the satisfaction of Aspinall. The word around Washington was that he planned to adjourn his Interior and Insular Affairs Committee on September 23 and do some campaigning in his Colorado district. After listening to Oberstar's account of Aspinall's concerns and intentions, Blatnik realized that if the committee adjourned on Aspinall's schedule, his park bill was dead, not only for that session but for good.

It was already September 18, which left little time to get Aspinall to delay adjournment of his committee until the Voyageurs bill was heard and reported out. Blatnik immediately tried to reach Aspinall at his Colorado home but was unable to make contact. His chances of meeting with Aspinall were better on the following Monday, September 21. There are slightly different accounts of what transpired over the period from September 21 through the day the Voyageurs bill finally won committee approval. But each one describes a remarkable effort on the part of Congressman Blatnik, his staff, NPS personnel, and VNPA leaders to keep the Voyageurs legislation on the path to final approval in the House.

Shemesh learned on September 21 of Aspinall's plan to "shut down" his committee from Joe Penfold, executive director of the Izaak Walton League. The only prospect of any reversal of Aspinall's intentions, according to Penfold, "would be if John Blatnik twists Aspinall's arm on a political basis." When she heard this, Shemesh said, "The wheels of the VNPA's infallible machinery were put in motion."[4]

Shemesh called Sigurd Olson, Elmer Andersen, Veda Ponikvar, her principal contact on the Iron Range, and key members of the Citizens Committee for Voyageurs Park and asked them to track down the congressman and urge him to move quickly to rescue the bill. Later that morning or early in the afternoon, Shemesh learned that Blatnik was scheduled to address a meeting of the AFL-CIO in Duluth later in the day. She made contact with him by phone and emphasized the urgency of the situation. Blatnik, as did many other veteran members of Congress, well remembered how Aspinall used delaying tactics to keep the wilderness bill bottled up for several years until it was finally passed in 1964. Blatnik did not want to see that happen to the Voyageurs bill. Unlike the wilderness bill, Voyageurs probably would not make it to the next Congress. Later in the afternoon of Monday, September 21, Blatnik began his aggressive effort to rescue the bill.

Blatnik reached Aspinall in his office that afternoon. He reminded Aspinall of his promise to report the bill out of his committee in that session. Aspinall refused to reconsider even after Blatnik assured him that the land donation matter could be resolved. Realizing that he was not getting anywhere with Aspinall, he angrily ended the conversation and called the Speaker of the House, John McCormack. Blatnik explained the situation to the Speaker and about Aspinall's refusal to reconsider his intention to adjourn the committee on September 23. McCormack quickly arranged a conference call whereby all three could discuss the problem.

According to Albert Eisele of the Knight-Ridder newspapers, Blatnik and Aspinall proceeded to engage in a shouting match, at which point McCormack asked Blatnik what he wanted Aspinall to do. Blatnik said he wanted him to turn the bill over to Representative Taylor, and he, Blatnik, would guarantee that the problems could be worked out. And contrary to Aspinall's angry claim, enough members of the full committee would be present to vote the bill out of committee.[5]

Blatnik's claim that he could deliver the necessary votes for committee passage was an unmistakable reference to his power as the chair designate of the Public Works Committee. Aspinall refused to budge on his intentions, whereupon Blatnik announced that he was flying to Washington and then abruptly ended the conversation, but only after telling Aspinall that he (Aspinall) would not treat a freshman congressman this way. Blatnik, who was Aspinall's senior in congressional service, said he never forgot the shabby treatment at the hands of the one person in the House who could have assured Voyageurs a smooth path through the House committee structure.[6]

Blatnik arrived in Washington shortly after noon on September 22 and went directly to the House floor to talk with Speaker McCormack. The Speaker told Blatnik that he "couldn't ask Aspinall to approve a park which he obviously felt didn't qualify for national park status."[7] Blatnik beckoned Representative John Saylor, the ranking minority member of the Interior and Insular Affairs Committee, and told Saylor, in the presence of McCormack, what Aspinall had said to the Speaker. Saylor said such a claim was simply not true and proceeded to recount the positive hearing testimony and the widespread public support for the park.

McCormack then set up a meeting in his office with Blatnik, Saylor, Taylor, and Aspinall. After a relatively short meeting that resulted in Aspinall backing off his earlier threat to discharge his committee, he agreed to Blatnik's request to have Taylor mark up the Voyageurs bill the next day *if* he could get a quorum for the session.[8] Blatnik later denied that he took advantage of the fact that he would be chairing the Public Works Committee in the next Congress. Aspinall needed no coaching on that subject. He knew well the power of a committee chair after twelve terms in Congress serving as chair himself. Aspinall also knew that his large district was dependent on federally financed projects that had to be approved by the Public Works Committee. Nor was the episode lost on other House members. They knew the power of the seniority system and the clout that goes with the chairmanship of any committee in the House.

The events just related were still well fixed in the memory of former Congressman Blatnik when interviewed fifteen years later.[9] As he described some of the details of his encounter with Aspinall, anger crept into his voice, especially when he told of the obstinate behavior of the representative from Colorado. Although he did not use the word, I got the impression that he took Aspinall's condescending manner as an insult, not just to himself, but to his home district in Minnesota. Blatnik said he spent some of his happier days as a young man working in and enjoying the border lakes region, which he regarded as some of the most beautiful scenery in the country. Aspinall inflicted a deep wound when he said this area in Blatnik's district was not qualified for designation as a national park.

As soon as Representative Taylor received the signal to move ahead with the markup of the bill, he called together his staff, NPS personnel, Oberstar, and McElvain to complete the assignment as soon as possible. A number of resource people were on hand to assist in the rewrite of the Blatnik bill so that it meshed with NPS requirements and also the requests of the two "clients"—Blatnik and Aspinall. Andersen and Wayne Olson from the VNPA flew to Washington to assist in the work, and Joe Penfold from the Izaak Walton League, and Doug Scott and Stewart Brandborg from The Wilderness Society joined them.[10]

Representative Aspinall had attached some conditions to his consent to hold off adjournment, as was soon discovered during the markup of the bill. He insisted that the legislation use precise language to clear up any confusion over the transfer of the 25,000 acres of state trust fund lands. He did not like what he interpreted as ambiguities contained in Governor LeVander's letter of September 5. Aspinall wanted the bill to say that the park would not be established by the secretary of the interior until the state lands were donated to the Department of the Interior. He also demanded that the legislation be clear on the prohibition of hunting in the park.

Congressman Blatnik continued to insist on the inclusion of the Crane Lake Recreation Area in the final version of the bill. (This was the major difference between the official NPS position on Voyageurs and the Blatnik bill.) As soon as the markup was completed, Taylor called his subcommittee together, and all but one of eighteen members showed up for the voice vote approving the legislation. Blatnik had contacted every member of the committee and asked them to be present at the subcommittee session. Senior members could not recall ever seeing so many members at a subcommittee session.

On the following day, September 24, the full Interior and Insular Affairs Committee met to review the product of the previous day's work. After making a few changes, including a reduction from $52 million to $45.2 million for land acquisition and development costs over a five-year period, the bill received unanimous approval. The dollar reduction was made so that the NPS would have to come back to the committee with detailed development plans for the Crane Lake area before the full amount was restored. (The original NPS master plan for Voyageurs did not include the Crane Lake Recreation Area addition.)[11]

Blatnik and others close to the Voyageurs issue were elated at the quick action by the Interior and Insular Affairs Committee. On Monday, September 21, the bill had seemed doomed for that session of Congress. But by Thursday it had cleared the committee. Prospects now looked brighter for passage before the close of the Ninety-first Congress. Passage of this bill in a *new* Congress was highly problematic given the uncertainties of the mood of a new Congress following the fall elections.

Even though approval by a House committee is generally considered the critical hurdle, Blatnik took no chances. To move the bill to the Senate as quickly as possible, he asked that the bill be placed on the House suspension calendar, which permits noncontroversial issues to be taken up under a suspension of rules. This meant that Blatnik's bill would avoid going through the Rules Committee, a time-consuming process normally required as a final step to full House consideration.[12] With that accomplished, Blatnik then asked Speaker McCormack to move the bill up from its fifteenth position if any of the bills ahead of it were removed. A friend and colleague from Ohio removed his own bill so that Voyageurs became the third one to be considered by the House on October 5.

On that date the House approved the bill on a voice vote. It was ready to move on to the Senate, where Walter Mondale would be its chief sponsor. Mondale had already asked Henry Jackson, chair of the Senate Interior and Insular Affairs Committee, to schedule hearings on the Voyageurs bill as soon as it came over from the House.

Ever watchful that the park bill not get caught up in scheduling delays and misunderstandings about the significance of the legislation to Minnesota, Shemesh, on the day following House passage, sent a letter to Alan Bible, chair of the subcommittee that would hear the Voyageurs bill in the Senate. In her letter she told the senator that the park proposal met all standards of the NPS, had been endorsed by all major conservation organizations and eighteen hundred other civic and professional groups, and had bipartisan support at all times. She urged him to schedule hearings quickly so that the bill could gain authorization before the close of the Ninety-first Congress at the end of December.[13] Shemesh encouraged VNPA supporters to write similar letters to the senator because many, like Shemesh, saw this Congress as the last chance for Voyageurs.

Shemesh's correspondence—the timely letter to Senator Bible, frequent letters to leaders of the Citizens Committee for Voyageurs, and the many personal notes of appreciation and concern about the welfare of individuals and families involved in the campaign—and her dedication and enthusiasm for this effort did not go unnoticed by friend and adversary alike. Within the VNPA, sincerity and enthusiasm for the Voyageurs cause were contagious and had an enormous impact on the final outcome of the campaign.

One of the conditions Aspinall insisted upon in the House bill was that the state must *donate* its lands within the boundaries of the proposed park to the federal government and that the transfer be accomplished *before* the park was established. Since much of the state land was classified as school trust fund land, the state legislature would be required to pass special legislation to reimburse the trust fund for the donated lands. Moving land donation legislation through the legislature required strong leadership from both parties but especially from conservatives who were in the majority in both houses.[14]

The two legislators who would assume key leadership roles on the land donation legislation would be Stanley Holmquist, majority leader in the senate, and Representative Thomas Newcome, chairman of the Minnesota Resources Commission (MRC), in the house.[15] Both had testified in favor of the park at the Washington hearings in July. Even though both were strongly committed to the park, they were well aware of the strong opposition within their own caucuses. Some who strongly opposed the park were senior leaders in the conservative-controlled legislature. For a number of them, the results of the fall primaries and the November elections caught them by surprise.

The Wednesday following the 1970 November elections saw the conservative majorities in the state legislature reduced significantly by liberal victories across the state. Wendell Anderson, a Democrat who had previous experience as a state senator, replaced Governor LeVander, who chose not to run for reelection. Anderson immediately launched a reorganization of the state administration that included the elimination of the Department of Conservation. It was replaced by a Department of Natural Resources and headed by Robert Herbst, no stranger to the capitol scene. He previously held the position of deputy to Clarence Prout, conservation commissioner in the Rolvaag administration.

Herbst returned to Minnesota from Washington, where he had been the national executive director of the Izaak Walton League. He and the new governor let it be known early on that they were committed to quick approval of state land donation legislation once the Senate passed and the president authorized the establishment of Voyageurs, thus removing the one remaining roadblock to full establishment of the park.

Holmquist won reelection and resumed his position as majority leader of the state senate, where the conservative margin had been reduced to only one vote over Democratic-Farmer-Labor liberals. The conservatives, who had held control of the senate since 1913, were able to retain control because one new senator, who had campaigned as an independent, decided to caucus with conservatives. Many supporters saw this as a fortuitous event because Holmquist, highly respected in both parties, would again be leading the effort for Voyageurs in the senate.

O. A. Sundet, chairman of the Senate Public Domain Committee and an opponent of Voyageurs, was defeated in the primaries. Senator Ray Higgins of Duluth, the most vocal and determined member of the anti-park faction, was defeated in the general election. His defeat came at the hands of Ralph Doty, a young college professor who had openly campaigned for Voyageurs and made Senator Higgins's negative stance on the park a major part of his campaign. Also going down in the liberal "landslide" were the state's senior lawmaker Senator Donald O. Wright and conservative Senator Gordon Rosenmeier, frequently called the most influential man in the state legislature.

As if to remove any chance that a senate committee would again be used as a forum for fighting the park, the committee structure for the 1971 session of the Minnesota Legislature no longer included a Public Domain Committee. Its duties were subsumed in a new senate committee, the Natural Resources and Environment Committee.

A *Duluth News-Tribune* editorial on the impact of the fall elections around the state said that the legislature had been changed significantly: "The state has witnessed a quiet revolution."[16] In looking for explanations for the philosophical shift, some observers speculated that the electorate expressed its preference for new and younger faces in the legislature, replacing some "pillars" of the old guard that had dominated the state legislature for many years. Others saw it as reflecting the increased public interest in environmental issues, which had begun throughout the nation in the 1960s, and a belief that legislative attention to these matters could best be dealt with by a new set of lawmakers. Shemesh had no doubts that it was the latter.

Just as soon as the election results were known, Shemesh sent congratulatory letters to Doty and Anderson, both strong supporters of Voyageurs. In a letter to Senator Mondale she said, "State Senators Higgins, Sundet and Rosenmeier and others were all defeated to a large degree, by virtue of their opposition to Voyageurs." Shemesh told him she believed the new crop of legislators was supportive of the park and could foresee "no problems at all in working out all the details on a state level *if* the park is authorized in the Senate session."[17] Shemesh's letter gave her the opportunity to tell the senator the good news for the park cause brought about by the election results and also to remind him, in not so subtle fashion, that park advocates in Minnesota were going to rely on him to help secure Senate passage of the House-approved bill. Little did she realize at the time she wrote the letter that the Voyageurs legislation would encounter unexpected opposition and delay in the Senate, and that the land donation legislation would meet with even more formidable resistance in the state legislature. In some ways the last few months of the legislative "ride" for Voyageurs National Park legislation were the roughest of the entire eight-year journey.

Senate hearings on the House-passed bill were scheduled for two half-day sessions on Friday, December 4, and Monday, December 7. Senator

Alan Bible of Nevada, chair of the Subcommittee on Parks and Recreation, presided at both sessions. Many witnesses at these hearings had appeared at the earlier House hearings and filed statements with the Senate that were essentially the same as those used at the previous hearings. The positions pro and con were known to both sides but not necessarily to all senators who participated in this hearing.[18]

Therefore, Blatnik, in his opening remarks, reviewed the history of the Voyageurs movement, the geographic setting of the proposed park, and in response to a question from Bible, his reasons for including the Crane Lake Recreation Area in his bill. As he had done in previous testimony in the House, he stressed the logic of single-agency jurisdiction over the entire park. Pointing to the map of the proposed park and particularly to the western third of Namakan Lake, he said, "To arbitrarily have a bisection here just wouldn't make any sense." He said it made no sense from an administrative point of view to have two federal departments involved in the management of an area he saw as a single geographic unit. Blatnik also reassured the committee that leaders of both houses of the Minnesota Legislature were committed to passing legislation authorizing donation of state lands in the proposed park.[19]

When Director Hartzog took his place at the witness table, he was accompanied by John Kawamoto, the park planner who had worked on the Voyageurs project from the beginning. By choosing Kawamoto, the NPS hoped to avoid the embarrassing experience of the House hearings when the director was subjected to thorough grilling by Representative McClure. McClure had made the most of the opportunity to embarrass the director by asking follow-up questions that called for fairly detailed knowledge of the area and the special circumstances surrounding the proposal. The director's office anticipated that the same tough questions would be asked by Idaho Senator Len Jordan, who was a member of the subcommittee's parent committee on Interior and Insular Affairs.

However, the questions Jordan might have asked, had he been able to attend the hearing, were put to Hartzog by Wyoming Senator Clifford Hansen. Kawamoto said later that Hansen "didn't quite understand the context of the questions so he asked them in such a way that they were easy to answer. So actually it was very easy. You answered the questions and that was the end of it."[20]

Director Hartzog's testimony included no new information, and adhering to the provisions of the "Treaty of the Potomac," it reaffirmed the

Interior Department's hands-off policy with respect to the Crane Lake Recreation Area. His stock answer to several questions on this subject was that the Interior Department deferred to the Agriculture Department on the issue. The Department of Agriculture chose not to send a representative to testify at the hearings, but in a prepared statement sent to the committee, Secretary of Agriculture Clifford M. Hardin strongly recommended that the Senate bill be amended to exclude any area within Superior National Forest from the proposed park.

Apparently the Agriculture Department felt their official position was well known and that any additional support for their stance on this matter would be made by other witnesses including the National Wildlife Federation, the American Forestry Association, the Wildlife Management Institute, St. Louis County commissioners, the Crane Lake Commercial Club, and private citizens in the affected area.

The subcommittee also heard several witnesses claim that designation as a national recreation area would be more appropriate than national park for the proposed Voyageurs. Alvin Hall, a member of the St. Louis County Board, spoke in favor of a "commission system" of management for the park that would rely on local and state representation, thereby keeping the federal government out of the area entirely. A variation of this type of management was described earlier as a product of the Charles Aguar study and the Allagash Wilderness Waterway model in Maine. Minnesotans would learn more about the proposed commission when park opponents pushed hard for approval of such an agency in the 1971 session of the state legislature.

The Washington Senate hearings attracted a new "entrant" to the Voyageurs controversy, William Essling, a former assistant U.S. attorney who worked with enforcement issues in the "Superior Roadless Primitive Area," now the BWCA, during the Truman administration. He appeared at the hearings as a landowner in the Crane Lake Recreation Area. Testifying without a formal written statement, Essling said that until the field hearings in International Falls in August 1969, the general public assumed that hunting and other uses more compatible with a national recreation area would be permitted in the proposed park. Hunting was advocated in Blatnik's legislation. He also said that land acquisition costs could run as high as $150 million and questioned the NPS's lack of information on property values. Once the park was established, Essling was successful in securing clients among the inholders and gaining generous awards for a number of these individuals.

Also appearing at the hearings was Dr. A. T. Banen, a dentist and the mayor of International Falls. A week before the hearings, several members of the city council learned that the mayor was intending to fly to Washington to testify in favor of the park. They reminded Mayor Banen that in July 1970 they had passed a resolution opposing the park by a six-to-one vote. His was the lone vote in opposition to the resolution. In his response Banen said, "The Council doesn't represent the city in the matter by simply passing a resolution."[21] He added that he had been invited to testify by the VNPA to represent the city, and that he intended to do just that and would be paying his own way. Banen also informed the council that he stood by statements he had made at previous meetings that council members who worked for Boise Cascade did not always think for themselves. During the course of the Senate hearings, Banen referred to the resolution opposing the park and noted that all six of those voting against the park were employees of Boise Cascade. He said he felt confident that sentiment for the park was shared by a majority of residents in International Falls, and as evidence of this view, he openly supported the park in his campaign for mayor and won by a two-to-one margin.[22]

Mayor Banen's belief that a majority of International Falls residents supported the park was shared by others who filed statements with the subcommittee. After the hearings on the first day, Senator Bible said that the many expressions favoring the park (at the hearings and from letters he had received) make "the green light for the park look pretty green."[23] But that was on December 4. By Thursday, December 10, the signal was on caution and moving slowly toward red. Just when the park legislation needed a barrier-free path with less than four weeks before the close of the Ninety-first Congress, obstructions began to appear along the right-of-way.

The results of a Senate vote had a negative effect on the park deliberations. One day before the subcommittee hearings, the Senate voted 52 to 41 against any new government spending on the supersonic transport (SST) program. Two of the senators voting with the majority to restrict funding were Minnesota's senators, Mondale and Eugene McCarthy. One of the chief sponsors of this legislation was Senator Henry Jackson from Washington State, where the health of the aircraft industry was always an important political issue. Jackson, who was chairman of the Interior and Insular Affairs Committee, which had to approve the Voyageurs bill in order to get Senate passage, was not at all happy with the lack of support for the SST from his colleagues in Minnesota. People close to Mondale said that Jackson had called him before the crucial vote, but Mondale stood firm in his opposition to further funding.

Rumors began to circulate in Washington that Jackson planned to hold up the park bill as retribution for Mondale's and McCarthy's lack of support on the aerospace legislation. Holding it up even a few days could have been lethal to the Voyageurs cause. What Blatnik needed was a Senate bill that was close to the House version, that is, a Senate bill without substantive amendments. Such a bill would not require House-Senate conference committee action and could go directly to the House floor for final action.

Getting a relatively "clean" bill out of the Senate in time to meet the deadlines for passage in the House would not be easy, as Blatnik's staff learned on December 10. On that day, Jackson's office notified Blatnik that the senator had a number of unanswered questions about his park bill. Along with his request for clarification on certain provisions in the bill came Jackson's assurance that he would not hold up the bill because of the SST issue. (Jackson always denied that it was ever his intention to use that issue to withhold his support for Voyageurs.)

Senator Jackson had three major concerns about the House bill: one, the use of snowmobiles in the park; two, state constitutional problems associated with the donation of state trust fund lands; and three, the inclusion of the Crane Lake Recreation Area. Jackson had been getting pressure from some conservation organizations as well as forestry industry representatives to remove these objectionable provisions from the bill. Blatnik immediately realized that if Jackson moved to satisfy these concerns, it would require substantive changes in the legislation and necessitate a conference committee to resolve differences.

The time remaining on the congressional calendar was insufficient to accommodate a conference committee process. The bill would be lost for the session and probably for good. If Blatnik were to save the Voyageurs bill, he would have to enlist the support of staff, colleagues in the House, and park advocates in a herculean effort. And this effort had to be compressed in a time period that included the Christmas holiday recess.

Blatnik began by calling for assistance from Elmer Andersen, Sigurd Olson, and other park supporters in Minnesota, and leaders of major conservation organizations to help him mount a "last-ditch" effort to move the Voyageurs legislation to final passage. If he failed, he and everyone else connected with the campaign over the previous six to eight years knew that it would be impossible to win approval in the new Congress. Voyageurs National Park would be a dead issue, a casualty of political wrangling, infighting, and indifference.

Congressman Blatnik asked Olson and Andersen to come to Washington as soon as possible to lobby for the bill. Before leaving for Washington, Olson, then president of The Wilderness Society, sent a telegram approved by the VNPA and eight conservation organizations with national memberships to Senator Jackson pleading for final Senate approval of the Voyageurs legislation: "We beg you and beseech you, please place the Voyageurs National Park bill on the floor of the Senate for passage before the session adjourns. We joined together sending this desperate plea for Voyageurs. Citizens all over the U.S. and the generations to follow will praise your wisdom forever."[24]

The rescue effort continued aggressively on Monday morning, December 14, when Blatnik contacted Jackson and Bible by telephone to tell them that he was confident that he and others outside the Congress who were familiar with the issues and the legislation could work out language and provisions in the bill that would satisfy the concerns of committee members. He believed he could do this and still come up with legislation close enough to the House version so that time-consuming conference committee proceedings would not be required. With members of his own staff, NPS personnel, and Senate Interior and Insular Affairs Committee staff working together to shape the legislation so that it would merit approval by the full committee, Blatnik then turned to another part of his plan to make the rescue effort a success.

After more than six years on the receiving end of relentless pressure from both sides of the Voyageurs issue, Blatnik decided to use the tactic on Jackson and his committee. He called on Senator-elect Hubert Humphrey and Senator Mondale to contact Jackson to stress the significance of the park bill to Minnesota and to note the legislation's broad support among the leading conservation organizations across the country. To make certain that these organizations were totally committed to the park bill as written and passed by the House, he called in representatives from six major conservation groups including the Sierra Club and The Wilderness Society to set aside their differences and let Jackson know they were behind the legislation 100 percent.[25]

While all of this was taking place, Andersen and Olson were making the rounds once again to drum up support for Voyageurs. Andersen, in an interview some years later, pointed out that normally national park bills are carried by the Congress member in whose district the park will be located, and the Senate will go along with the legislation as it comes over from the House. But, he said, in this case some western senators, including Jackson, were getting pressure from park opponents including Boise Cascade and others in the forest industry. Also, Andersen felt that Minnesota's senators were not as helpful as they should have been.[26]

When Andersen and Olson arrived in Washington on December 13, the Voyageurs bill was in deep trouble. Andersen learned that Jackson's staff had "looked at the Voyageurs proposal as immature and considered it dead."[27] He realized that the best course of action would be for he and Olson to meet with Jackson and his staff as soon as possible. Andersen then called a friend, Senator Gordon Allott, former lieutenant governor of Colorado and ranking Republican member of Jackson's committee, and asked him to arrange a meeting with Jackson. The meeting was arranged for December 14 in Jackson's office. Andersen recalled, "We talked fast and furious for an hour describing the park. Jackson asked his staff what they thought and they replied that they had been misinformed. Jackson then said let's do it. Sig and I left the meeting elated."[28]

Andersen continued to meet with Republican members of the Senate committee, and Blatnik and his team of staff people and park supporters continued to work on modifying the bill to make it acceptable to the committee. On Tuesday, December 15, Blatnik learned that Jackson had scheduled a committee meeting for Thursday to consider Voyageurs and two other park proposals, the Chesapeake and Ohio Canal National Historic Park and Gulf Islands National Lakeshore. Blatnik's optimism was short-lived, however. By Wednesday morning Voyageurs legislation had hit yet another snag. Once again it was caught up in the SST controversy.

Following the normal procedure, the Senate version of the SST bill, which included cuts the Senate imposed earlier in December, went to conference with the House. But when it returned to the Senate, SST opponents noticed that the conference committee had restored much of the money the Senate had earlier removed. Almost immediately, Senator William Proxmire of Wisconsin, a leading opponent of the SST, launched a filibuster with the intent of keeping the Senate tied up until the end of the session.[29]

The Interior and Insular Affairs Committee meeting that had been scheduled to consider the three park bills was promptly canceled, as Jackson was busy assessing the impact of a long filibuster on the SST legislation. Press accounts said that committee staff were told the meeting was canceled because Senator Bible was not available. This may have been the case, but certainly the fate of the SST bill had to be uppermost in Jackson's mind at the time. To ease the anxiety of supporters for all three parks, Interior Department staff felt certain that the committee meeting would be rescheduled for early the next week. True to assurances given by Jackson's office, the committee session took place on Monday, December 21, at which time the bill was approved and quickly sent to the full Senate for final action.

While these events were under way in the Senate, Blatnik met with Roy Taylor, chair of the House Subcommittee on Parks and Recreation, to go over alterations made in the Senate on the Voyageurs bill. The changes were happily determined to be minor, and Taylor agreed to the changes, including one that went beyond the House requirement that the park would not be established until all state lands were donated. The Senate had added another line that prohibited federal purchase of any privately owned land for park purposes until all state lands had been donated.[30] Upon appeal to the secretary of the interior and under certain extenuating circumstances, some purchases could go forward, but the intent was to firmly place the burden on the state legislature to expedite the land donation process.

With Taylor's agreement, the usual House-Senate negotiations were avoided, and the legislation was ready for Senate action. Setting aside the SST issue for a brief period, the Senate passed the Voyageurs legislation on December 22. Blatnik hoped to get action on his bill before the Christmas recess, but it was late getting over from the Senate to the

House side, which delayed final action until the House reconvened after the Christmas break.

On the afternoon of December 29, with only sixty members in attendance, Representative Taylor asked for unanimous consent to accept the minor Senate changes in H.R. 10482. Following several questions and comments regarding game management and state land donation, the bill was passed by voice vote without opposition. In the waning hours of the Ninety-first Congress, the eight-year campaign for Voyageurs came to a close. President Nixon signed the authorizing legislation on January 8, 1971, at the "western White House" in San Clemente, California.

It all began on June 27, 1962, with a trip along the shores of the Kabetogama Peninsula and with a consensus statement drafted by Andersen on behalf of the director of the NPS, the director of the Midwest Region of the NPS, Minnesota Department of Conservation officials, the director of the Minnesota Historical Society, a representative of the Minnesota and Ontario Paper Company, the largest landowner on the Kabetogama Peninsula, and naturalist Sigurd Olson, declaring that the beautiful Kabetogama Peninsula and surrounding lakes should be made available to a larger public, "while preserving its wilderness character for posterity. Establishing it as a national park would be an excellent way of accomplishing these objectives."[31] Only one hurdle remained before Voyageurs National Park could officially join the others in the National Park System—approval of the land donation process in the 1971 session of the Minnesota Legislature.

CHAPTER ELEVEN

The Final Step to Establishment

Land Donation and the State Legislature

News that the president had signed the legislation authorizing the establishment of Voyageurs National Park was greeted across Minnesota as a major triumph for conservation and environmental protection. There were many expressions of pride that national recognition had finally been given to the historical significance and the beauty of the westerly segment of the state's border lake region, just as it had been some years earlier to the Boundary Waters Canoe Area Wilderness to the east. That this recognition came through designation as the nation's thirty-sixth national park was especially significant. Press accounts appearing in newspapers around the state generously commended the leadership, dedication, and perseverance of Elmer Andersen, Congressman John Blatnik, Judge Edwin Chapman, Sigurd Olson, State Parks Director U. W. Hella, Rita Shemesh, and many others in and outside of government, who steadfastly insisted that the Kabetogama area satisfied the strict criteria for designation as a national park.

The eight-year effort led by these individuals was in some ways similar to a political campaign. The latter requires that campaign leaders be in general agreement with the political philosophy of the candidate and then be willing to devote the time, effort, and persistence to see the campaign to its successful conclusion. In the campaign for Voyageurs, however, the commitment was not to an individual but to the uniquely American concept of a national park where carefully selected landscapes possessing outstanding natural and cultural resources are set aside by the Congress as national areas in the public interest. Park proponents conducted a statewide informational campaign explaining the objectives of the NPS and why its management program for such areas was superior to alternative schemes. In this effort they were eminently successful in winning endorsements for the park from hundreds of civic and professional organizations in the state and nation. Early in the campaign, however, park proponents discovered that many people around the state took an entirely different position on the proposal for the Voyageurs National Park.

A great many park opponents saw the national park as an unwarranted intrusion of the federal government into an area long enjoyed as a recreation area unfettered by restrictive rules and regulations. This opinion was most strongly held by many residents living close to the newly authorized park in the communities of International Falls, Ranier, Ray, Kabetogama, and Crane Lake. Also, a hundred miles to the south, in the cities and towns along the Mesabi Iron Range, many residents never embraced the notion of a national park in the Kabetogama area, a popular recreation area less than two hours from home. By contrast, in the Duluth area, with the largest concentration of population in St. Louis County—just sixty miles south of the Iron Range—the park proposal met little opposition, with many local social, political, and civic organizations officially endorsing the park. The St. Louis County Board, whose membership reflected the population distribution patterns of the county, opposed the park, thereby expressing the sentiments of their rural constituents in the northern third of the county. The county board held firm in its opposition to the national park even after the park legislation had cleared Congress. It gave clear evidence of its feelings when, just two days before the president signed the authorizing legislation on January 8, it voted to send a telegram to President Nixon, reaffirming its opposition to the national park bill. One commissioner, Joseph Priley of Duluth, voted against the resolution, thus attesting to his consistent support for the national park.[1]

Many county residents living closest to the park boundary agreed with park advocates that this relatively unspoiled area was certainly worthy of special recognition and even special management status to protect its natural and cultural features. But the prospect of more federal control in the border region to accomplish this task was unwelcome and unthinkable. Those who owned cabins, resorts, or other properties on the peninsula and islands in the park area were particularly disturbed.

Most realized they might eventually have to sell their holdings to the NPS, thus severing the close connections, some going back several generations, with the big lakes. They listened when NPS personnel explained in public meetings the long acquisition process, which was described as fair and equitable for all property owners. But it is doubtful their spirits were lifted by the message. At this late hour many were still hoping for an alternative to NPS control over the area. After examining the authorizing legislation, opposition leaders realized that they would have one more opportunity to press their position that protection of the resources in the Kabetogama area could be accomplished just as effectively at the state or regional level.

The Congress had authorized the park, but it attached conditions in the first section of the federal bill, where two provisions were specified as conditions that had to be met before *formal establishment* of the park could be accomplished: (1) the state was required to donate all of its land within the park boundaries to the NPS, and (2) the secretary of the interior was prohibited from purchasing any private lands inside the park boundaries until the state had complied with the donation requirement.[2] In the opinion of the Senate Committee on Interior and Insular Affairs, these conditions were necessary because the School Trust Fund lands and other state and county holdings "are substantial and essential to a viable national park."[3] Additionally, and perhaps just as important to some congressmen, was the concern that Governor LeVander's successor might not exert the kind of leadership required to see donation legislation through the next session of the legislature. They also recalled the summer 1970 hearings in Washington when, with full knowledge that the NPS requires donation of state lands for new park creation, Governor LeVander expressed strongly that the *federal government* purchase the state's school lands so that the trust fund account could be reimbursed with the proceeds of the sale. Now with the land donation requirements clearly stated in the authorizing legislation, the Congress had shifted the responsibility for securing a Voyageurs National Park to the halls of the Minnesota state legislature and a new state administration. Of course, the entire process of state land donation to the NPS would have to be spelled out in legislation approved by the state legislature, and this was the opportunity individuals, organizations, and some legislators long opposed to the park had been looking for—hearings and debate on Voyageurs in the state legislature.

Aside from the several Public Domain Committee hearings previously noted, all formal discussions before legislative bodies were held at the federal level. However, despite the advantage of "home turf," opposition leaders recognized that they were dealing with an issue that was popular across the state. Proof that the Voyageurs proposal enjoyed widespread support came in the early part of the legislative session when the *Minneapolis Tribune* published results of a statewide opinion poll on the question of land donation, taken in the second week of February 1971. People were asked if they were in favor of donating state lands to meet the requirements of the federal legislation. Seventy-eight percent answered, yes. The same poll showed that even in northern Minnesota more than two-thirds supported land donation legislation.[4] In the face of such widespread public approval for donating state land to bring about a national park, it was clear to those opposed to the park that blanket opposition would not be effective in winning support for their position. Counter proposals, however, such as a state park in the Kabetogama area or a regional park managed by a state-local commission might be seen by legislators as a more desirable alternative to simply giving up state lands to the NPS, which by law and general practice would be required to impose more restrictive management policies.

In retrospect, it seems unlikely that leaders of the opposition to land donation thought such proposals would win approval in the legislature, but they knew that each would require hearings and have to run the gamut of the legislative process. For some, the real motive was to take advantage of the often slow, deliberate legislative routine to the point where session deadlines would force the bill into the next session. Several proponents had long experience in and with the legislature and were well aware of the consequences of protracted debate and political maneuvering in both houses. They realized that failure to pass the donation bill in the 1971 session could effectively kill the Voyageurs' bill. Therefore, they urged Wendell Anderson, the new governor, to get a donation bill to the legislature as soon as possible. The governor wasted no time in responding to the wishes of park advocates. Just two days after the president signed the park bill, Anderson, from a hospital bed where he was recovering from bronchitis, asked his staff to draft appropriate land donation legislation requiring the transfer of some 36,000 acres of state land to the NPS.[5]

Approximately 25,000 acres, or 70 percent of the total donation package, were lands constitutionally tied to the state's School Trust Fund.[6] It was this block of land that LeVander wanted the federal government to purchase outright. LeVander reasoned that the proceeds could then be deposited in the School Trust Fund account, and the issue neatly resolved. It was this procedure that LeVander presented so forcefully during the Washington hearings in July 1970. However, members of the House Subcommittee on Parks and Recreation rejected the governor's proposal, noting that long-standing congressional practice required states to donate prospective national park lands to the federal government. Just to make certain that Minnesota followed through with the land transfer required in the house bill, the Senate added another provision in the legislation that forbade government acquisition of lands from private parties until the land transfer process was complete, and the appropriate legal documents delivered to the federal government.

By early February, it became evident to the governor and his staff that certain key issues had to be addressed in the land donation legislation before the bill could be placed on the legislative calendar. The state had determined that park boundaries would enclose about 36,300 acres of state land, which would have to be donated to the federal government before Voyageurs National Park could become a reality. This land was divided into three categories, each requiring special attention in the donation legislation: 24,976 acres of School Trust Fund lands, 5,902 acres of tax-forfeited land, and 5,459 acres in Kabetogama State Forest.[7] The state forest lands posed no significant legal problems in making the transfer. However, the school lands and tax-forfeited lands were a different matter.

To expedite the legislative process, the donation bill would have to identify the public interests served by transfer of lands to the national government; determine how to free the school land from its constitutional constraints, and how to fund the acquisition of this land; determine whether or not to compensate local taxing districts for the market value of any tax-forfeited lands donated for inclusion in the park; and if the decision was to reimburse the local units, determine what would be the source of funds for the compensation. Governor Anderson, with advice from his staff, determined that the best way to focus on these questions would be for he and members of his staff to meet with the legislative leaders from both houses, who would be responsible for carrying the land donation bill in the legislature. This conference would examine these issues and try to come to general agreement as to their resolution. The meeting, held during the first week of February, did produce ideas and consensus on several of the key issues that proved to be useful in shaping the content of the land donation legislation.[8]

Participants in the discussion included the governor; Robert Herbst, newly appointed commissioner of the Department of Natural Resources (DNR); State Senator Gene Mammenga of Bemidji; Philip Olfelt, special assistant to the attorney general; Representative Thomas Newcome, who was also chair of the Minnesota Resources Commission, which was preparing a "fact book" on the park to help legislators understand the issues in the land donation legislation; and several liberal legislators including Irvin Anderson of International Falls, Jack Fena of Hibbing, and House Minority Leader Martin Sabo of Minneapolis.[9] The individuals attending the governor's "conference" were generally committed to successfully moving the land donation bill through the legislature to final passage. But even though the bill would enter the legislative stream with bipartisan support, the intuitive skepticism of the politician told them that concerted efforts could and in all likelihood would be made by opponents to extend debate on some of the more controversial issues, present alternative proposals that had little chance of acceptance by the legislature, and through parliamentary gimmicks and maneuvers cause delays that could place the legislation in a difficult position in the closing days of the session. To combat such tactics, park supporters both in and outside the state legislature believed it was essential that a tight piece of legislation be drawn that responded clearly and concisely to the central legal and fiscal questions regarding donation of state lands for inclusion in the park.

The land donation bill, or "land transfer" bill, was ready for formal introduction less than three weeks after the meetings in the governor's office. But as an indication of things to come, the legislation encountered the first of many diversions when a disagreement arose between house conservatives and Governor Anderson over who would be designated chief sponsor of the bill in the house. The governor's choice was Representative Irv Anderson, a liberal from International Falls, in whose district a segment of the new park was located. However, the conservatives, who controlled the house, chose Representative Thomas Newcome as the bill's chief sponsor. Aside from party loyalty, there was fundamental logic behind their choice. Newcome, who also served as chair of the MRC, the research group charged with preparing a ready reference book of "facts" on Voyageurs, was also one of the most knowledgeable legislators, irrespective of party, on matters related to the park. He, along with Senator Stanley Holmquist, majority leader in the senate, was a key witness in support of the park proposal at the congressional hearings in late 1970. After a bit of political sparring between the governor and the house leadership—and a delay of more than a week—Newcome was named principal author and sponsor of the donation bill for the house.

Senate Majority Leader Holmquist was the principal author of the land donation bill in the senate, where conservatives had emerged from the November elections in a tie with the liberals. Fortunately for the conservatives, the tie-breaking vote for control of the senate was cast by freshman Senator Richard Palmer of Duluth, who campaigned as an independent but chose to caucus with the conservatives when he arrived in St. Paul. As the hearings on the land donation legislation progressed, it became clear that Holmquist had been placed in a weakened position by the razor-thin conservative margin in the senate.

On March 9, the *International Falls Daily Journal* carried an Associated Press story announcing the filing with the state legislature of bills authorizing the donation of state lands to the United States to meet the congressional requirements for establishment of the park.[10] Identical bills were submitted for this purpose in both chambers, H.F. 1337 and S.F. 1026. In St. Paul, the filing was announced at a news conference at the governor's office with a statement read by Herbst, commissioner of the DNR. Commissioner Herbst identified eleven provisions in the legislation that would meet the land donation requirements of the authorizing legislation and also the interests of the state and local tax districts required to donate land within the park area.[11] Three of the provisions would be particularly significant in the coming debate: donation and conveyance of all state lands inside the park to the United States, condemnation of trust fund lands and reimbursement to the trust fund, and reimbursement of local taxing districts for tax-forfeited lands.[12] Also on March 9, the VNPA formally launched its campaign of support for the land transfer legislation in a statement by Elmer Andersen, president of the VNPA. Andersen's message stressed the park's importance and historical significance to Minnesota and expressed confidence "that Minnesotans, once again, will support and urge positive action on this so that all the details may be completed during this session."[13] This reference to completing the legislature's work on land donation in the 1971 session was emphasized later that month in an informational bulletin prepared by the Minnesota Division of the Izaak Walton League for distribution at the annual sports show in Minneapolis. The handout, which sought citizen interest and support for the land transfer legislation, warned, "It is vital that this legislation be adopted *before* the end of the session! Opponents of the Voyageurs Park are trying to get the Park defeated by delaying action on these bills."[14]

A valuable document, useful in the debate on the land donation issue, appeared eight days after the bills were filed. *Voyageurs National Park Fact Book*, researched, printed, and distributed by the MRC legislators and staff personnel, provided information on twenty-one topics, ranging from camping to zoning and planning.[15] The one topic not included in the *Fact Book* was the appraised value of all state lands proposed for donation. This information was essential to committees charged with recommending ways to reimburse the school trust fund account following condemnation of these lands. Representative Newcome, chairman of the MRC, referred to this matter in his cover letter to the members of the legislature: "The Commission is attempting to establish a 'ball park' estimate of the value of the school trust fund and tax-forfeited lands within the boundaries of the Voyageurs National Park as background information for the Appropriation committees. With the cooperation of the Department of Natural Resources the Commission has obtained the services of professional foresters to attempt to provide this information by May 1."[16]

On the day the legislation was entered, Newcome, chief sponsor in the house, briefly noted some of the legislature's responsibilities during the session. He said that once an "estimate of value" was determined, the legislature could then determine how to repay the school trust fund account for school lands involved. They could either choose to reimburse out of general funds or issue bonds, thus spreading the cost over a period of years. The federal government would purchase the private lands in the park area.[17] On the same day, Holmquist, majority leader and chief sponsor of the legislation in the senate said, "We anticipate little difficulty in getting affirmative action by the House and Senate." He predicted speedy passage of the Voyageurs bill.[18] Holmquist's remarks could be interpreted as the kind of political rhetoric expected from a party leader shortly before the critical vote is taken on an issue. In reality, however, he had good reason to be confident. The Voyageurs issue had generated endorsements from more than one thousand organizations across the state. A statewide poll conducted the month before the first hearing on the donation bill showed that 78 percent of the respondents favored donation of state land to fulfill requirements for establishment of the park. The park project consistently enjoyed bipartisan support in the administrations of four governors—two Republican and two Democrat—and always received unanimous support from the Minnesota congressional delegation.[19]

Even Rita Shemesh, whose VNPA would coordinate the proponent's efforts during the hearings, could express a bit of optimism about the prospects for the land donation legislation. In a March 10 memorandum to VNPA board members, she said that "although we do not anticipate that this bill will have too much opposition, I know that the usual foes will be lurking in the halls trying to sabotage Voyageurs." Mindful of the need to keep park advocates alert and active participants in the campaign, she concluded her memo by encouraging them to make their opinions known to members of the key committees in both houses: "It may be that as time goes on, we may have to send directives to our members and endorsing organizations so that they can make their opinions known to their legislators."[20]

Senator Holmquist's optimism on bill filing day was destined to be short-lived. One day before the hearings commenced, Robert Ashbach, a senate colleague, entered two bills that, in the view of some proponents, were intended to slow the progress of land donation legislation. One of Ashbach's bills required a constitutional amendment to transfer school trust fund lands for Voyageurs, and the second bill authorized creation of a state park on the Kabetogama Peninsula. Companion bills were introduced in the house. On the surface, a reading of the constitutional amendment proposal seemed helpful to the park cause. However, it would take at least two years to go through the amending process, including a statewide vote of approval required of all amendments to the constitution. There is no record of this bill ever receiving serious attention during the 1971 session. On the other hand, the state park proposal resonated with some legislators who were opposed to a national park primarily because of the federal attachment. For them, a state park was an agreeable alternative. Senator Ashbach, of course, had similar views. He admitted that his state park proposal faced an uphill battle, but he explained, "I think the people of Minnesota will favor the idea when they realize that a state park would keep the area as a wilderness without purchasing expensive public lands and turning them over to the federal government."[21]

Senator Ashbach, along with two other conservatives, Rollin Glewwe and Harold Krieger, were joined by two liberals, A. J. and George Perpich, in most actively opposing the land donation legislation in the senate. They were all members of the Natural Resources and Environment Committee, and their opposition to turning over state trust fund lands to the federal government to fulfill requirements for a national park were frequently and forcefully expressed. With more than 20 percent of the twenty-two committee members actively opposed, it was evident to legislators and the interested public that the fate of the land donation issue would be settled in that committee.

With the land donation bills properly filed in both houses, the *Fact Book* in the hands of the legislators, and the promise of a professional appraisal to determine the value of the school trust fund lands by May 1, the legislature was poised for the hearings to begin on March 18. Opening statements and posturing by both sides during the first session gave onlookers an indication of the direction the process would take, but in no way did they reveal the intensity of the debate and the sometimes embarrassing behavior of the participants on both sides of the issue.

The chair of the Natural Resources and Environment Committee, Senator Cliff Ukkelberg, called the hearing to order in a meeting room packed with individuals on both sides of the land donation question. Most in the room realized then that this was really a "showdown" battle over Voyageurs, regardless of the title of the bill. Because of time constraints at this first session, a continuation meeting took place on March 29 so that proponents could complete their testimony.[22] Some of the statements made by proponents at this hearing were similar to those presented at congressional hearings held earlier in International Falls and Washington, D.C. Again, the economic advantage of having a national park in northeastern Minnesota was stressed a number of times. For example, the president of the International Falls Chamber of Commerce, Ernest Rousseau, after noting that the national park would "pre-serve the natural beauty, history and romance of the area," declared that establishment would mean his city would become the largest tourist center on the Canadian border.[23] Reference was made by witnesses and by others in letters to editors to the advantage of a second industry in International Falls, a community so dependent on the health of the paper industry. Proponents emphasized that the NPS's multimillion-dollar investment in facilities proposed for Voyageurs plus private in-vestments stimulated by the new park would more than offset the prop-erty tax losses due to donation of state and county lands and the sale of private lands to the federal government.[24]

Opponents frequently asserted that the state and the two counties in the park area would lose significant tax support if the land transfer to the federal government occurred. The MRC's *Fact Book* contained tax data provided by the offices of the county auditors for St. Louis and Koochiching Counties, showing that the annual income to the state from school trust fund lands it owned in the park was about $3,000 each year, and the real estate taxes collected in 1970 by the two counties in the park area totaled $64,345.84.[25]

On March 30, the day after the proponents completed their testi-mony, VNPA board members met at the Holiday Inn near the state capi-tol. Executive Secretary Shemesh gave them a status report on the orga-nization's efforts to secure quick passage of the land donation bills. Her comments, summarized in a memorandum to the board the next day, were a straightforward and sobering assessment of a situation that she believed to be serious: "Clearly, the Park proponents are doing very badly in the State Legislature! The opposition has organized itself as effec-tively as the proponents did for the Washington hearings!"[26] She also cited the appearance of numerous letters to the editors around the state and evidence that many property owners in the Kabetogama area had joined organizations this time to represent their interests. She then listed opposition claims and arguments the VNPA would have to deal with throughout the legislative session:

1. Why a national park at Kabetogama? Why not to the east in already federally owned lands?
2. One or two million people in the area would devastate the wilderness aspect of the park.

3. The cost of developing the area.
4. The cost to the state in "giving away forever" the trust fund lands, and the usual arguments about the sanctity of the state trust fund lands, cheating the education funds, and so on.
5. The mineral value of the area.
6. This land should be for Minnesota—that is, "Minnesota for Minnesotans."
7. Too much federal ownership.
8. Lack of legislative relationship—legislature not consulted enough.
9. Defeat of Higgins, Sundet, and others, and claims that park supporters used strong-arm tactics to defeat legislators.

Her memo also included recommendations for combating this challenge from what was now an organized and energized opposition. She cited measures that had been so successful in the congressional campaign, such as an aggressive letter-to-the-editor campaign, fact sheets responding to specific opposition arguments, contact with endorsing organizations in communities where legislators resided, and personal contact with key people in the legislature.[27]

Following the meeting at the Holiday Inn, board members walked over to the capitol to attend the hearing on land donation conducted by the House Committee on Natural Resources. Shemesh had considerable experience organizing and conducting campaigns involving controversial issues, and she certainly knew what was required to train, motivate, and lead a group through a successful and satisfying campaign. What she saw and heard at this hearing was an adversary much better positioned to move its cause against the park than in the earlier congressional hearings. What she observed was an organized and systematic approach in the opponent's presentation, and she believed it was paying dividends for them. The group of witnesses, led by Dr. Alvin Hall, St. Louis County Commissioner from Ely, included, among others, landowners, loggers, a statement by a schoolteacher in the Kabetogama area, and St. Paul attorney William Essling, who was a landowner on Namakan Lake. Essling, a member of the Boundary Waters Landowners Association, lobbied aggressively for the newly formed organization, which proved to be a persistent opponent of the state land donation legislation for Voyageurs.

Shemesh realized that changes would have to be made in the campaign, including more witnesses from the area around the park and greater participation in the entire process by VNPA members. With these ideas still fresh in her mind, she dictated a statement that was attached to her March 30 memo to the VNPA board. She sent both documents to other VNPA leaders as well. Shemesh described the house hearing as "a devastating experience for the Park proponents! Our sense of victory was far too premature! We *MUST* have a good representation from the Park area at all the *committee hearings!* After all our years of hard work we *can't* stop now! If the Land Transfer bills are *defeated* the opposition will have *two (2) more years* to propagandize their opposition. PLEASE HELP!!"[28] VNPA members responded to the impassioned plea for letters and personal contacts as they sought to offset the high-energy campaign of their opponents. Nevertheless, the forthcoming senate hearings in April gave them little cause to celebrate.

Textbooks on American government tell their readers that the real work of a legislative body takes place in the committee rooms. The chamber floor may be the place for the occasional display of eloquence by members participating in floor debate, but the difficult work of shaping a piece of legislation, including the search for resolution of troublesome side issues, has already been accomplished in committee. But unlike a textbook version, S.F. 1026 often traveled a stormy, acrimonious, and indirect course through nine committee sessions. Each such episode raised doubts in the ranks of park advocates that the bill would survive.

The Senate Committee on Natural Resources and Environment scheduled two sessions, April 5 and 12, to hear from those opposed to the land donation legislation. A number of witnesses were affiliated with organizations or associations opposed to land donation and spoke on their behalf. Leading the opposition effort was Hall, who had served in the same capacity at the house hearings the week before.[29] Hall, an Ely chiropractor, had established a reputation as an articulate spokesperson on issues affecting northern St. Louis County. He was primarily responsible for coordinating the opposition testimony during the legislature's public hearings on the Voyageurs. Testimony by opponents was wide-ranging and touched on most of the issues listed in the Shemesh memo of March 30 to the VNPA board. The record and press commentary show that the opponent's agenda focused on four areas: presentations proposing alternatives to a national park, proposals for delaying action on the legislation in the 1971 session to permit further study of the issues, expressions of environmental concerns related to high visitation to the new park, and costs associated with the purchase of lands for donation plus the loss of tax revenue from private lands purchased for inclusion in the park.

F. T. Frederickson, Minnesota woodlands manager for Boise Cascade, made a proposal for an alternative to a national park on the first day of hearings. Speaking for the company, he said that "in the public interest, we have committed ourselves to a cooperative, multi-use program administered by a commission of federal, state, county and private land owners."[30] Frederickson also explained that Boise already had a multi-use development program on the Kabetogama Peninsula that could continue under its proposed joint management scheme.

In the week following Frederickson's presentation, R. V. Hansberger, president and chairman of Boise Cascade, repeated his company's commitment to the plan and added, ". . . such a plan, if adopted would save taxpayers millions of dollars in the cost of acquiring lands and millions of tax dollars in the cost of development and maintenance of the area by the National Park Service."[31] The complexities of Boise's plan and details as to how several levels of governmental and private participants would interact to manage the area were not offered. There is no indication in the record that key legislators were drawn to support the plan. Also, however laudable its objectives, not enough time remained in the session for serious evaluation of the plan's potential as an alternative to a national park. On the other hand, Senator Ashbach's state park proposal was mentioned frequently during the hearings in both houses as a more suitable alternative.

The belief that at least some portion of the Kabetogama Peninsula should be included in the state park system was held by personnel in the state parks department long before the planning team from the NPS was invited to evaluate the area for such status. Impressed by what they saw on their trip on and around the peninsula, they suggested that NPS personnel do further studies to explore the area's potential for national park status. After several years of field studies and historical research, the NPS recommended a Voyageurs National Park. But the state parks department's earlier interest in a state park was not forgotten, and twenty years later when Voyageurs was one step from meeting the requirements for formal establishment, Senator Ashbach, along with colleagues in both houses of the state legislature, offered it as a viable alternative to a national park. For some, including a number of members on the natural resources committees of both houses, handing over land to the federal government for a national park was just too much to ask. For them, the state park was a way of declaring support for a *park* on Kabetogama and one controlled by the state, not the federal government.

One of the first to testify before Senator Ukkelberg's Natural Resources and Environment Committee in strong support of the state park alternative was a longtime foe of the national park proposal, former state senator Ray Higgins from Duluth. Higgins, who opposed the proposal at every opportunity as an active member of the senate's Public Domain Committee, was a casualty of the liberal sweep in the 1970 election and spoke as a private citizen. In his testimony he explained why he supported a state park proposal: "The area as a state park would be preserved. It would be available to the public, and it would be managed at home rather than from Washington, D.C. . . . Give Minnesota a chance to show that we in Minnesota can out-preserve, out-manage and out-promote this great area for the benefit of all. Do not give away the area for all time without providing Minnesota a chance to show what they can do."[32]

Higgins's testimony is best remembered for his criticism of Senator Holmquist's statements during the House congressional hearings on Voyageurs in Washington, D.C. During those hearings, Holmquist was asked by Congressman Roy Taylor, "Now the State owns a sizeable amount of land involved. Do you know whether or not it is the State's intention to donate that [state lands] to the Federal Government or any part of it?" Holmquist said in reply, "It is my judgment that the State of Minnesota, either through private funds or through legislative action, would be glad to accommodate the Voyageurs National Park."[33] Higgins was still angered that Holmquist had chosen to ignore the work and conclusions of the old Senate Public Domain Committee on Voyageurs and instead had used his position as chair of the Rules Committee to assure the congressional committee of Minnesota's supposed willingness to donate the state lands.

Higgins followed this assertion with a rhetorical question, "Could it be possible that Senator Holmquist finds himself somewhat at cross purposes, torn between his responsibility to the Minnesota Senate, which he tended to ignore, and responsibility to his brother-in-law, Elmer L. Andersen, the chief proponent of the national park?"[34] Holmquist later interpreted this as a personal attack and added, "There wouldn't have been a national park in the United States if we had yielded to a small minority. As for former Governor Andersen, I am proud to be his brother-in-law. He and I displayed good judgment in marrying sisters."[35]

Appeals for state park status continued to be made throughout the meetings and hearings on the land donation legislation. In an effort to dispel notions that the state would be advantaged by choosing the state park alternative, Director of the Division of Parks and Recreation U. W. Hella filed a statement with the committee on natural resources in both houses, explaining why the best interests of the state would be better served through a national park designation. He said that although state park designation would preserve many of the amenities of the park area, "We, however, question that the best interests of the state would be served considering that a national park will attract nationwide attention and provide a substantial second industry to augment the present single industry economy of this region. The congressional act requires the state to deliver approximately 32,000 acres of land for the purposes of a national park at an estimated cost of $4 million, whereas the estimated cost of acquiring 79,000 acres of private lands by the National Park Service totals $20,300,000; a liability which would accrue to the state if these lands were to be acquired for the purposes of a state park. It has been estimated by the National Park Service that the cost of development over a 5-year period will total $19,179,000 and, should this area be established as a state park, this also would be a state liability. The total liability, including land and property acquisition, development, and maintenance operation and protection which will accrue to the National Park Service in the first 5 years, is estimated at over $41.2 million. I reiterate—the best interest of Minnesota will be served if this area is established as the Voyageurs National Park."[36]

On the first day of the hearing on the land donation question, Senator Holmquist, lacking a more precise figure, said, "A rough estimate of the value of state-owned lands is $3 or $4 million."[37] Finally, on April 22, the MRC reported that the value of these public lands was $3,833,000.[38] Still called an estimate, this figure was the result of the work of professional appraisers hired by the MRC. This professional valuation should have placed advocates and opponents of land donation on "the same page" with respect to the state's cost for land acquisition. Whether deliberate or not, speculation by opponents as to the value of these lands ranged from $8.4 million to $60 million. Even after the official appraised value was announced, the speculation continued. The $8.4 million figure, for example, came from Ed Chilgren, former speaker of the house, and Hall, St. Louis County commissioner, both residents of northeastern Minnesota, after the MRC value was known. In announcing their estimate, Chilgren said the MRC number was the "most unrealistic figure to come out of the controversy."[39] On the same day that Holmquist announced the MRC estimate of $3.8 million, Senator Ashbach estimated "the cost of giving the land to the federal government at a minimum of $25 million."[40] And Essling, a leader in the Boundary Waters Landowners Association, made the $60 million estimate in a letter to the editor of the *International Falls Daily Journal.* Essling said, "Now these insensible zealots plan to give away the children's priceless heritage."[41] Such grossly inflated land costs left the average citizen who was trying to understand the land donation process only more bewildered than before. But the MRC figures did help legislators who had repeatedly heard and read of the wide-ranging estimates of the opponents. The MRC report was also important to the finance committee members and staff in both houses as they studied ways to finance the acquisition of lands targeted for donation to the federal government.

Senate Majority Leader Holmquist came to the Natural Resources Committee hearing on April 22 looking to get quick approval of the bill and movement over to the finance committee. After a brief review of the legislation by Holmquist, Senator Ashbach made several motions that some observers viewed as calculated to delay action on the bill. His first motion that the bill be sent to subcommittee for further study failed on a ten to eight vote.[42] Later he suggested postponement of the legislation and that the entire issue be studied by an interim legislative commission, with a request that the commission report back at the beginning of the next legislative session—a period of two years. Ashbach and a conservative colleague then disputed the $4 million estimate of the value of the lands to be acquired, saying $11 to $13 million was more realistic. Angered by Ashbach's delaying tactics, Holmquist said, "A militant minority has been assembled before this committee to create doubt"; in other words, it was in Ashbach's interest to create doubt, and it was not in the public's interest. At this, an angry Ashbach said he resented the insinuation.[43]

Later in the meeting, Ashbach tried to amend the bill to put a $6-million ceiling on state land costs for the park. Chairman Ukkelberg said the amendment should be made in the finance committee. Ashbach protested, and amid a shouting match among other members of the committee, Ukkelberg banged his gavel and promptly adjourned the meeting and stalked out of the room.[44] Shortly after the aborted meeting, the majority leader said he was not going to give up and would press for a vote at the next meeting. He felt secure in that prediction because he believed there were only four members who were firmly opposed. The slim two-vote margin that kept the bill from the subcommittee showed that Holmquist's estimation of numerical support was generous, to say the least.

The Natural Resources Committee reassembled two days later for another "round" of debate. Senator Holmquist's hope for a quick vote of approval at this meeting was also doomed from the start. Members opposed to the park began raising questions about the costs for land acquisition, lack of information about what the NPS planned to do, and "how are we going to put 1.2 million people in that park each year and still protect the environment?"[45] Members who said they had serious environmental concerns had seized on an estimate of annual visitation of 1.4 million visitors for Voyageurs. The estimate was made by the Minnesota Department of Economic Development and was published just ten days before the April 24 meeting of the Natural Resources and Environment Committee.[46] This number was quickly incorporated in opponent's letters to the editor and in committee debate as evidence of the conflict between arguments for preservation of wilderness values through the national park and the potential for the destruction of these same values because of overcrowding. Senator Harold Krieger said, "Nobody has yet told me how we are going to put 1.2 million people in that park each year and still protect the environment."[47]

It should be remembered that this debate in the legislature took place at the height of the environmental movement in the United States. The National Environmental Policy Act (NEPA) was less than two years old, and the first Earth Day was celebrated in April 1970, one year before the land donation debate in St. Paul. And it was also a time when the public was beginning to learn that some of our national parks were under considerable stress from the pressures of increased visitation. Newspapers and magazines carried alarming and sometimes frightening stories about overcrowding, traffic congestion, and even crime in some of the larger western parks. Park opponents seized on these stories and warned that the Kabetogama area as a national park could be subject to the same problems.[48]

But even these concerns were overshadowed by a totally unsuspected parliamentary stratagem, which resulted in sending the land transfer legislation to a subcommittee for further study. Just a few days before, Senator Ashbach's motion to do the same thing failed on a vote of ten to eight. But this time the motion carried twelve to eight. Because Ashbach was on the losing side in the first attempt, he was unable to move to reconsider. However, George Conzemius, a liberal and avowed supporter of the bill, made the motion and was joined by two other liberals and one conservative, enough to produce a most embarrassing setback for Senator Holmquist. He pleaded with the committee not to take such action but to no avail. With only six days remaining on the legislative calendar for the committee to complete its work, the park bill was in serious trouble.[49]

Realizing the seriousness of the situation, Chairman Ukkelberg acted quickly to appoint a special five-member subcommittee, four of whom were friendly to the park. This meant bypassing the standing subcommittee, where the membership might be disposed to kill the bill. In this move, Ukkelberg was calculating that in a few days the bill would be discharged from the subcommittee, get back to the full committee, and placed again on the path to passage.[50] Of course, this reversal sent shock waves through the ranks of park advocates, who from the very beginning of the bill's journey through the legislature feared this kind of delay, especially near the end of the session in the rush to meet deadlines. But what motivated *supporters* of the bill to take actions placing it in such jeopardy? Members of the committee knew the answer to that question on the very day of the event, and the public found out by reading their Sunday newspapers.

Senator Holmquist was leading his conservative caucus with a one-vote margin over the liberals, and on this piece of legislation he had trouble with some members in his own party. But it was DFLers (liberals) looking for a way to embarrass the majority leader who were behind this move. They knew Holmquist would need their help to pass the land donation bill out of committee and also with other bills before the session ended. And they were especially upset over an earlier decision by Holmquist to exclude them from membership on a conference committee dealing with congressional reapportionment. So this move by liberals had little or nothing to do with the need for further study of Voyageurs or the land donation requirement. The park question had been thoroughly studied for almost a decade. It was an intrusion of partisan politics into a debate over legislation essential to the establishment of Voyageurs. One account said it was a message from the liberals to Holmquist that "you are going to need us to pass some of your major legislation in the closing days of the session."[51]

Over the weekend, Governor Anderson heard plenty from the leadership of the VNPA and leaders of organizations that had endorsed the park. He called in a few liberal members of the subcommittee and told them he was totally committed to seeing the bill passed during the *current* session and to get it back to the full committee so that could happen. Because at that time the legislature met only in odd years, the next session would occur after the 1972 election, in 1973. The uncertainties of a scenario in which the bill would have to deal with new members and changes in leadership in a session two years away were so unattractive that for all advocates—and especially the governor—the message was to get the bill back to the full committee as soon as possible and avoid the confusion of the last days of the session.

The subcommittee held its only meeting on the evening of April 28. If the members had seen the editorial in the St. Paul newspaper that morning, they would have read some scathing remarks about their behavior in recent committee sessions: "... bills to make the park a reality through transfer of state lands are in jeopardy through a series of political delaying maneuvers. The delayers include not only diehard opponents but some legislators who have professed to favor it." At another point, the writer emphasized the statewide public support for the park legislation and the consistent bipartisan effort it had enjoyed: "Yet today, with the national park needing only legislative approval of land transfers to come into being, carping critics are still out to kill the project."[52]

The subcommittee spent three hours in an orderly session settling matters relating to contrasting land appraisal values of private, state, and county lands. Senator Ashbach's amendment limiting the state's cost for land acquisition to $6 million was approved. The committee then voted to approve and send the bill back to the full committee on Natural Resources and Environment.[53]

The full committee met two days later to give the legislation a final review before sending it on to the full senate. This session, like the one preceding, was not without its anxious moments. Senator Krieger, an outspoken opponent, again offered an amendment to refer the bill to an interim legislative committee for further study. A voice vote on the amendment was deemed too close for a ruling, so Chairman Ukkelberg delayed a call for a show of hands until a senator known to be favorable to the park was called from another meeting to vote against the amendment. The vote was twelve to eight against, and a subsequent motion to approve and send the bill to the finance committee was approved fourteen to eight. This was really the deciding vote for the land donation legislation because the House Natural Resources Committee had approved its version of the legislation the day before.[54]

Compared to the rough journey in the senate, the bill in the house had a more tranquil experience. Most of the action on the land bill took place in a subcommittee of the Natural Resources Committee, and the only serious debate occurred in one committee meeting. The subcommittee lost some of its decorum and comity when the chair, conservative Roger Scherer, challenged an amendment made by Jack Fena, a liberal from northeastern Minnesota. The amendment, approved by the subcommittee, required the state to reimburse Koochiching and St. Louis Counties for tax revenue lost by land acquisition for the park. The "in lieu of taxes" payment, $128,000 over a five-year period, was challenged by the chair as a way to get state money for the two counties without justification. Another member, Newcome, opposed the amendment because he reasoned that the economic benefits from the park development would exceed the loss in tax revenue. Chairman Scherer then countered with his own amendment, which would have removed from the bill the section authorizing reimbursement of local taxing districts for the market value of land donated for the park. Immediately after that amendment was approved, Representative Irvin Anderson from International Falls said, "What you have done by this amendment has effectively stopped establishment of Voyageurs National Park." He said he would go back to his county board and recommend that it not donate Koochiching County lands for the park.[55] Anderson's charge that the chairman's amendment could kill the park led to reconsideration and its prompt removal from the record. Because both parties wanted credit for securing the national park, the pressure was on to compromise.

Although some were still upset with the proceedings, the subcommittee voted approval and sent the amended bill to the full committee on natural resources. That committee accepted the subcommittee's "in lieu of taxes" amendment for the two northern counties in the park. It also heard from the executive secretary of the State Board of Investment, Robert Blixt, who described a plan to reimburse the trust fund from revenue generated from the sale of state bonds. Blixt's plan was to invest these funds in securities bearing a higher yield than the state would pay in interest on its bonds. The gain would be used to pay off the principal and interest, and in twenty years the bonds would be paid off. The state would also appeal to the IRS to grant tax-exempt status to the interest on the bonds, which would make them more attractive to investors.[56] The committee then approved the amended version and sent the bill over to the House Appropriations Committee, which acted quickly to approve and send it to the house floor.

Debate on the house floor on May 12, 1971, lasted about one hour, just long enough to receive an amendment by a representative from northeastern Minnesota seeking a two-year legislative commission to study the impact of the park proposal. By then it had become a familiar proposal that was always rejected, and it was turned aside once more, 118 to 9. A motion to approve the land donation legislation followed this action, and it carried by a lopsided vote of 108 to 26. Only four representatives from the northeastern part of the state voted against the legislation authorizing donation and transfer of lands for the park.[57]

Over in the state senate, the Finance Committee hearings offered opponents another opportunity to go on record in opposition to legislation authorizing the state to donate lands for Voyageurs. After the failure of a motion to lay the bill over until the next session, Senator Krieger expressed his concerns about the adequacy of sanitation facilities to serve over a million park visitors a year. He said the bill was "moving too hurriedly in the direction of a very dirty mistake."[58] He proposed an amendment requiring construction of a sewage treatment plant to accommodate 1.5 million visitors. The amendment failed, but in the final version of the legislation, matters such as water, land, and air quality were covered in a separate section on environmental protection. Others testifying during the two-hour meeting repeated concerns and objections heard before at previous hearings in both houses. One witness, Lieutenant Governor Rudy Perpich, wondered why there was such hurry on the bill. He also expressed concern that the two counties in the park area "did not have the tax base to pay for additional services required by park visitors." Finally, Blixt, from the State Board of Investment, explained again the bonding strategy for reimbursing the trust fund account. The committee then voted approval by a wide margin and sent the bill to the senate floor.[59]

True to the pattern of many of the senate committee hearings on the Voyageurs bill, the debate during the final session on the floor turned contentious at times but occasionally humorous as well. At one point, a senator from southeastern Minnesota said, "Any of the fur traders who had stumbled into the 219,000-acre park area were lost because the area was not on the Voyageurs route."[60] At another point, this same senator took a parting shot at the majority leader when he accused Holmquist with "misleading the legislature on the importance and effect of the bill. The Pied Piper from Grove City... will lead us down the shores of Kabetogama right into the drink."[61]

Senator Holmquist told the senate at the beginning of the session that he accepted the amendments made by committees in both houses and urged approval of the legislation that would pave the way for final establishment of the national park. After four hours of "debate," including the threat of a filibuster by an Iron Range senator, the bill passed on May 15 on a vote of forty-nine to sixteen, and within a few days was considered by a conference committee to deal with several noncontroversial amendments. One was to adopt Minnesota Pollution Control Agency standards for air and water quality in the park, and another permitted St. Louis and Koochiching Counties to petition the Ramsey County District Court for a determination of the value of county lands to be acquired for the national park. Committee agreement came quickly, and the bill was returned to the legislature for final approval. The bill was "repassed" on May 21, 1971.[62]

The legislature's record on the park issue is clear. Supporters and opponents had a final opportunity to be heard, and though the committee and floor debate was often stormy, the final tally in favor of donation and land transfer of state lands to the federal government was decisive. One hundred ninety-nine legislators voted on the measure, and 157 voted in favor, a margin of almost 4 to 1. But those attending committee sessions might have gained an entirely different impression as opponents made repeated efforts to delay or scuttle the measure by proposing a state park alternative or postponing a final decision for two years until an interim commission could study the matter. Proponents countered with reminders that they had the opportunity to make the legacy of the 1971 legislative session one of support for the long-term benefits of protection through preservation of this timeless natural asset in northern Minnesota, and that the best way to assure that this would be accomplished was through a Voyageurs *National Park*. The leadership in both political parties and most of the legislators favored that option. All that remained was for the governor to sign the land donation bill, so that the process of donation and transfer of state lands could go forward, private lands could be acquired, and the secretary of the interior could certify that the requirements for establishment imposed by Congress had been met.

CHAPTER TWELVE

The Four Years to Establishment

Bill signing ceremonies are always pleasant occasions in the life of a politician after a victorious legislative battle. Politicians gather around the political leader and listen while he or she congratulates those who led the effort to see the legislation successfully through the political process. In the legislative history of Voyageurs National Park, the date was June 4, 1971, the political leader was Governor Wendell Anderson, and the bill to be signed was authorization for the state to donate and transfer lands within the boundaries of the park to the federal government. Many of the state's newspapers carried a picture of the governor seated at a table with three of his predecessors, all of them instrumental in moving the Voyageurs project forward during their administrations: Elmer L. Andersen and Harold LeVander, Republicans; and Karl Rolvaag, a Democrat. Behind the governors and next to a banner that read, "Historic Voyageurs National Park, America's 36th—A Great Opportunity for Minnesota," stood Eighth District Congressman John Blatnik, a Democrat.[1] In his remarks, the governor said, "This park is set in one of the most ruggedly beautiful regions of North America. It is the only national park in the nation situated in the forest and lake country in our northern border region."[2] He also had special praise for Andersen and Blatnik for their untiring efforts on behalf of Voyageurs.

The scene around the governor's table dramatically illustrated the importance of bipartisanship in the quest for approval of a project, which had as its central objective the protection and preservation of a natural resource. Bipartisan cooperation was not unusual during the 1960s and

1970s, particularly on environmental issues in the state legislatures and Congress during those years. It was an explicit response to public awareness and concern over the health of the nation's environment and the management and preservation of its natural resources. The environmental movement was without precedent in American history. With the encouragement and new directives during the Kennedy-Johnson years, the NPS saw major change and expansion. Most of the changes and additions to the system came during what NPS historian Barry Mackintosh called the Hartzog years, 1964–72.[3] George Hartzog, associate director of the NPS, succeeded retiring Conrad Wirth as director in 1964. Wirth, who was familiar with Minnesota's geography and history from his boyhood years as the son of the superintendent of Minneapolis parks, helped initiate the Voyageurs project during his final two years as director. Hartzog, no stranger to the NPS, said in his memoirs that the operation of the NPS is not nearly as smooth as the organizational chart.[4]

Director Hartzog's recommendations for changes in the management policies of the NPS were reflected in Interior Secretary Udall's policy memorandum in July 1964. This document established three categories of NPS units: natural, historical, and recreational. Under this tripartite scheme, sixty-nine new units were added to the NPS between 1964 and 1972, "nearly three quarters as many as had been permanently added in the preceding thirty years."[5]

It was during this period of environmental activism that the concept of a Voyageurs National Park, like so many other federal park facilities, was born and eventually realized.[6] New national parks and recreation areas received broad support from the general population with the exception of those people residing in communities and rural areas peripheral to the new units. This exception certainly included people residing near Voyageurs who were not happy to be caught up in this wave of environmentalism, new jargon, and new parks—especially if it was a federal park. Understandably, many had serious concerns about possible impacts the new park would have on existing socioeconomic conditions, land use patterns, and recreational activity. As noted in chapter 6, the purchase of private property to accommodate management objectives of the NPS at Voyageurs produced real hardship and anxieties for many in the local communities.

For new units like Voyageurs, it fell to the first park official assigned to the new facility to explain and interpret the management philosophy of the NPS and allay fears of unreasonable intrusion on existing recreational practice. At Voyageurs, this task became the responsibility of the "project manager," a title used instead of superintendent until the park was formally established.

Anticipating the approval of land donation legislation, the NPS began to look for someone to serve as project manager at Voyageurs. Sometimes the first person at a new unit was one schooled in land acquisition but with little experience in park management. For Voyageurs, however, the NPS selected a person with managerial experience who could deal with the public "in the types of problems that come up in relation to the actual management of the park. . . ."[7] That person was Myrl Brooks, a veteran NPS employee who had the credentials and a thorough understanding of the NPS management philosophy. Eight days after Governor Anderson signed the donation law, Congressman Blatnik announced the appointment of Brooks as project manager. In his statement Blatnik said, "This appointment right on the heels of the state bill becoming law is a definitive indication that the federal government is moving ahead vigorously on the park."[8]

Brooks, born in Roanoke, Virginia, had the manner of a soft-spoken southerner. He was thoroughly familiar with NPS policy and politics, and with more than twenty years experience in the field and in the Washington office, he knew his way around the institution. In an interview in his Washington office before leaving for Minnesota, Brooks said, "Our endeavor there will be to be a good neighbor."[9] Upon his arrival in St. Paul, he spent several days making contacts and getting acquainted with key people familiar with the park and the efforts to secure its authorization. Most helpful was U. W. Hella, state director of Parks and Recreation and an early supporter of the park. Recalling those first days, Brooks said he met one person in the capitol area he did not forget— Lieutenant Governor Rudy Perpich. Brooks said, "he was very cordial but informed me that he had been opposed to the park and continues to be opposed to it and really didn't plan to change his mind. . . ." Looking back at that meeting, Brooks said, "He certainly lived up to all expectations in that regard."[10]

Brooks delighted in telling of his arrival at the International Falls airport on his first visit to the park in mid-June 1971. From the plane window, he could see a group of people, several television cameramen, and press personnel standing on the tarmac. As he got off the plane, he wondered who the VIP was that was on the same flight with him. He walked around the knot of people and into the terminal to rent a car, when he heard himself being paged. The waiting group had relied on George Esslinger, a local resort owner, to recognize Brooks. Esslinger assured them that he knew the new superintendent because he had worked for him when the NPS did its initial study of the area several years before. The man Esslinger recalled was *Chester* Brooks, who Esslinger thought was to be the park's superintendent. Myrl Brooks said they were all amused, and although Esslinger was embarrassed, it turned out to be a friendly welcome to the community.[11]

Brooks soon became a familiar figure on the streets of International Falls, and he quickly learned to check the *International Falls Daily Journal* to find out how well he was doing at his new job. He was no doubt happy to read a timely editorial written by Erik Kendall of the *Midland Cooperative* (Wisconsin) and reprinted by the *Daily Journal* on June 16, 1971. In this piece, Kendall recalled the oratorical overkill employed by both sides in the debate over the park and concluded by saying, "it is time for proponents and opponents of the national park to shake hands in friendship, turn the grimaces into smiles, and to pull together."[12]

There was certainly nothing ostentatious about the project manager's first office. During the first six weeks, it was a room in a motel and the back of a station wagon. His next office was a small, modest space across the Rainy River from the sometimes odorous Boise Cascade paper mill in Ft. Frances. He remained in the downtown area until a prefabricated structure was erected in 1975 on U.S. Highway 53 on the south edge of International Falls.

For Voyageurs and the NPS, there were both good news and bad for the balance of 1971. The presence of the NPS would soon be felt in Duluth with the announcement that a land acquisition office would be opening soon to function as headquarters for processing the paper involved in the purchase of private lands in five new park units in Minnesota, Michigan, and Wisconsin. But purchases could not be made for Voyageurs until all state lands within the park boundaries were donated to the federal government.[13] In September, the Internal Revenue Service approved tax-exempt status for the interest on bonds sold by the state to reimburse the education trust fund for land donated to the park.[14] In St. Paul, the state was beginning to do the legal work to prepare state lands for donation to the federal government.

For VNPA members, one of the most enjoyable events of the year was a recognition ceremony held in August during their annual meeting. The meeting was held at the historic Kettle Falls Hotel, located at the east end of the Kabetogama Peninsula. The president of the association, Elmer Andersen, recognized people who had worked for almost ten years at the state and national levels to gain national park recognition for this scenic and historic area. Those present in turn thanked Andersen for his leadership of the park movement. He was finishing his term as the president of the association at this meeting and was succeeded by Martin Kellogg. Before stepping down, Andersen sent a letter and certificate of appreciation to friends of Voyageurs who had worked for its establishment. In his letter, Andersen warned that opponents might mount efforts to stall development of the park. He made an appeal for membership renewal so that the association would be able to ward off such attempts.[15]

Within days of the VNPA meeting and the Andersen letter warning of possible obstructionist moves to thwart park development, a suit was filed in the U.S. District Court challenging the disposition and value of school trust fund lands located in the park.[16] In effect, the suit asked the court to rule that the legislature's action authorizing donation and transfer of school lands to the NPS be invalidated. A ruling accepting the plaintiff's position could have stopped the donation process in its tracks. Park supporters hoped for a speedy court decision, and it came on November 15, 1971, when Judge Edward Devitt ruled against the plaintiff.[17] However, as some expected, the decision was appealed by the plaintiff, a landowner in the park area, and the case went to the Eighth Circuit Court of Appeals. That court denied the appeal in early June 1972, ruling that the case did not belong in the federal courts.[18] For over ten months, a cloud hung over the state's efforts to complete the required donation process and transfer the lands to the federal government. The challenge was not only costly to the state in time and money, but it confirmed Andersen's warning that efforts would be made to block establishment of the park. Some believed the legal action against the state, though costly to the plaintiff, was best classified as a delaying maneuver.

Although Brooks could watch this court challenge from the sidelines, other matters drew his attention and involvement. One of these was a planning program for the area peripheral to the park. Park planning naturally focuses on the spaces within the boundaries of the park unit.

Planning in areas on the periphery is the responsibility of local and state governments. But bad planning and zoning are all too obvious to the visitor approaching some parks. State and local officials were determined not to let this happen around Voyageurs. Within two months after the passage of the land transfer legislation, the Minnesota Resources Commission (MRC) held a conference on perimeter planning and toured the area around the park and International Falls.

During the conference, MRC Chairman Thomas Newcome said he "hoped local governments would be able to control development near recreation sites but if they don't I'm sure the state will feel it's important enough to usurp home rule."[19] Anticipating the need for better planning and zoning, Koochiching and St. Louis Counties had already worked out a bi-county agreement to develop compatible zoning ordinances. The chair of the Koochiching County Planning Commission said that "our main aim is to protect our people from the bad development."[20] But it soon became evident that the goal of developing new zoning and planning ordinances was beyond the reach of Koochiching County because of the limitations of funding and staff and the research required. Further, because a number of state, county, and local agencies would have to be involved, the governor believed it would be necessary to coordinate the efforts of the several agencies to accomplish the goals of good planning in the perimeter area. He therefore called on the state planning director to form a management committee, which would serve as a contact point for a joint effort by the three levels of government.[21] From the work of this committee, a four-year planning effort commenced, resulting in a completed plan for the perimeter of Voyageurs. This plan was transmitted to the State Planning Agency in November 1975. In his letter of transmittal, the executive director of the Arrowhead Regional Development Commission, which did much of the plan, said it was the first time that state, local, and county units of government had coordinated their planning efforts before a national park was opened.[22]

During a meeting with the Koochiching County Board, Brooks said that he had plenty of work to do with the planning of the park, but he had made time to review the perimeter plan and make comments to planners. He said he was critical of the NPS for frequently designating a national park without giving much thought to its impact on the periphery: "The Service should recognize that a park cannot exist in a vacuum detached, independent and unaware of what's going on around it."[23]

As the calendar year 1971 drew to a close, two events occurred that affected Voyageurs. The NPS, in a move better understood by those familiar with the NPS administrative maneuvering, shifted upper management of Voyageurs from the Midwest Regional Office in Omaha, where it had been for thirty-four years, to the Northeast Regional Office in Philadelphia. This arrangement lasted only twenty-six months before Voyageurs was back under the wing of the Omaha office.[24] Brooks did not think the moves affected the park very much, although at the regional level the change occasionally proved awkward. For example, during early discussions regarding a request to move the boundary at Black Bay on Rainy Lake, Midwest Regional Office Director Merrill Beal had to delay responding to the commissioner of the Minnesota DNR regarding boundaries until he could retrieve the necessary maps from the Northeast Region.[25]

But it was the second event that took Brooks by surprise. He attended a meeting initiated by members of the Koochiching Sportsmen's Association, DNR Area Game Manager Jim Schneeweis, and state Representative Irv Anderson. The meeting was held in December 1971 to discuss "the possibility of moving the proposed park boundary to retain waterfowl hunting in the Gold Portage area."[26] Schneeweis noted in a memorandum written in February 1972 that the Gold Portage area of Black Bay had traditionally been the best place for International Falls duck hunters. He concluded by stating, "I believe the Department of Natural Resources should take immediate action at the highest level to have the proposed Voyageurs National Park boundary moved east so that the state can retain control of hunting rights in the Gold Portage area."[27] The Schneeweis memorandum was followed by a letter sent to DNR Commissioner Herbst from the Sportsmen's Club president, and five days later a memorandum from an area employee of the DNR, Milt Stenlund, to a DNR game supervisor. In his letter, Stenlund said, "It is unfortunate that absolutely no consideration was given to the hunters during proceedings establishing the park."[28] During the first congressional subcommittee hearing at International Falls on August 21, 1969, Congressman Taylor was very specific when he said that public hunting would not be permitted in a national park. No one testified at that time to call attention to what in 1971, just two years later, was declared a special duck hunting area. No representative from the DNR appeared to testify at this hearing, nor did the agency file a statement with the subcommittee relating to any natural resource issue arising from the location of the boundaries of the proposed park.

Commissioner Herbst, apprised of the Black Bay situation by personnel from the International Falls area, sent a letter to Director Hartzog recommending a boundary adjustment to remove the affected area from the park. He received a response to his letter from Associate Director Stanley Hulett stating that the suggested change "is, we believe, not minor and is not the type for which Congress delegated authority, therefore, only Congress can bring about the change you suggest."[29] Schneeweis took Hulett's response as a no and to mean that there was little hope of working directly with the NPS on the matter. In a memorandum he wrote, "It is apparent that our best course of action would be to go directly to our congressional delegates through the Commissioner."[30] From this point in spring 1972 until 1983, more than ten years, the Black Bay issue was a major concern for staff at Voyageurs and the Midwest Regional Office. The general public first became aware of the dispute during the fall 1975 hunting season, when duck hunters challenged NPS authority on Rainy Lake's Black Bay.

Schneeweis was correct in his assessment of the situation and also the remedy. Before long, state representatives from the area, especially Irvin Anderson from International Falls, Congressman Jim Oberstar (elected after Blatnik's retirement), Senator David Durenberger, Governor Anderson, and Commissioner Herbst carried the appeal to the highest levels of the NPS and the Department of the Interior, urging changes in the boundary of the park to exclude the Black Bay waterfowl area and place it under the management of the DNR. At the park, Brooks and two of his successors, along with the small staff of rangers, had to confront firsthand the challenge to federal jurisdiction at Voyageurs. Sometimes it was simply a matter of explaining park policy and their task in carrying out the mandates of the authorizing legislation. On several occasions it was issuing citations.

When Brooks told the reporter before leaving Washington that his first endeavor would be to establish a good neighbor relationship with the people in International Falls, he meant it. Of course, good neighbors talk to each other, and Brooks began the dialog with a presentation in January 1972 at a forum sponsored by the Rainy Lake Women's Club. He used slides from other national parks to familiarize his audience with NPS policy in place at these parks. He told them, for example, that limited development within the park would be a goal for Voyageurs. Only 2 percent of the land area would be developed, and private enterprise would be encouraged to provide overnight accommodations outside the park. He said no overuse of park facilities would be permitted, and he emphasized that there would be seasonal management and safeguards of the forest, wildlife, and natural features to protect park values.[31] Brooks's presentation was followed by four other programs in the forum series related to park issues, which included wilderness, commercial development, perimeter planning and zoning, and state highway department plans for roads to the park.

A few months later, Brooks made a similar presentation to the Izaak Walton League chapter in Grand Rapids, Minnesota. During his talk he said, "We are determined that Voyageurs Park will become a living symbol of a nation that treasures its natural heritage and conserves its natural resources."[32] This was the NPS mission for all of its units, and it was also Brooks's mission. He could have expressed as much in the first person—"*I* am determined that Voyageurs Park . . ." He was personally committed to seeing that management policies would allow Voyageurs to reach the goal of full restoration of its eighteenth-century natural state. Brooks believed these policies should be implemented in its early years as a national park. These early discussions explaining the mission of the NPS and how park policies would apply to Voyageurs also gave the public an opportunity to meet the man whose responsibilities included the administration of those policies at Voyageurs.

On June 25, 1972, almost one year to the day of his arrival at Voyageurs, a three-person park evaluation team from the Northeast Regional Office greeted Brooks. In their final report, they acknowledged that there were some who opposed the park, especially summer homeowners whose property was within the park, but that aside, they wrote that Brooks "has established an excellent rapport with the local people. Myrl is a first class 'missionary' for the park and the Service so that public attitudes toward Voyageurs is the envy of many newly established areas."[33] Perhaps had the team returned two years later, its final assessment would have been less effusive.

The evaluation report, divided into operational categories, stated that "the organization at Voyageurs is a 'one man band' which is the Project Manager, with the able assistance of a Secretary."[34] The office secretary was convalescing following surgery when the team visited the park. She died several weeks later, and Brooks found himself manager of a national park with no clerical assistance and no land to manage. But he still carried the awesome responsibility of explaining to a large number of local skeptics what national parks were all about and what to expect at Voyageurs when it was finally established, on a date he could not give because it had not been set. Voyageurs was a demanding assignment, even for a veteran ranger and administrator like Brooks.

Under the heading "legislation," the evaluation report stated that the authorizing law "is a landmark piece of legislation which prevents the Secretary [of the Department of the Interior] from establishing the Park and acquiring private lands until the lands owned by the state of Minnesota and its political subdivisions have been donated to the federal government."[35] Although long delays between authorization and establishment happened at other parks, the postponement at Voyageurs was especially difficult. The four-year lag time led to a quarrelsome session in the state legislature, delayed land acquisition and development of visitor facilities, and increased confusion and mistrust among local residents. Visitors who traveled many miles to see the park became angry when they discovered there were no directional signs to the park, no visitor center or other facilities common to a national park, and few people who could give them a proper explanation for the situation.

Who was to blame for the conditional clause in the authorizing legislation? The answer can be found in the record of the House subcommittee hearings on the park in summer 1970. Serious doubts had arisen among committee members over the ability of the state administration to deliver on the required donation of state land to the federal government. Chairman Aspinall of the House Interior Committee therefore insisted the restrictive clause be added to the bill. Congressman Aspinall's grip over the Interior and Insular Affairs Committee, which he had used to very nearly kill the Voyageurs legislation, ended with his defeat in the primary of fall 1972. Aspinall encountered strong opposition from constituents in his home district in Colorado over environmental matters, and he was the target of several national environmental groups who were upset with inaction on legislation in the House by powerful House committee chairmen.[36] A *New York Times* editorial saw Aspinall's defeat as an indication that voters "do not share its [the House of Representatives] built-in reverence for seniority...."[37]

Finally, there was some good news regarding land acquisition for Voyageurs. In fall 1972 during his governor's "Tour of the Park," Governor Anderson presented a deed for more than five thousand acres of state land within the park to NPS Deputy Director Ray Freeman. The NPS also announced that contracts had been awarded for mapping the area, an abstract company had been engaged to do legal work to prepare lands for transfer to the NPS, and appraisal of Boise Cascade lands had begun.[38]

The park was also able to announce the addition of a chief ranger, Bob Walker, in November 1972, and in February 1973, Joe Cayou came as district ranger. With two experienced rangers on his staff, Brooks no longer had to shoulder the administrative duties by himself. He could devote more time to contact with the public. In January 1973, he released a statement of management objectives for the park and informed the local and regional public that work on the park's master plan was under way.[39] Both are standard documents for new units of the NPS that convey the philosophy and mission of the NPS and engage the public in helping to plan for the park's future. At Voyageurs, it was hoped that these documents would be especially useful because the neighboring population was less familiar with the NPS than people in the western part of the country. Many in the local area believed that a summer vacation traveling many miles to a national park could not be compared to weekends and a two- or three-week stay at a summer cabin on an area lake. And some were amazed that people would travel hundreds of miles to visit Rainy or Kabetogama Lakes just because they were now within a national park. But it was no mystery to the inveterate national park visitors around the country and the world. They came not only because of the beauty of the parks but also because of the interpretive services, the emphasis on historical and scientific research that supported the park programs, and the professional staff in attendance. Visitors had come to appreciate and expect a standard of excellence at a national park, and Voyageurs was to be a participating unit in the park system. As Brooks began his third year at the park, he hoped many neighbors of the park would come to feel the same way.

A few days after Brooks attended a special meeting of the VNPA in Minneapolis, a story appeared in the *Duluth News Tribune* describing what had quickly become a routine activity at the park since the project manager arrived—picking up trash. The article, written by the newspaper's outdoor writer Jim Blubaugh, records a boating journey through the park with Brooks. Blubaugh wrote, "... one of our biggest surprises while touring Voyageurs was the amount of trash piled on many of the islands. There was a nice sand beach, seemingly a great place to camp or swim or whatever. But only a few feet back of the sand was garbage—a pile of unbelievable proportions—similar to a small landfill. Only this spot isn't supposed to be a landfill."[40] Brooks said that in 1972 the park hauled out eight hundred large bags of trash, and more than a hundred other sites needed to be cleaned up. He said it was a "monumental task," a monument to an era that man could never afford again. Most of the dumps were created by summer residents and resort and houseboat operations in the days when there was less concern about environmental standards. Brooks believed that with stricter standards being implemented, accumulation like those observed in the early 1970s would not occur again. The presence of so many unsightly dumps belies the claim frequently made by residents at public hearings that they had taken good care of the park area but now feared pollution on a grand scale if it became a national park.

Not long after Voyageurs was authorized by Congress, the Conservation Foundation, on the one-hundredth anniversary of Yellowstone National Park, published an important volume on the future of national parks in America. One of the book's recommendations was that "the National Park system be used as a showcase of man's proper stewardship of land, water and air."[41] Mindful of this charge to the NPS, Brooks told his guest from the newspaper that although Voyageurs did not have a distinctive feature like Old Faithful, "This is a composite of land, water and blue skies ... a combination of these things for now and the future." By implication, Brooks saw the park as equal to or even more significant than some of the other parks in the system. He saw Voyageurs as a challenge to the NPS to help restore the area to the full natural glory of the fur trade era, and he believed early implementation of NPS standards to be the key to meeting that challenge. He said, "We have the same old problem of providing uses with conflicts. We can't make everybody happy. We have to look at what is reasonable and fair and fulfill responsibilities Congress has given us to preserve the area."[42]

In mid-August 1974, the directors of the VNPA held a special meeting at the Normandy Inn in downtown Minneapolis to hear from federal and state officials on the status of land acquisition, perimeter planning, and master plan preparations for the park. President Lloyd Brandt announced that condemnation of state trust fund lands had been completed, and "it is now possible to complete the transfer to the NPS, representing a major milestone towards establishment of park operations."[43] Once the state lands were transferred to the NPS and added to other lands acquired from the USFS and earlier private donations, the secretary of the interior could seriously consider formal establishment of Voyageurs. In a 1990 interview, Brooks said that he, along with Midwest Regional Director Merrill Beal and staff people from the NPS legal department in Washington, advised the secretary as to when a sufficient amount of land and water had been donated to warrant full establishment in accordance with the authorizing legislation. The actual transfer of 32,000 acres of state and local land took place during a ceremony at the state capitol on December 12, 1974, when Governor Anderson presented deeds to NPS Deputy Director Russell Dickenson.[44]

The August meeting of the VNPA also included discussion of the proposed master plan, which Brooks said would be ready for public hearing in early 1975. Maurice Chandler from the State Planning Agency announced that his agency had a contract with the Arrowhead Regional Planning Commission in Duluth to complete the perimeter planning in 1975. Before adjournment, Brooks was asked about the proposal to delete the duck hunting area in Black Bay. His response was brief. He simply said that a deletion of the size proposed would require congressional action.

The Black Bay issue was very much alive at the time of this meeting, and Brooks certainly had more information on the subject but chose not to provide greater detail at that time. Few stories on the subject appeared in the press, but many memos and letters were exchanged within the DNR and between some DNR personnel and elected officials in Minnesota and Washington. The decision by International Falls area DNR staff and local sportsmen in spring 1972 to press their case for a boundary change by pressuring elected officials and key staff people in the DNR and NPS worked well, no doubt way beyond their expectations. A key figure in this campaign was DNR Commissioner Herbst, who had recommended deletion to Director Hartzog.[45] The response from Washington was always the same—it would take congressional action to make the change. From July through October, Congressman Blatnik was confronted with letters and calls from DNR personnel and an International Falls legislator to move the request along in Washington. By October, Blatnik had had enough, and in a letter to Director Hartzog, he made two suggestions: one, that the NPS get a legal opinion from the solicitor as to whether Voyageurs' legislation permitted deletion of acreage from the park by executive action by the secretary of the interior or by congressional action; and two, that the NPS conduct a study of the Gold Portage area of Black Bay to determine its value as a waterfowl breeding ground and hunting area.[46] The NPS agreed to these suggestions, and as Blatnik had hoped, the issue cooled down and did not surface again until spring 1974.

The hunting study was carried out in fall 1973 in a cooperative spirit between the NPS and the DNR. Then in spring 1974, an article appeared in the International Falls newspaper saying that the DNR and its local game manager backed a change in the park boundary to accommodate local duck hunters.[47] The same article urged local sportsmen to get strongly behind the effort to remove Gold Portage from the park. Now, for the first time, the issue was out in the open, and the Blatnik-inspired "quiet time" had expired. But because Blatnik had announced his intention to retire, his successor and former administrative assistant, Jim Oberstar, would handle the next rounds in the Black Bay fight. Not long after the *Daily Journal* article about the DNR's support for the boundary change, the Hibbing newspaper carried the news that the MRC had also agreed to support the proposed change. This was the same commission whose chairman, Thomas Newcome, had testified in support of the park during the congressional hearings in summer 1970. The difference in 1974 was the presence of International Falls Representative Irv Anderson on the commission.[48]

The next episode in the "saga" of Black Bay took place in the fall when two park rangers confronted hunters on the first day of duck season. Brooks said later that the solicitor's office had informed him the day before the season opened that the land adjacent to the bay had been donated to the government, and therefore park laws prevailed, and he was required to enforce no-hunting regulations. Chief Ranger Walker said, "Our purpose is not to write citations, but to work with and help hunters understand Park Service regulations."[49] The ranger's policy and hunter cooperation kept the scene peaceful. Earlier in July, during a telephone conversation with the Midwest Regional Director and an NPS official in the Washington office, Brooks said, in reference to the Black Bay issue, that while there was a good deal of smoke, there really was not much fire, and that the NPS should keep its cool and ride it out. He said the park had not received a single letter on the matter.[50] As the 1975 fall hunting season drew near, Brooks would have a different view.

At long last Brooks could announce that the long-awaited master plan to revise the 1968 plan would be ready for public hearing in June. However, the people in International Falls were given a preview of its principal contents at a public meeting in February. Brooks said everything should be considered tentative until the public hearing process had run its course. But he could tell them that the main visitor center would be located on Black Bay rather than Sullivan Bay, and that the plan proposed deletion of the Gold Shores (Neil Point) development. The 1968 plan had shown a main facility development on a peninsula jutting into Rainy Lake about a half mile north of Highway 11 and one and a half miles northwest of the newly proposed main visitor center site on Black Bay. The area, known locally as Gold Shores, was identified as the site of a large campground, marina, and visitor center. In the 1975 revision, the NPS decided to delete this area for several reasons, including the cost of acquiring a number of private homes and properties and the decision to develop wilderness campsites on islands and shoreline within the main body of the park rather than near entrances to the park. The NPS hoped the private sector would provide camping facilities at sites on the park's periphery. Other matters, such as NPS tenancy options for continued occupancy of property scheduled for inclusion in the park, were also outlined at this meeting.[51]

The February meeting was one of many public sessions that Brooks held during his tenure at Voyageurs. In my opinion, Brooks was at his best at such public meetings. Unfortunately, he frequently had to tell his audiences things that some did not want to hear. He knew he was often being judged as the bearer of bad news, informing people of policy matters whose origin he had little to do with. But as time passed, even his bitterest enemies came to respect him for his forthrightness and courage even in the midst of hostile audiences.

Now that the state's land had been duly transferred to the federal government, and the secretary of the interior had been advised by his committee of Brooks, the Midwest Regional Director, and members of his legal staff that the state had met the conditions of the authorizing

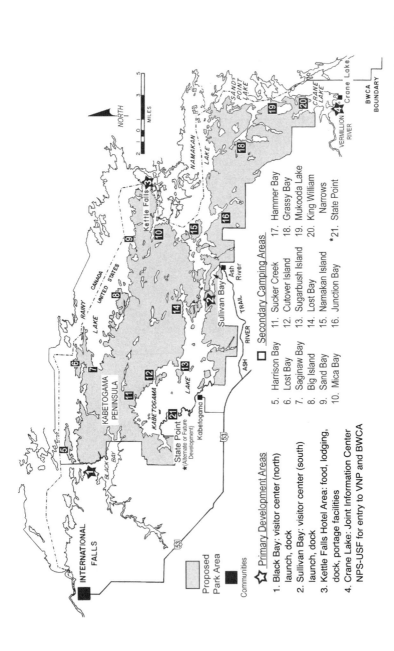

Primary Development Areas

☆

1. Black Bay: visitor center (north) launch, dock
2. Sullivan Bay: visitor center (south) launch, dock
3. Kettle Falls Hotel Area: food, lodging, dock, portage facilities
4. Crane Lake: Joint Information Center NPS-USF for entry to VNP and BWCA

Secondary Camping Areas

☐

5. Harrison Bay
6. Lost Bay
7. Saginaw Bay
8. Big Island
9. Sand Bay
10. Mica Bay
11. Sucker Creek
12. Cutover Island
13. Sugarbush Island
14. Lost Bay
15. Namakan Island
16. Junction Bay
17. Hammer Bay
18. Grassy Bay
19. Mukooda Lake
20. King William Narrows
*21. State Point

Draft master plan for Voyageurs National Park, 1975. This plan incorporated three major changes from the 1968 plan: the elimination of Neil Point as the principal visitor center on the north, the designation of the west side of Black Bay as the new site for the northern visitor center, and the designation of Crane Lake as the location for a proposed joint information center and Forest Service station to serve visitors entering either Voyageurs or the BWCA.

act, he could issue the order formally establishing Voyageurs National Park. In a manner about as low key as imaginable, the secretary's order was published, as required, in the Federal Register on April 8, 1975, and the official announcement was made by Congressman Oberstar the following day.[52] As soon as Brooks learned that the secretary had authorized publication in the Federal Register, he called his good friend and local park supporter Wayne Judy and told him the good news. Then he celebrated.[53]

Voyageurs National Park was only the thirty-sixth national park established since Yellowstone in 1872. It was classed as a "natural area" by the NPS, the same category as the country's largest and most popular western parks. The human connection was its link to the French Canadian voyageurs, who for more than a century used the large lakes in the park as part of what Sigurd Olson called the "Voyageurs Highway." Al Eisele of the Ridder News Service, who followed closely the events leading to the park's authorization said, "The long-sought dream of northern Minnesota, Voyageurs National Park became a reality—as the National Park Service formally established the 220,000 acre land and water reserve as the nation's 36th national park."[54]

Establishment came more than four years after the president signed the authorizing legislation. To park supporters, it seemed like an interminable delay, due in part to efforts by some to modify park policies and even request that a segment of the park be removed. Also, four years of restrictions on land acquisition set park development back. But four years is certainly no record. Great Smoky Mountains and Shenandoah National Parks waited twice that long between authorization and establishment, primarily because of land donation requirements. Also, both parks had a large number of inholders who had to be bought out, and in the years before the Land and Water Conservation Fund, the money simply was not there for ready purchase by the federal government.[55]

Events before and after establishment were clear indications that making Voyageurs a full member of the National Park System would not protect park officials from challenges to their judgment and authority. Brooks would have his hands full. Five weeks before the park was established, a bill was introduced in the state legislature by Majority Leader Irv Anderson to create a Citizens Council on Voyageurs National Park. The committee members would serve without compensation but would be reimbursed by the state for expenses. Anderson said the committee was necessary to provide citizen input as decisions concerning the park's operation were made.[56] President Lloyd Brandt of the VNPA quickly challenged the need for the committee since the VNPA was a "true citizens organization," with no allegiance to anyone or any group. Its sole purpose was the establishment of a national park "that will preserve the beauty of an area and serve the best interests of Minnesota."[57] In a letter to Brooks, Midwest Regional Director Merrill D. Beal said the new committee would have no official relationship to the park and no preferred status so far as the NPS was concerned.[58]

Brooks would soon get better acquainted with the citizens committee. His chief concern after the park was established was to prepare for the five master plan hearings in June 1975. These meetings were scheduled for International Falls, Orr, Virginia, Duluth, and Minneapolis, in that order. In the years to follow, park superintendents could always expect things to "brighten up" after the sessions on the Iron Range. That pattern was established during this set of hearings on the master plan.

Reading the press accounts after more than twenty years have passed is truly an alarming experience. Few at the first three meetings spoke a favorable word for the national park or its project manager. At International Falls, only George Esslinger, a resort owner and early supporter of Voyageurs, spoke up for the national park. Intemperate remarks against park regulations, the federal government, and the plan were frequently made. At Virginia, one speaker said, "They call this a master plan for the park but it's a master plan to control people."[59] But as with all park documents of this type, it was essentially a passive one. It described the area, gave a brief legislative history, and described park concepts, interpretive concepts, park access and circulation, land classification, visitor facilities, and proposed locations of main entrances and proposed development areas.

Brooks, soon to become the park's first superintendent, had to listen to ten hours of vituperative, sometimes abusive remarks. He and two rangers found themselves in the midst of very unhappy people. Brooks once said that after occasions like that, he would return to International Falls and take refuge in the quiet of the park. Once, while sitting with friends on the porch of his home on Rainy Lake, someone said, "this place is too pretty to fight in." He agreed.[60]

A major challenge to the park's authority came in fall 1975 when a number of duck hunters threatened to challenge NPS regulations against hunting in park waters of Black Bay. According to Brooks, many hunters were led to believe that the state had jurisdiction over the waters around the park. As a show of concern by the NPS, two additional rangers were sent from the St. Croix and the Ozark Scenic Riverways to assist the Voyageurs' rangers. Brooks said later that the plan was to issue citations to deliberate challenges, and the park rangers would pick an appropriate time. A citation was issued several days into the season to one person, who proceeded to challenge the park's authority in the courts. On appeal, the Supreme Court refused to hear the case, thus upholding the lower court's ruling that the NPS did have jurisdiction over the waters in the park.[61]

Also in October, meeting for the first time, the Citizens Council on Voyageurs National Park (CCVNP) passed a resolution asking the NPS to consider modifying its policy prohibiting all hunting in national parks and urged that 960 acres of prime duck hunting land at Black Bay be deleted from Voyageurs.[62]

Voyageurs had not been "official" eight months, and its superintendent and small staff faced challenges and problems of major significance to the future of the park. An opportunity for superintendents to list these problems came on November 11, 1975, when the Midwest Regional Director relayed a memorandum he had received from the Washington office. It read in part, "We are again requesting that you survey the programs under your jurisdiction and report to us events or projects which will force decisions by the Washington office or by the Secretary's office."[63] Brooks's response identified seven issues that in his judgment would become even more difficult in the future. I believe the first four are the most significant for Voyageurs:

1. Continued pressure for the deletion of lands or waters in the Gold Portage area of Black Bay to accommodate duck hunting.
2. Increasing activity to redesignate Voyageurs National Park as a national recreation area.
3. A contention by the State of Minnesota and a state legislator that the legislative boundary line across the east end of Black Bay was not located in accordance with planning intent, that the line was intended to be further east.
4. Almost any action on the part of the National Park Service which establishes a park presence which is not in agreement with State Representative Irv Anderson's or special interest desires.
5. Policy review of the Master Plan and Environmental Impact Statement for Voyageurs National Park.

6. Pressure to delete part of the D. J. McCarthy lands within the Black Bay development site.
7. Possible ownership or operation of the Kettle Falls Dam by the National Park Service would result in serious legal problems, public relations problems, and the future likelihood of torts from resort owners and others.[64]

In January 1976, Brooks filed his annual report for 1975. Under the category, "The Future," Brooks continued to identify troublesome issues for the young park: "There will be a continuing local relations problem as we establish a park identity. The enforcement of hunting, trapping, aircraft, snowmobiling and water safety [regulations] necessitates strong support from the courts." But in his concluding statement, he recognized that to counter criticism, he had to take the offensive: "The best way to establish a park identity is through interpretive and education programs and stronger emphasis needs to be given as soon as protection activities approach standards." Under the heading "Public Relations," Brooks said that the park was a target of county (Koochiching) and state politicians who seemed bent on destroying Voyageurs as a national park and having a national recreation area designated instead: "This activity generates, feeds and encourages through a receptive news media, which exemplifies yellow journalism at its best; opposition which otherwise would not be as strong or as hard to work with."[65]

Under "Wilderness Management" in the annual report, Brooks wrote, "The status of land acquisition and master planning for Voyageurs National Park complicate the management of land in relation to potential wilderness. Motorized use [snowmobile and aircraft] in much of the land area is in conflict and cannot be allowed to become a traditional use in portions of the established park."[66]

The 1975 report may well have been written when Brooks was feeling his lowest about accomplishments at Voyageurs and the future of the park. It was a "cranky" document revealing a mood of exasperation over the course of events that he most certainly believed were not in the best long-term interests of the park. Most administrators of any private business or public institution would admit to similar misgivings about their accomplishments from time to time. As Brooks wrote his annual report, he knew that Black Bay was lost. He had letters in his file that showed that the leading politicians with interests and responsibilities for Voyageurs had already taken positions advocating deletion, including Congressman Oberstar, Commissioner Herbst, Governor Wendell Anderson, and Representative Irvin Anderson. He also knew that eventually the NPS would agree to a compromise permitting deletion of a portion of Black Bay in exchange for road access to the Ash River Visitor Center near Sullivan Bay, and the deletion of the Neil Point area in exchange for the addition of land for a visitor center at the north end of Black Bay. He believed that some of these events represented capitulation and appeasement. He did not agree with some in and out of the NPS who believed these moves would lead to tranquility at Voyageurs. He also saw the new CCVNP as a major negative factor in the park's future. And he saw these and other changes simply leading eventually to a move to change the park's designation from national park to national recreation area.[67]

The annual report for 1976 was short and with the exception of a comment on the CCVNP, was relatively routine. Brooks said the CCVNP's primary function "has been to serve special interest groups or individuals opposed to the park or national park management for the area."[68] The 1977 report was prepared by the chief ranger in a short, narrative style and included park statistics for the year.

In 1978, Brooks was granted his request for a transfer. He assumed his new duties as superintendent of Padre Island National Seashore in Texas on October 15, 1978. After several years in Texas, he retired to a home in the country outside Chattanooga, Tennessee.

In this last chapter, about the four years between authorization and establishment of Voyageurs National Park, I have emphasized the experiences, dedication, and efforts of its first superintendent. By any measure, he was the dominant figure and the guiding force for the park. Toward the close of his tenure at Voyageurs, he said his assignment to the park was the biggest challenge of his life—but not likely the most pleasant years of his career. Former NPS Director George Hartzog wrote after his retirement, "The National Park Service is operated with three levels of management: The director's office in Washington, which is responsible for translating the Secretary's objectives into action; the regional offices [six during his tenure] which are responsible for coordination of field management; and the parks, each in the charge of a superintendent responsible for on-site accomplishment of the service mission, namely, preserve the park resources and serve the visitor." Hartzog also made this observation, "Park people are intensely committed to their mission, hard-working, strong-willed and fiercely independent."[69] This is an excellent characterization of Myrl Brooks, first superintendent of Voyageurs National Park.

Epilogue

During the month of August 2000, Voyageurs National Park celebrated its twenty-fifth anniversary since establishment in 1975. Visitors to the park who had not been there for several years were surprised by the numerous visible changes, especially in park access and facilities. Arriving from the south on U.S. 53, they saw the first of several national park signs near the town of Orr, about fifty-five miles south of International Falls. The signs announce directions to the four entrance points to the park: Crane Lake, Kabetogama, Ash River, and Rainy Lake, eleven miles east of International Falls. Except for Crane Lake, each has a professional staff, interpretive displays, literature, and other facilities of the type visitors to all national parks are accustomed to seeing. The park provides visitors with an official guide, the *Rendezvous,* a complimentary park newspaper that describes activities, accommodations, and special events in the park for the entire year. The publication of the *Rendezvous* is now supported financially by individuals and businesses in the area. Also, many of the resorts and other food and lodging businesses distribute colorful literature, including maps of the park, at locations throughout the park area. By contrast, in 1975 little mention was made about the new park in tourist promotional material. But that has gradually changed, especially in the past fifteen years.

The completion of the large and impressive visitor center on Rainy Lake in 1987, subsequent improvements at the Kettle Falls Hotel and the Kabetogama and Ash River visitor centers, and the completion of new access roads to the centers help explain the difference. Significant

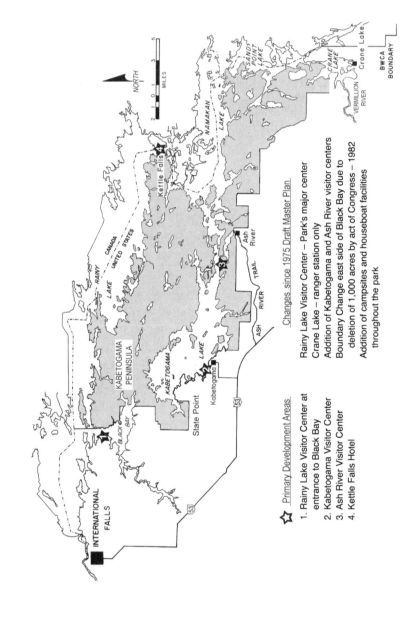

NORTH

MILES
2 1 0 1 3 5

INTERNATIONAL
FALLS

BLACK BAY

RAINY LAKE

CANADA
UNITED STATES

KABETOGAMA
PENINSULA

KABETOGAMA

KABETOGAMA
LAKE

State Point

Kabetogama

53

53

Kettle Falls

NAMAKAN
LAKE

SANDY
POINT
LAKE

ASH RIVER TRAIL

ASH

Ash
River

CRANE
LAKE

VERMILLION
RIVER

Crane Lake

BWCA
BOUNDARY

☆ Primary Development Areas

1. Rainy Lake Visitor Center at
   entrance to Black Bay
2. Kabetogama Visitor Center
3. Ash River Visitor Center
4. Kettle Falls Hotel

Changes since 1975 Draft Master Plan

Rainy Lake Visitor Center – Park's major center
Crane Lake – ranger station only
Addition of Kabetogama and Ash River visitor centers
Boundary Change east side of Black Bay due to
   deletion of 1,000 acres by act of Congress – 1982
Addition of campsites and houseboat facilities
   throughout the park

Voyageurs National Park, 2001.

federal, state, and local funding for these facilities sent the message to the nearby resort communities that the park was adding and would continue to add facilities like hiking trails, groomed snowmobile and cross-country ski trails, campsites, boating facilities, and navigation aids, and numerous interpretive programs and other features their guests could enjoy on a visit to their resort. New access roads and improvement of existing roads to the park entrance communities represented a significant change since the park was established.

A first-time visitor during the anniversary year might have taken an early morning stroll near the Rainy Lake visitor center to watch the sun rise over Black Bay. He would have noticed the activity at the new boat launch as local sport fishermen prepared to place their boats in the water. Not far away a few visitors might have been looking over the tour boat that would take them on a day trip along the shores of Rainy Lake to the Kettle Falls Hotel at the east end of the Kabetogama Peninsula. Continuing his walk through the picnic area and standing at the waters edge, he could not imagine a more peaceful scene. Placed in the same setting, a longtime park visitor would certainly marvel at the beauty of his surroundings but also at how much the park had changed in terms of facilities and accommodations. Then, sadly, he would recall the previous twenty-five years as a period of acrimonious wrangling over challenges to NPS authority and jurisdiction: bitter resentment by some over land acquisition issues, the pace of federal funding for park development, why a national park instead of a national recreation area, wilderness or the status quo, snowmobiling or no snowmobiling on the peninsula, and park superintendents who were said to be lacking in ability to communicate with local people and should be replaced.

This is not the place to make judgments about the merits or veracity of the claims for or against the NPS, but it is essential to state that these were not tranquil times at Voyageurs National Park. Is Voyageurs with its bouts with local officials and vocal critics the exception among national parks in this regard? Hardly. A study was done on parkland politics in 1981, and the findings are enlightening. The author stated that "the importance of media, of activity by *ad hoc* environmental groups, and intervention by national conservation groups pale in comparison to the role of the local community in park affairs." At Voyageurs, as at other parks, the local community and particularly individuals in the community whose economic and political well-being is closely tied to the park have a special interest in the park's policies. The power of the local community was demonstrated when, as discussed briefly in the last chapter of this book, a group marshaled the support of local, state, and national political figures to cause the NPS to acquiesce to demands to delete 1,000 acres of park territory at Black Bay, a reversal of park policy on this matter. On other issues community support has worked to the park's advantage.

We frequently hear the phrase, "it's time to move on," or "we must put this behind us." Either expression is appropriate for Voyageurs. The park has seen significant growth in its facility requirements in recent years and continual pressure for policy revision in matters that affect its fundamental mission. Following nearly three years of discussion, public review, and hearings, a new general management plan became law in November 2001. This document replaces a 1980 plan, and the expectation is that the new plan will carry the park forward through the next fifteen to twenty years. With this plan in place, the park can now look forward to a better public understanding of its goals and to stewardship of the park's resources for the long term.

APPENDIX A

Voyageurs National Park Legislation

An Act to authorize the establishment of the Voyageurs National Park in the State of Minnesota, and for other purposes. (84 Stat. 1971)

Be it enacted by the Senate and House of Representatives of the United States of America in Congress assembled, That the purpose of this Act is to preserve, for the inspiration and enjoyment of present and future generations, the outstanding scenery, geological conditions and waterway system which constituted a part of the historic route of the Voyageurs who contributed significantly to the opening of the Northwestern United States.

Establishment

Sec. 101. In furtherance of the purpose of this Act, the Secretary of the Interior (hereinafter referred to as the "Secretary") is authorized to establish the Voyageurs National park (hereinafter referred to as the "park") in the State of Minnesota, by publication of notice to that effect in the Federal Register at such time as the Secretary deems sufficient interests in lands or waters have been acquired for administration in accordance with the purposes of this Act: *Provided,* That the Secretary shall not establish the park until the lands owned by the State of Minnesota and any of its political subdivisions within the boundaries shall have been donated to the Secretary for the purposes of the park: *Provided further,* That the Secretary shall not acquire other lands by purchase for the park prior to such donation unless he finds that acquisition is necessary to prevent irreparable changes in their uses or character of such a nature as to make them unsuitable for park purposes and notifies the Committees on Interior and Insular Affairs of both the Senate and the House of Representatives of such findings at least thirty days prior to such acquisition.

Sec. 102. The park shall include the lands and waters within the boundaries as generally depicted on the drawing entitled "A Proposed Voyageurs National Park, Minnesota," numbered LNPMW-VOYA-1001, dated February 1969, which shall be on file and available for public inspection in the offices of the National Park Service, Department of the Interior. Within one year after acquisition of the lands owned by the State of Minnesota and its political subdivisions within the boundaries of the park the Secretary shall affix to such drawing an exact legal description of said boundaries. The Secretary may revise the boundaries of the park from time to time by publishing in the Federal Register a revised drawing or other boundary description, but such revisions shall not increase the land acreage within the park by more than one thousand acres.

Land Acquisition

Sec. 201. (a) The Secretary may acquire lands or interests therein within the boundaries of the park by donation, purchase with donated or appropriated funds, or exchange. When any tract of land is only partly within such boundaries, the Secretary may acquire all or any portion of the land outside of such boundaries in order to minimize the payment of severance costs. Land so acquired outside of the park boundaries may be exchanged by the Secretary for non-Federal lands within the park boundaries. Any portion of land acquired outside the park boundaries and not utilized for exchange shall be reported to the General Services Administration for disposal under the Federal Property and Administrative Services Act of 1949 (63 Stat. 377), as amended. Any Federal property located within the boundaries of the park may be transferred without consideration to the administrative jurisdiction of the Secretary for the purposes of the park. Lands within the boundaries of the park owned by the State of Minnesota, or any political subdivision thereof, may be acquired only by donation.

(b) In exercising his authority to acquire property under this section, the Secretary shall give immediate and careful consideration to any offer made by any individual owning property within the park area to sell such property to the Secretary. In considering such offer, the Secretary shall take into consideration any hardship to the owner which might result from any undue delay in acquiring his property.

Sec. 202. (a) Any owner or owners (hereinafter referred to as "owner") of improved property on the date of its acquisition by the Secretary may, if the Secretary determines that such improved property is not, at the time of its acquisition, required for the proper administration of the park, as a condition of such acquisition, retain for themselves and their successors or assigns a right of use and occupancy of the improved property for noncommercial residential purposes for a definite term not to exceed twenty-five years, or, in lieu thereof, for a term ending at the death of the owner, or the death of his spouse, whichever is later. The owner shall elect the term to be retained. The Secretary shall pay to the owner the fair market value of the property on the date of such acquisition less the fair market value on such date of the right retained by the owner.

(b) If the State of Minnesota donates to the United States any lands within the boundaries of the park subject to an outstanding lease on which the lessee began construction of a noncommercial or recreational residential dwelling prior to January 1, 1969, the Secretary may grant to such lessee a right of use and occupancy for such period of time as the Secretary, in his discretion, shall determine; *Provided,* That no such right of use and occupancy shall be granted, extended, or continue after ten years from the date of the establishment of the park.

(c) Any right of use and occupancy retained or granted pursuant to this section shall be subject to termination by the Secretary upon his determination that such use and occupancy is being exercised in a manner not consistent with the purposes of this Act, or upon his determination that the property is required for the proper administration of the park. The Secretary shall tender to the holder of the right so terminated an amount equal to the fair market value of that portion which remains unexpired on the date of termination.

(d) The term "improved property," as used in this section, shall mean a detached, noncommercial residential dwelling, the construction of which was begun before January 1, 1969, together with so much of the land on which the dwelling is situated, the said land being in the same ownership as the dwelling, as the Secretary shall designate to be reasonably necessary for the enjoyment of the dwelling for the sole purpose of noncommercial residential use, together with any structures accessory to the dwelling which are situated on the land so designated.

Sec. 203. Notwithstanding any other provision of the law, the Secretary is authorized to negotiate and enter into concession contracts with former owners of commercial, recreational, resort, or similar properties located within the park boundaries for the provision of such services at their former location as he may deem necessary for the accommodation of visitors.

Sec. 204. The Secretary is authorized to pay a differential in value, as hereinafter set forth, to any owner of commercial timberlands within the park with whom the State of Minnesota has negotiated, for the purpose of conveyance to the United States, an exchange of lands for State lands outside the Park. Payment hereunder may be made when an exchange is based upon valuations for timber purposes only, and shall be the difference between the value of such lands for timber purposes, as agreeable to the State, the Secretary, and any owner, and the higher value, if any, of such lands for recreational purposes not attributable to establishment or authorization of the park: *Provided,* That any payment shall be made only at such time as fee title of lands so acquired within the boundaries is conveyed to the United States.

Administration

Sec. 301. (a) Except as hereinafter provided, the Secretary shall administer the lands acquired for the park, and after establishment shall administer the park, in accordance with the provisions of the Act of August 25, 1916 (39 Stat. 535) as amended and supplemented (16 U.S.C. 1–4).

(b) Within four years from the date of establishment, the Secretary of the Interior shall review the area within the Voyageurs National Park and shall report to the President, in accordance with subsections 3(c) and 3(d) of the Wilderness Act (78 Stat. 890; 16 U.S.C. 1132 (c) and (d)), his recommendation as to the suitability or nonsuitability of any area within the lakeshore for preservation as wilderness, and any designation of any such area as a wilderness may be accomplished in accordance with said subsections of the Wilderness Act.

(c) All mining and mineral activities and commercial water power development within the boundaries of the park shall be prohibited, and further, any conveyance from the State of Minnesota shall contain a covenant that the State of Minnesota, its licensees, permittees, lessees, assigns, or successors in interest shall not engage in or permit any mining activity nor water power development.

Sec. 302. (a) The Secretary shall permit recreational fishing on lands and waters under his jurisdiction within the boundaries of the park in accordance with applicable laws of the United States and of the State of Minnesota, except that the Secretary may designate zones where and establish periods when no fishing shall be permitted for reasons of public safety, administration, fish and wildlife management, or public use and enjoyment. Except in emergencies, any regulations of the Secretary pursuant to this section shall be put into effect only after consultation with the appropriate agency of the State of Minnesota.

(b) The seining of fish at Shoepack Lake by the State of Minnesota to secure eggs for propagation purposes shall be continued in accordance with plans mutually acceptable to the State and the Secretary.

Sec. 303. The Secretary may, when planning for development of the park, include appropriate provisions for (1) winter sports, including the use of snowmobiles, (2) use by seaplanes, and (3) recreational use by all types of watercraft, including houseboats, runabouts, canoes, sailboats, fishing boats and cabin cruisers.

Sec. 304. Nothing in this Act shall be construed to affect the provisions of any treaty now or hereafter in force between the United States and Great Britain relating to Canada or between the United States and Canada, or of any order or agreement made or entered into pursuant to any such treaty, which by its terms would be applicable to the lands and waters which may be acquired by the Secretary hereunder, including, without limitation on the generality of the foregoing, the Convention Between the United States and Canada on Emergency Regulation of Level of Rainy Lake and of Other Boundary Waters in the Rainy Lake and of Other Boundary Waters in the Rainy Lake Watershed, signed September 15, 1938, and any order issued pursuant thereto.

Sec. 305. The Secretary is authorized to make provision for such roads within the park as are, or will be, necessary to assure access from present and future State roads to public facilities within the park.

Appropriations

Sec. 401. There are authorized to be appropriated such sums as may be necessary to carry out the provisions of this Act, not to exceed, however, $26,014,000 for the acquisition of property, and not to exceed $19,179,000 (June 1969 prices) for development, plus or minus such amounts, if any, as may be justified by reason of ordinary fluctuations in construction costs as indicated by engineering cost indices applicable to the types of construction involved herein.

Approved January 8, 1971.

Legislative History

House Report No. 91-1552 (Committee on Interior and Insular Affairs). Senate Report No. 91-1513 (Committee on Interior and Insular Affairs). Congressional Record, Vol. 116 (1970):

Oct. 3, considered and passed House.

Dec. 22, considered and passed Senate, amended.

Dec. 29, House concurred in Senate amendments.

APPENDIX B

Legislative Chronology for Voyageurs National Park, 1891–2001

1891   The Minnesota State Legislature passed a concurrent resolution requesting that the president of the United States establish a national park between Crane Lake and Lake of the Woods.

1899–1908   A campaign for a national park led by the Minnesota Federation of Women's Clubs was begun. Following compromise with competing proposals, the effort resulted in congressional action in 1908 establishing the Minnesota National Forest in north-central Minnesota between Bemidji and Grand Rapids. The name was changed in 1928 to Chippewa National Forest.

1909   President Theodore Roosevelt established the Superior National Forest in northeastern Minnesota.

1926   The secretary of agriculture issued a policy statement establishing a roadless primitive area within the Superior National Forest, thereby recognizing the significance of recreational values in the management of the forest.

1927   The Quetico-Superior Council, a conservation coalition dedicated to protection of the natural resources in the Minnesota-Ontario boundary waters area, was formed. Ernest Oberholtzer from northern Minnesota was the council's most active supporter and its first president.

1930   The Shipstead-Newton-Nolan Act was passed by Congress to conserve for recreational use the natural beauty of shorelines on all federal lands in the boundary waters area. Logging was forbidden on all shores to a depth of 400 feet from the natural waterline. Three years later Minnesota passed similar legislation pertaining to state lands.

1933–37   On several occasions during the depression years, the St. Louis County Board wrote to the governor favoring federal purchase of its tax-delinquent lands in the Kabetogama area.

1938–39   Working with the state, the NPS conducted a "State Park, Parkway and Recreation Area" study in Minnesota. A report in 1939 included a plan that eventually led to eight new units in the Minnesota State Park system. The Kabetogama Peninsula (west half) was looked at for its potential as a state park but was not included in the recommended list.

1957–58   The NPS was asked by the state to assist in updating the 1939 "State Park, Parkway and Recreation Plan." The NPS was also asked to evaluate the Northwest Angle area as to its potential as a unit in the National Park System. After study, the Northwest Angle area was not recommended, but the Kabetogama Peninsula did interest NPS personnel.

1959–61   NPS personnel carried out reconnaissance surveys of the Kabetogama Peninsula to determine its potential as a national park. The state continued to withhold Kabetogama state lands from sale pending possible state park status.

Fall 1961   NPS Director Conrad Wirth authorized advanced studies of the Kabetogama area, as recommended by NPS staff.

1962   Minnesota Governor Elmer L. Andersen hosted a tour of the Kabetogama area with guests NPS Director Conrad Wirth, State Parks Director U. W. Hella, Minnesota Historical Society Director Russell Fridley, naturalist Sigurd Olson, and George Amidon, the official representing the Minnesota and Ontario Paper Company, the principal landowner on the Kabetogama Peninsula. Governor Andersen wrote a consensus statement for the group recognizing the potential of the area as a unit of the National Park System. Olson suggested the park be named Voyageurs National Park. The Advisory Board on National Parks, Historical Sites, Buildings and Memorials approved a resolution to the secretary of the interior, recommending Voyageurs be added to the National Park System.

1963   The NPS completed a report on a proposed Voyageurs National Park extending from Rainy Lake to the mouth of the Vermilion River at Crane Lake. This proposal, which included lands and water under the jurisdiction of the USFS, was an "in-house" document circulating between the NPS and the USFS. The USFS strongly objected to the inclusion of their lands in the proposed park.

1964   The first official park proposal was published for public information. It described a park located on the Kabetogama Peninsula and adjacent waters on Rainy Lake and Kabetogama Lake.

1965   Voyageurs National Park Association was organized to promote the establishment of a national park on the Kabetogama Peninsula.

October 1967   A Citizens Committee for Voyageurs National Park was established to generate public support for the park proposal across the state; five thousand signed the park petition at the Minnesota State Fair.

November 1967   Governor Harold LeVander sponsored a special workshop on Voyageurs National Park in Virginia, Minnesota, where positions on both sides of the park proposal were invited and discussed.

December 1967   Governor LeVander endorsed the NPS proposal for a national park on the Kabetogama Peninsula and made the case for extending the boundaries southeasterly to include Namakan and Sand Point Lakes.

1968   The NPS published a master plan for the proposed Voyageurs National Park on the Kabetogama Peninsula; Minnesota's Eighth District congressman, John Blatnik, joined by the entire state congressional delegation, introduced legislation authorizing a Voyageurs National Park extending from Rainy

Lake on the northwest to Crane Lake on the southeast. The Blatnik proposal was quite similar in extent to the original plan completed by the NPS staff in 1963.

April 1969   Representative John Blatnik reintroduced his Voyageurs National Park bill in the Congress.

August 1969   The House Subcommittee on Parks and Recreation held field hearings in International Falls, Minnesota, on the Voyageurs National Park legislation.

July 1970   The House Subcommittee on Parks and Recreation held hearings in Washington, D.C.

October 1970   The House of Representatives approved Voyageurs National Park legislation.

December 4, 1970   The Senate Subcommittee on Parks and Recreation held hearings on the Voyageurs National Park bill in Washington, D.C.

December 22, 1970   The Senate approved Voyageurs National Park bill after adding amendments.

December 29, 1970   The House agreed with Senate amendments, and the Voyageurs National Park bill was sent to the president for signature.

January 8, 1971   President Richard M. Nixon signed the bill authorizing Voyageurs National Park.

May 1971   The Minnesota State Legislature approved donation of state lands for Voyageurs National Park to comply with congressional requirements.

June 1971   Myrl Brooks was appointed project manager for Voyageurs National Park. Brooks became the first superintendent of the park after its formal establishment.

April 8, 1975   Voyageurs National Park was formally established as the thirty-sixth national park.

1975   In spring, the state legislature approved funding for a Citizens Council on Voyageurs National Park. The Legislation was opposed by the Voyageurs National Park Association.

1977   The federal court affirmed park jurisdiction over waters in Voyageurs National Park.

1978   The park's first visitor center opened on Highway 53, International Falls.

1980   A local resident challenged Voyageurs' land acquisition program. The first master plan and final environmental assessment for the park was completed.

1983   Congress deletes 1,000 acres on Black Bay following an appeal by duck hunters. The Cruiser Lake trail on Kabetogama Peninsula was completed.

1985   The Locator Lake trail was completed from the south shore of Lake Kabetogama to the peninsula's interior at Locator Lake.

1987   Rainy Lake Visitor Center was dedicated. Public meetings were held on a fire management plan and water level issues.

1988   Construction was completed of the Kabetogama Lake visitor center and a new access road to Rainy Lake; rehabilitation of Kettle Falls hotel was completed.

1989   Environmental education programs began.

1990   The United States paid V. Davis $1.2 million for land.

1992   The park designates winter protection areas to protect gray wolves and eagles.

1993   The Little America Island Mine trails and exhibit opened; a gold rush celebration took place.

1994   Friends of Voyageurs National Park was established.

1996   A thirteen-member citizen panel began efforts to resolve problems facing management of Voyageurs National Park. Discussions were refereed by the Federal Mediation and Conciliation Service.

1997   The federal court affirmed the NPS's mandate to manage park wildlife. The Ash River visitor center road was dedicated.

1998   Work on the General Management Visitor Use and Facilities Plan began.

1999   The federal court *reaffirmed* the NPS's jurisdiction over park waters. The park has constructed 214 campsite/day-use sites, 25 miles of hiking trails, 110 miles of snowmobile trails, and 15 miles of ski trails.

1999   The governor ended state funding for the controversial Citizens Council on Voyageurs National Park.

2000   The twenty-fifth anniversary of Voyageurs National Park was celebrated in August 2000.

November 2001   The new "Voyageurs National Park General Management/Environmental Impact Statement/Visitor Use and Facilities Plan" was completed and became law on November 11, 2001.

Notes

Preface

1. The Boundary Water Wilderness Act of 1978 extended to the Boundary Waters Canoe Area (BWCA) full wilderness status and enlarged the BWCA to 1,075,500 acres. Since 1978, it has been called the Boundary Waters Canoe Area Wilderness (BWCAW).

2. Remarks made at the dedication of the Lindbergh House on the site of the Lindbergh Interpretive Center, Little Falls, Minnesota, September 1973. This site is managed today by the Minnesota Historical Society as a state historic site.

3. Wallace Stegner, "The Best Idea We Ever Had," *Wilderness Magazine,* spring 1983, 4–13.

Introduction

1. Wallace Stegner, "The Best Idea We Ever Had," *Wilderness Magazine,* spring 1983, 4–13.

2. Sterling Brubaker, *Rethinking the Federal Lands* (Washington, D.C.: Resources for the Future, 1984), 49–50.

3. John R. Borchert, *Minnesota's Changing Geography* (Minneapolis: University of Minnesota Press, 1959), 24.

4. "Land Grabber's Scheme," *Duluth News-Tribune,* 5 December 1891.

5. *Duluth News-Tribune,* 9 December 1891.

6. R. Newell Searle, "Minnesota National Forest," *Minnesota History* 42 (1971): 249.

7. R. Newell Searle, *Saving Quetico-Superior: A Land Set Apart* (St. Paul: Minnesota Historical Society Press, 1977), 16.

8. R. Newell Searle, "Minnesota Forestry Comes of Age: Christopher C. Andrews, 1895–1911," *Forest History* 17, 2 (July 1973): 23–24.

9. Michael Frome, *The Battle for Wilderness* (New York: Praeger Publisher, 1974), 118; David Backes, "Wilderness Visions," *Forest and Conservation History* 35 (July 1991): 128–37.

10. Frome, *The Battle for Wilderness*, 118.

11. Backes, "Wilderness Visions," 132.

12. Searle, *Saving Quetico-Superior*, 26.

13. Samuel T. Dana, *Minnesota Lands* (Washington, D.C.: American Forestry Association, 1969), 121–22.

14. Ibid., 122.

15. Statement of Charles S. Kelly, chairman of the president's Quetico-Superior Committee on May 22, 1964, at a Quetico-Superior Institute held in St. Paul, Minnesota. Although the leadership of the council was dominated by Minnesota men, its advisory board included many prominent Americans representing a variety of interests and professions. For a detailed account of the organization and early efforts of the Quetico-Superior Council, see Searle, *A Land Set Apart*.

16. For more on the life of Ernest Oberholtzer, see R. Newell Searle, "Ober's Long Shadow," *Living Wilderness* 41 (January/March 1978): 5–11; "Ernest C. Oberholtzer – 1884–1977," *Wilderness News*, Quetico Superior Foundation, summer 1977, 2; and Joe Paddock, *Keeper of the Wild* (St. Paul: Minnesota Historical Society Press, 2001).

17. President's Quetico-Superior Committee, *An International Peace Memorial Forest in the Quetico-Superior Country* (Chicago: 1948), 10. President Franklin Roosevelt established this committee by executive order in 1934 to consult and invoke the aid of federal and state agencies and other nongovernmental organizations concerning the use and preservation of the Quetico-Superior area in the public interest.

18. Ibid., back cover. The plan was endorsed by the American Legion and the Canadian Legion in 1929. In 1944 the Ontario Legion urged dedication of the forest to veterans of both world wars, and the American Legion endorsed the concept by re-endorsing the Peace Memorial Forest in 1948.

19. Ernest C. Oberholtzer, "A University of the Wilderness," *American Forests* 35, 11 (November 1929): 692. In the same article, Oberholtzer referred to three other "principles" of the Quetico-Superior Council's international memorial forest. They spoke to modern forest practices to ensure maximum timber supply, game and fish management for maximum natural production, and an international board of forest, park, and biological authorities to monitor the program. The Quetico-Superior Council was committed to what today is commonly called a multiple-use policy.

20. Dana, *Minnesota Lands*, 123.

21. Ibid. The legislation was originally entered in the House as the Shipstead-Newton Act, recognizing then Congressman Walter H. Newton from Minneapolis. Newton later accepted a position in the Hoover administration and was replaced by William I. Nolan, also from Minneapolis.

22. Ernest C. Oberholtzer, interviewer unknown, accession #9529, reel 3, Minnesota Historical Society Archives, St. Paul.

23. Ibid., 35.

24. Ernest C. Oberholtzer, "Attention Please, for Quetico-Superior, *National Parks Magazine* 78 (July–September 1944): 15.

1. The National Park Service in Northeastern Minnesota

1. Mathew E. Mattson to Frederick Winston, Chairman, Executive Committee for the Quetico-Superior Council, 21 March 1936, Quetico-Superior files, Minnesota Historical Society Archives, St. Paul.

2. St. Louis County Board of Commissioner's resolution to the governor advocating purchase of forest lands in St. Louis County, 15 December 1933, Superior National Forest files, Duluth, Minn.

3. Leslie S. Bean to R. V. Harmon, 19 August 1937, Superior National Forest files, #5510.

4. Senior Administrative Assistant R. C. Slye, Superior National Forest, memorandum for the files, 12 December 1938, Superior National Forest files, #5501. The memorandum is an account of the debate held on 9 December 1938 sponsored by the St. Louis County Club and Farm Bureau.

5. Assistant Chief of the USFS L. E. Kniepp to Regional Forester Leslie Bean in Milwaukee, Wis., 15 May 1941, Superior National Forest files.

6. The Civilian Conservation Corps was originally called the Emergency Conservation Work Administration when it was established in 1933.

7. Conrad Wirth, *Parks, Politics and People* (Norman: University of Oklahoma Press, 1980), 75–76.

8. U. W. Hella, *Quest for Excellence: A History of the Minnesota Council of Parks, 1954–1974* (St. Paul: Minnesota Parks Foundation, 1985), 41; U. W. Hella, interview by author, 17 August 1990.

9. Hella, interview.

10. The Northwest Angle is the peculiar northward projection of the state's boundary with Ontario and Manitoba. This boundary anomaly resulted from the requirement contained in treaties with Britain in 1783 and 1818 that in delimiting the international boundary, surveyors must utilize the northwestern corner of Lake of the Woods, the 49th parallel, and the entry point of Rainy River into Lake of the Woods on the southeast. Samuel Dana, *Minnesota Lands* (Washington, D.C.: American Forest Association, 1960), 64–65.

11. Hella, interview; Hella, *Quest for Excellence*, 18.

12. NPS Acting Chief of the Division of Recreational Resources Planning Sidney S. Kennedy to Bureau of Land Management, 16 July 1958, Voyageurs National Park Archives, International Falls, Minn.

13. Bureau of Land Management Acting Director Charles P. Mead to NPS Acting Director Jackson Price, 21 May 1959, Voyageurs National Park Archives.

14. John A. Blatnik, obituary, *New York Times*, 19 December 1991, D23; *Minnesota Legislative Manual, 1945–46* (St. Paul: State of Minnesota).

15. Evan Haynes report, July 1959, Minnesota Department of Conservation files, #56C95B, Minnesota Historical Society Archives, St. Paul.

16. Clarence Prout to Minnesota Conservation Department directors, 30 March 1961, Minnesota Department of Conservation files, #56C95B.

17. U. W. Hella to Manager of the International Falls Chamber of Commerce Claude Blais, 26 July 1961, Minnesota Department of Conservation files, #45A77B.

18. U. W. Hella to Governor Elmer L. Andersen, 21 September 1961, Minnesota Department of Conservation files, #45A77B.

19. Chronology on Voyageurs National Park, February 1966, Voyageurs National Park Archives. Items 10 and 11 summarize an October 1961 memorandum from the NPS midwest regional director to the NPS director recounting the events of his Minnesota visit.

20. Ibid., item 11.

21. Ibid., item 12.

22. Governor Elmer L. Andersen to Representative Albert Quie, 11 December 1961, Voyageurs National Park Archives; Representative Walter Judd to NPS Director Conrad Wirth, 18 December 1961, Voyageurs National Park Archives.

23. Broderick, Richard, "Minnesotan of the Year—A Generous Spirit," *Minnesota Monthly,* December 1989.

2. Developing a Proposal for Voyageurs National Park

1. NPS Assistant Midwest Regional Director Chester C. Brown memorandum to NPS Midwest Regional Director Howard Baker, 21 June 1962, Voyageurs National Park Archives, International Falls, Minn.

2. Ibid.

3. Ibid. Before 1958 the canoe country wilderness area in the Superior National Forest was called the Roadless Primitive Area. In that year a more appropriate name, the Boundary Waters Canoe Area (BWCA), was adopted. After the passage of the Wilderness Act in 1964, the BWCA became a unit of the National Wilderness Preservation System, and in 1978 the BWCA became the Boundary Waters Canoe Area Wilderness (BWCAW) to formally recognize its wilderness nature.

4. John Kawamoto, interview by author, Voyageurs National Park, International Falls, Minn., 21 June 1979.

5. Brown to Baker, 21 June 1962.

6. *International Falls Daily Journal,* 28 June 1962.

7. Elmer L. Andersen, interview by author, Arden Hills, Minn., 23 October 1990.

8. Ibid.

9. NPS Midwest Regional Director Howard Baker memorandum describing a plane trip over the border lakes region, 28 June 1962. The memorandum includes a chronology of NPS activities in northern Minnesota, undated, Voyageurs National Park Archives.

10. When Regional Forester George James referred to the Crane Lake area, he was identifying USFS lands adjacent to Namakan, Sand Point, and Crane Lakes. From 1963 to 1971, when Voyageurs National Park was authorized by Congress, the common reference to this area was "the Crane Lake area." However, during the entire eight-year effort for establishment of the park, the waters of Crane Lake were never included on maps *published* by the USFS or the NPS as being part of the territory under their jurisdiction. The NPS did produce a *planning* document (1963) for internal use only that showed a proposed Voyageurs National Park with Namakan, Sand Point, and Crane Lakes included. This map also showed a short stretch of the Vermilion River from its mouth on the south shore of Crane Lake to the river gorge a few miles south. The NPS included the river segment because of the historical significance of this location during the fur trade era. *But the map was never published.* When the Superior National Forest established its Crane Lake Recreation Area in 1966, it kept Crane Lake and its lakeside community *outside* its jurisdictional boundaries. Crane Lake, though outside the boundaries of the Voyageurs, continues to be a common reference point for the *southeastern* segment of the park.

11. Regional Forester George James to NPS Midwest Regional Director Howard Baker, 17 August 1962, Voyageurs National Park Archives.

12. NPS Midwest Regional Director Howard Baker to NPS Director Conrad Wirth, 22 August 1962, Voyageurs National Park Archives.

13. Ibid. Department of the Interior Secretary Stewart Udall in April 1962 established the Bureau of Outdoor Recreation (BOR). Such a bureau was one of the recommendations contained in the Outdoor Recreation Resources Review Commission's report, completed earlier in 1962. The BOR was to carry out nationwide recreational planning and coordinate recreation activities among federal agencies. Because these had been primary responsibilities of the NPS since the 1930s, the BOR was seen by many in the NPS, including Director Wirth, as challenging its long-standing reputation as the preeminent federal recreation agency. Nevertheless, personnel and funds were transferred from the NPS to the BOR to help launch the new bureau. Wirth was severely criticized by some in the Kennedy administration for not supporting the BOR, and this may have caused him to move up the date of his retirement, which took place in January 1964. Lacking the supportive constituency of agencies like the NPS and the USFS, the BOR's role diminished through the remainder of the 1960s and 1970s until it was abolished early in the Reagan administration. Ronald A. Forestra, *America's National Parks and Their Keepers* (Washington, D.C.: Resources for the Future, 1984); Edwin M. Fitch and John F. Shankland, *Bureau of Outdoor Recreation* (New York: Praeger, 1970); Conrad Wirth, *Parks, Politics and the People* (Norman: University of Oklahoma Press, 1980).

14. Advisory Board on National Parks, Historic Sites, Buildings and Memorials Chairman Harold Fabian to the Secretary of the Department of the Interior Stewart Udall, 17 October 1962, Voyageurs National Park Archives.

15. Ibid.

16. *International Falls Daily Journal,* 20 September 1962. Speech delivered on September 19, 1962, by Governor Elmer L. Andersen at a gathering at the Rex Hotel in International Falls, Minn.

17. The gubernatorial election in 1962 was more vigorously contested by both parties than in previous contests because the state was moving from two- to four-year terms for that office. The race became very close in the closing weeks of the campaign. It was then that a charge was made by a Minnesota Highway Department inspector that concrete was poured on a segment of I-35 near Hinckley at below-standard temperatures in order to rush the road to completion. The implication was that the governor saw political advantage in quick completion and had something to do with that decision. Governor Andersen vehemently denied the charge. Andersen's staff later discovered that the inspector was a brother of a person working on the Rolvaag campaign staff. Eighth District Congressman John Blatnik called for an investigation by the Bureau of Public Roads, a move calculated to further embarrass the governor. (Mr. Blatnik would later introduce legislation to authorize Voyageurs National Park.) Andersen challenged Blatnik to answer questions regarding what Andersen maintained were false charges. Blatnik chose not to respond. Political observers at the time believe this event tipped the election in Rolvaag's favor.

18. Andersen, interview.

19. Superior National Forest staff, J. B. White memorandum, 21 November 1962, Superior National Forest files, Duluth, Minn. The memorandum summarizes the November 15 meeting in Duluth with NPS personnel.

20. L. P. Neff, memorandum to USFS Regional Forester George James, 27 November 1962, Superior National Forest files.

21. E. M. Bacon, memorandum to USFS Regional Forester George James, 5 December 1962, Superior National Forest files. Bacon was the leader of a special task force, apparently out of Washington, D.C., to assess the NPS intentions in Minnesota. He reviewed NPS plans with Assistant Regional Director Chester C. Brown in Omaha. In his report to James, Bacon stated that the NPS had not determined if its proposal would call for a national park or a national recreation area. His personal opinion was that the proposed plan more nearly resembled a recreation area than a national park, which emphasizes preservation.

22. Ibid.

23. *The Voyageurs Route and a Proposed Voyageurs National Park* (Omaha: National Park Service, March 1963). First of several drafts prepared by the NPS for internal use and interagency review. A copy of what the USFS called a *Plan of Management-Namakan Lake Area* was appended to this report. Voyageurs National Park Archives.

24. Ibid.

25. *Crane Lake Recreation Area*, Superior National Forest, Duluth, Minn., 1966. A brochure prepared for public information by the Superior National Forest.

26. Conservation Commissioner Clarence Prout to NPS Midwest Region Chief of Park and Recreation Planning Henry Robinson in Omaha; and Prout to USFS Regional Forester George James in Milwaukee, 21 January 1963, Minnesota Department of Conservation file #45A810F, Minnesota Historical Society Archives, St. Paul.

27. The official announcement of the agreement was made jointly by the two departments and included a congratulatory letter from the president dated January 3, 1963. Governor Harold LeVander file #55668F, Minnesota Historical Society Archives.

28. Director of Minnesota State Parks U. W. Hella to Sigurd Olson, 11 February 1963, Minnesota Department of Conservation file #56C95B, Minnesota Historical Society Archives.

29. Sigurd Olson to Judge Hella, 15 February 1963, Minnesota Department of Conservation file #56C95B, Minnesota Historical Society Archives.

30. Howard Baker to Conrad Wirth, report on St. Paul meeting with Governor Andersen, regional USFS staff, and Minnesota Department of Conservation staff, 11 February 1963, Superior National Forest files.

31. George S. James, Regional Forester, memorandum for files summarizing the St. Paul meeting with Governor Andersen, National Park Service officials, and Minnesota Department of Conservation staff, 11 February 1963, Superior National Forest files.

32. Baker to Wirth, 11 February 1963; James, memorandum, 11 February 1963. Both documents pertain to the St. Paul meeting on 8 February 1963.

33. Baker to Wirth, 11 February 1963.

34. "The Voyageurs Route and a Proposed Voyageurs National Park," draft proposal (Omaha: Midwest Regional Office, National Park Service, March 1963), Voyageurs National Park Archives.

35. Judge Hella to Clarence Prout, 3 March 1963, Minnesota Department of Conservation file #56C95B, Minnesota Historical Society Archives.

36. Governor Elmer L. Andersen to Clarence Prout, 1 March 1963, Minnesota Department of Conservation file #56C95B, Minnesota Historical Society Archives. The memorandum informed Prout of the content of his conversation with Wirth.

37. USFS Chief Forester Edward P. Cliff to NPS Director Conrad Wirth, 28 March 1963, Voyageurs National Park Archives.

38. Sigurd Olson to U.S. Department of the Interior Secretary Stewart Udall, 13 May 1963, Voyageurs National Park Archives.

39. U.S. Department of the Interior, National Park Service, *Proposed Voyageurs National Park,* revised draft (Omaha: September 1963), 45.

40. Olson to Udall, 13 May 1963.

41. Sigurd Olson to NPS Assistant Director Theodore Swem, 6 June 1963, Sigurd Olson file #32B810F, Minnesota Historical Society Archives.

42. U.S. Department of the Interior, National Park Service, *Proposed Voyageurs National Park* (Omaha: 1964), 37, Voyageurs National Park Archives.

43. USFS Chief Forester Edward Cliff to NPS Director Conrad Wirth, 15 September 1964, Voyageurs National Park Archives.

44. U.S. Department of the Interior, National Park Service, *Proposed Voyageurs National Park* (Omaha: 1965), Voyageurs National Park Archives.

45. U. W. Hella to Clarence Prout, 4 April 1963, Minnesota Department of Conservation file #56C95B, Minnesota Historical Society Archives. Hella's reference to a national recreation area instead of a Voyageurs National Park was no doubt prompted by statements in the joint declaration of the Interior and Agriculture Departments "Treaty of the Potomac," which supported the creation of national recreation areas. In some cases these areas would be managed by the USFS, in others by the NPS, and in some instances, joint management would be appropriate.

3. Delay and Frustration

1. "National Park Service Proposal Will Be Discussed," *International Falls Daily Journal,* 23 April 1963.

2. NPS Acting Assistant Midwest Regional Director Harry Robinson to Minnesota Conservation Commissioner Clarence Prout, 20 June 1963, Voyageurs National Park Archives, International Falls, Minn. Letter requests information on existing ecological studies pertaining to the Kabetogama area. Of special concern was information on deer and beaver populations on the peninsula.

3. Eliot Davis to NPS Acting Assistant Midwest Regional Director Robinson, 21 June 1963, on "Kabetogama Trip"; Davis, memorandum to NPS Regional Director Baker, 25 June 1963, on "Land Values" in the proposed area. Voyageurs National Park Archives.

4. Davis to Robinson, 21 June 1963.

5. *Minnesota Legislative Manual 1963–1964* (St. Paul: State of Minnesota), 153, 191–93.

6. Howard Baker to W. Olson, 4 September 1963, Minnesota Department of Conservation files.

7. "Expect Endorsement for Voyageurs National Park," *International Falls Daily Journal,* 8 October 1963.

8. "City to Write 'Stronger' Letter on National Park," *International Falls Daily Journal,* 13 November 1963.

9. Editorial, "National Park Question," *International Falls Daily Journal,* 14 November 1963.

10. Clarence Prout, memorandum regarding telephone call from Vice President of the Minnesota and Ontario Paper Company's Woodland Division George Amidon, 2 December 1963, Minnesota Department of Conservation file #56C95B, Minnesota Historical Society Archives, St. Paul.

11. Minnesota Department of Conservation Deputy Commissioner Robert J. Brown to Director of Minnesota State Parks U. W. Hella, 9 December 1963, Minnesota Department of Conservation file #56C95B, Minnesota Historical Society Archives.

12. Eliot Davis, memorandum to NPS Midwest Regional Director Lemuel Garrison, 2 January 1964, Voyageurs National Park Archives.

13. John Kawamoto, oral history interview by Voyageurs National Park Historian Mary Lou Pearson, 12 June 1979, Voyageurs National Park Archives.

14. George Amidon, oral history interview by Voyageurs National Park Historian Mary Lou Pearson, 12 July 1976, Voyageurs National Park Archives. Once before, in the late 1940s, the M&O offered to exchange its Kabetogama lands for state lands closer to its mill. The governor supported the offer as did the Minnesota commissioner of conservation, but the plan ran into heated opposition by some who said the state would be giving up valuable trust fund lands for a "worthless rock pile." The M&O later withdrew its offer.

15. Minnesota and Ontario Paper Company Woodlands Division Vice President George Amidon to NPS Acting Assistant Regional Director Harry Robinson, 24 March 1964, Minnesota Department of Conservation file #56C95B, Minnesota Historical Society Archives.

16. Kawamoto, interview, 56–57.

17. Wayne Judy to Conservation Commissioner Wayne Olson, 20 October 1964, Minnesota Department of Conservation file #56C95B, Minnesota Historical Society Archives.

18. Kawamoto, interview, 59–60.

19. Barry Mackintosh, *The National Parks: Shaping the System* (Washington, D.C.: National Park Service, U.S. Department of the Interior, 1984), 62–75.

20. Kawamoto, interview, 62.

21. Ibid., 64.

22. Ibid., 64.

23. Ibid., 15–16.

24. Interoffice memoranda, 10 September 1963 and 4 October 1963, Minnesota Department of Conservation file #56C95B, Minnesota Historical Society Archives.

25. U. W. Hella to Sigurd Olson, 6 June 1964, Minnesota Department of Conservation file #56C95B, Minnesota Historical Society Archives.

26. Chronology on Voyageurs National Park prepared by the National Park Service, 1966, Voyageurs National Park Archives.

27. "Area Sentiment Strongly against Kabetogama Park," *International Falls Daily Journal*, 28 August 1964.

28. Ibid.

29. National Park Service news release from the Midwest Regional Office in Omaha, 17 September 1964, Legislative and Congressional Office files, Department of the Interior, Washington, D.C.

30. Northeast Minnesota Organization for Economic Education press release, 2 September 1964; Jeno Paulucci to Governor Karl Rolvaag, 17 September 1964.

Minnesota Department of Conservation file #56C95B, Minnesota Historical Society Archives.

31. Congressman Blatnik to Jeno Paulucci, 6 September 1964, Blatnik file #45A810F, Minnesota Historical Society Archives.

32. Editorial, "Take a Hard Look at National Park Idea," *International Falls Daily Journal*, 17 September 1964.

33. Kawamoto, interview, 56–58.

34. *International Falls Daily Journal*, 22 September 1964; reprint of Associated Press account of the Minneapolis hearing.

35. "Claim Park Would Be Economic Detractor," *International Falls Daily Journal*, 23 September 1964.

36. Kawamoto, interview, 58.

37. Jeno Paulucci to Governor Karl Rolvaag, 23 September 1964 and 25 September 1964, Minnesota Department of Conservation file #45A810F, Minnesota Historical Society Archives.

38. Governor Karl Rolvaag to Mrs. Floyd Breneman, Littlefork, Minn., 25 September 1964, Minnesota Department of Conservation file #45A810F, Minnesota Historical Society Archives.

39. Editorial, *International Falls Daily Journal*, 23 September 1964. The reference to road access referred to a causeway and bridge connection from the mainland across Black Bay to the peninsula. The Kabetogama Peninsula would then no longer be isolated and would lay open to the kind of resort development found around most Minnesota lakes.

40. Editorial, "Voyageurs National Park Idea Should Be Dropped," *Duluth News-Tribune*, 24 September 1964.

4. Progress on Voyageurs Stalled

1. In 1958 the USFS chose the name Boundary Waters Canoe Area, a more suitable name for its "Roadless Primitive Area" in the Superior National Forest. The new name more accurately recognized the area's recreational use and value. To reduce the conflicts between wilderness recreational uses and logging activity, Secretary Freeman, on January 12, 1965, ordered a 250,000-acre no-cutting zone added to the original 362,000 acres designated in 1941. For additional information, see R. Newell Searle, *Saving Quetico-Superior: A Land Set Apart* (St. Paul: Minnesota Historical Society Press, 1977); and Sierra Club, North Star Chapter, *A Wilderness in Crisis: The Boundary Waters Canoe Area* (Minneapolis: Sierra Club, 1970), 11–15.

2. "Fast Action Planned on Canoe Area," *Duluth Herald*, 14 January 1965.

3. NPS Midwest Regional Director Lemuel Garrison to NPS Director George Hartzog, 20 January 1965, Voyageurs National Park Archives, International Falls, Minn.

4. Transcript of Elmer Andersen speech to Rotary Club, International Falls, Minn., 27 January 1965, Voyageurs National Park Archives.

5. Minnesota and Ontario Paper Company President Robert Faegre to Governor Karl Rolvaag, 18 February 1965, Minnesota Department of Conservation file #45B17B, Minnesota Historical Society Archives, St. Paul; "Mando Favors National Park at Crane Lake," *International Falls Daily Journal*, 19 February 1965.

6. John Kawamoto, oral history interview by Voyageurs National Park Historian Mary Lou Pearson, 12 June 1979, Voyageurs National Park Archives; Ernest Oberholtzer to NPS Midwest Regional Director Lemuel Garrison, 30 March 1965, Voyageurs National Park Archives. Shortly after M&O announced its opposition to the Kabetogama site, Garrison received a letter from Oberholtzer, a longtime advocate of public ownership of the boundary waters region. He explained that M&O had acquired the peninsula lands in the late 1930s after much of it had been logged and burned over. The USFS had hoped to purchase the lands and put them under its management program, thus bringing them under public control—a long-sought goal of the Quetico-Superior Council. However, Governor Stassen, using newly acquired authority granted him by the Minnesota Legislature, vetoed the USFS plan that allowed M&O to purchase the lands at a very low price. Shortly thereafter, M&O offered to exchange these lands for more valuable state forest lands in an adjoining county but with the provision that M&O retain the flowage rights on the peninsula's shorelands, which would rid them of any necessity to pay flood damages on any shorelines that passed out of their hands. (M&O owned the power plant and dams that regulated the level of Rainy Lake.) Oberholtzer said these lands would all be sold subject to that reservation and the owner would be helpless to ask for recompense. This advantage to the M&O was revealed in public hearings. In the course of the hearings, those opposed to the trade said Minnesotans were giving up good forest land for a rock pile. In the hearings on the park issue during the 1960s, M&O representatives would remind the public that the state could have acquired these lands in 1940 but rejected the offer. However, they did not mention that retention of flowage rights was a condition for the proposed exchange.

7. Planning Associates Aguar, Jyring, and Whiteman, *Report of Preliminary Multiple-Use Plan for the Kabetogama Peninsula*, 24 February 1965, Voyageurs National Park Archives.

8. NPS Division of National Park System Studies Chief Chester Brown memorandum to NPS Director Hartzog, 18 March 1965, Voyageurs National Park Archives. This memorandum covered items discussed in a meeting with Secretary Udall.

9. NPS Midwest Regional Director Lemuel Garrison to NPS Director Hartzog, 20 April 1965, final recommendations for Voyageurs National Park, Voyageurs National Park Archives.

10. Ibid.

11. Ibid.

12. At midcentury, Minnesota's reserves of high-grade natural iron ores, which had been the mainstay of its iron mining industry since the 1890s, were rapidly declining. The industry began to turn to its vast reserves of leaner, low-grade ores, called taconite, as a replacement for the richer ores. However, taconite required an elaborate beneficiation (upgrading) process before it could be used in the blast furnaces. Because of the large investment required to construct the processing plants, the industry, complaining of the onerous tax policy on its activities, asked for a constitutional change in the state's iron ore taxing policies that would introduce some stability and fairness to the system. Resolving this problem became a precondition for making major investments in the new taconite industry. Initially there was strong resistance to the amendment proposition in northeastern Minnesota's iron ranges. But former Governor Andersen led a successful statewide educational

campaign to convince voters that passage of the amendment would lead to major investments on the iron ranges, thus revitalizing an ailing industry and at the same time benefiting the entire state. Within twenty-four hours of its passage, U.S. Steel Corporation announced a plan to build one of the largest iron ore beneficiation plants in the world on the Iron Range.

13. Chronology for Voyageurs National Park prepared by the National Park Service, February 1966, Voyageurs National Park Archives.

14. United Northern Sportsmen resolution, 16 February 1965.

15. Greater Minneapolis Chamber of Commerce report on Voyageurs National Park, 18 February 1965, Governor LeVander file #55G681, Minnesota Historical Society Archives.

16. Wayne Judy to Minnesota Department of Conservation Commissioner Wayne Olson, 24 March 1965, Minnesota Department of Conservation file #45B17B, Minnesota Historical Society Archives.

17. Robert Watson to Lloyd Brandt, 23 August 1975, Minnesota Department of Conservation file #45B17B, Minnesota Historical Society Archives.

18. Sam Morgan to Robert Watson, 6 May 1965, and 17 May 1965, Minnesota Department of Conservation file #45B17B, Minnesota Historical Society Archives.

19. NPS Deputy Assistant Director for Resources Studies Howard Stagner, "Why a Voyageurs National Park," speech delivered at the first general membership meeting of the Voyageurs National Park Association held in St. Paul on May 15, 1965, Minnesota Department of Conservation file #45B17B, Minnesota Historical Society Archives.

20. Editorial, "Suspend Land Exchange, for Cool-off and Study," *Duluth News-Tribune*, 9 March 1965.

21. Howard Stagner to NPS Director Hartzog, 21 May 1965, Voyageurs National Park Archives.

22. NPS Associate Regional Director George F. Baggley to Garrison, 30 June 1965, Voyageurs National Park Archives. Baggley's memorandum was a report on the Minnesota Outdoor Recreation Review Commission's hearing on June 18, 1965.

23. Lemuel A. Garrison to Robert Treuer, 28 March 1978, Voyageurs National Park Archives.

24. Northland Multiple Use Association resolution forwarded to administration officials including President Lyndon Johnson, 27 May 1965, Voyageurs National Park Archives.

25. Lemuel Garrison to Boise Cascade Vice President Robert Faegre, 11 June 1965, Voyageurs National Park Archives.

26. Letters from the Secretary of the Department of Agriculture Orville Freeman to Kabetogama Lake Association President Herbert Townsend, 21 June 1965, and State Senator and Chairman of the Minnesota Outdoor Recreation Resources Commission Henry Herren, 13 July 1965, Voyageurs National Park Archives.

27. Secretary of the Department of the Interior Steward Udall to Senator Walter Mondale, 16 August 1965, Voyageurs National Park Archives.

28. Wayne Olson to Walter Mondale, 13 July 1965, Minnesota Department of Conservation file #45B17B, Minnesota Historical Society Archives.

29. Draft statement by NPS Midwest Regional Director Lemuel A. Garrison and Sigurd Olson that declared no further studies were required beyond those already

made by the NPS and approved by the Department of the Interior proposing a national park in the Rainy Lake–Kabetogama Peninsula region, 23 September 1965, Voyageurs National Park Archives.

30. Chief of the Division of National Park System Studies Chester C. Brown to NPS Director George Hartzog, 24 September 1965, Legislative and Congressional Affairs Office files, Department of the Interior, Washington, D.C., memorandum regarding a Blatnik telephone call to Brown.

31. Ibid.

32. John Blatnik, interview by author, Washington, D.C., March 1985. Blatnik was living in retirement in Arlington, Virginia, at the time of this interview.

33. NPS Midwest Region Planner Harold R. Jones to NPS Assistant Director for Cooperative Activities, 1 December 1965, Legislative and Congressional Affairs Office files, Department of the Interior, Washington, D.C. Jones met with Oberstar in Blatnik's Washington office on 30 November 1965.

34. "Lumber Executive Hits Kabetogama Park Supporters," *Duluth News-Tribune*, 23 December 1966. The article was a response by George Amidon of Boise Cascade to Edwin Chapman's criticism of Boise's position on the Voyageurs National Park proposal. Chapman was president of the Voyageurs National Park Association.

35. House Committee on Interior and Insular Affairs, *Field Hearings on H.R. 10482 before the Subcommittee on Parks and Recreation, 91st Cong., 1st sess., International Falls, Minn., 21 August 1969, 78.*

36. NPS Assistant Director Theodore Swem to Congressman Joe Karth, 1 March 1966, Voyageurs National Park Archives.

37. Malcolm O. Watson to Congressman John Blatnik, 17 January 1966, Minnesota Department of Conservation file #45124, Minnesota Historical Society Archives. Shortly after the ads appeared, Congressman Blatnik received a letter from Watson stating the advertisements were misleading because they did not accurately state the source of funds used to pay for them. He noted that the money actually came from the Border Lakes Association, an organization of lakeshore property owners who had received a cash settlement from the M&O Paper Company for flood damages in 1950. (Flooding occurred due to faulty operation of the M&O dam at the west end of Rainy Lake.) M&O preferred a lump sum payment to an organization of claimants rather than settling a host of individual suits. Watson, who represented his father's interest on the board of directors of the Border Lakes Association, stated that the lump sum payment had grown to $40,000 by 1965. According to Watson, late that year some anti-park board members were successful in voting a $10,000 donation to the newly organized Northland Multiple Use Association, which then used the funds to support the full-page advertisements and other activities of the association.

38. Assistant Secretary of the Interior Stanley Cain to U. W. Hella, 8 August 1966, Minnesota Department of Conservation files, Minnesota Historical Society Archives.

5. State Administration Leads National Park Cause

1. Wayne Olson to Walter Mondale, 13 July 1965, Minnesota Department of Conservation file 45B17B, Minnesota Historical Society Archives, St. Paul.

2. Archie D. Chelseth, interview by author, Cloquet, Minn., 19 January 1990. Chelseth was a staff assistant to Governor LeVander from 1965 to 1969 with special

responsibilities for the Voyageurs National Park project. At the time of the interview, Chelseth was an officer in the Potlatch Corporation in Cloquet.

3. Roger Williams, conversations with author between 1989 and 1992, primarily in St. Paul, Minn. Williams was Governor LeVander's special staff coordinator for the Voyageurs National Park project.

4. Aguar, Jyring, and Whiteman, Planning Associates, *Report of Preliminary Multiple-Use Plan for Kabetogama-Rainy Lake Area,* February 1965, rev. December 1966, Voyageurs National Park Archives, International Falls, Minn. Aguar chose to use the term *natural area* instead of *national park* in his report to the county boards in January 1967. Natural areas, in the system nomenclature of the NPS, are those that possess outstanding natural, scenic, scientific, and cultural resources of national significance. In the classification hierarchy of the NPS, national parks must meet these criteria. The NPS determined that the Kabetogama Peninsula lands and adjacent waters met these conditions and if established as a national park, would be managed in a more restrictive manner than other units in the system such as national monuments, historic sites, or national recreation areas. Aguar believed that his county board clients and the residents on the periphery of the proposed park preferred a management plan that was *less* restrictive, thereby permitting a use pattern similar to the one in existence. His plan, therefore, recommended a national recreation area rather than a national park. Aguar based his plan on analysis of aerial photographs and maps and a boat and aerial reconnaissance of the Kabetogama area. His classification consisted of four categories: General Outdoor Recreation, Natural Environment Areas, Outstanding Natural Areas, and Historic and Cultural Sites. The report noted that recommendations for a management plan centered on the multiple-use concept would require more detailed study including the work of federal and state agencies active in the border lakes region.

5. Charles Aguar to NPS Midwest Regional Director Frederick Fagergren, 27 January 1967, Voyageurs National Park Archives.

6. Courtland Reid, memorandum to Theodor Swem, 24 January 1967, Voyageurs National Park Archives.

7. "Park Service Proposal for Kabetogama Unchanged," *Mesabi Daily News,* 23 March 1967.

8. Raymond Naddy, "Park Group Acts to Halt Land Sale," *Duluth News-Tribune,* 7 March 1967.

9. "Board Eyes Decision on Land Sale," *Duluth News-Tribune,* 11 March 1967.

10. "County Contends Land Sale Legal," *Duluth News-Tribune,* 16 March 1967.

11. Ibid.

12. Einar Karlstrand and Richard Skophammer, "Board to Refund Purchase Money," *Duluth News-Tribune,* 28 March 1967.

13. "Park Backers Buy 113 Acres for Voyageurs," *Minneapolis Tribune,* 13 September 1967.

14. NPS Northeast Regional Director Lemuel A. Garrison to Midwest Regional Director Fagergren, 9 February 1967, Voyageurs National Park Archives. This memorandum was written following a visit in Minneapolis in early February 1967 with park supporters and other close to the park issue.

15. "A Profit Lovely as a Tree," *Time,* 21 July 1967, 69.

16. "Resort Plans May Block Voyageurs Park," *Minneapolis Tribune,* 26 July 1967.

17. Ibid.

18. "Senator Mondale Calls for Establishment of the Voyageurs National Park," *Congressional Record*, 20 September 1967, 90th Cong. 1st sess. 113: 26214–15. This was the text for Mondale's address to the Minnesota Conservation Federation, Duluth, Minn., on 16 September 1967.

19. Ibid.

20. John Heritage, "Blatnik Pressed to Submit Bill for Voyageurs Park," *Minneapolis Tribune*, 18 September 1967.

21. Minnesota Poll, "Most State Residents Want National Park," *Minneapolis Tribune*, 16 July 1967.

22. Editorial, "It's Time to Decide on Voyageurs Park," *Minneapolis Tribune*, 16 July 1967.

23. Richard Kleeman, "Frazer to Offer Voyageurs Park Bill," *Minneapolis Tribune*, 12 July 1967.

24. Albert Quie to Hartzog, 14 July 1967, Voyageurs National Park Archives.

25. "Udall Hopes Minnesota Will Have a National Park," *Minneapolis Tribune*, 12 August 1967.

26. John Kawamoto to Theodor Swem, Assistant Director of Cooperative Activities, 7 August 1967, Legislative and Congressional Affairs Office files, Department of the Interior, Washington, D.C.

27. Russell E. Dickenson, Chief, Division of New Area Studies and Master Planning, memorandum to Chief, Office of Resource Planning, WSC, 21 September 1967, Legislative and Congressional Affairs Office files, Department of the Interior, Washington, D.C.

28. Kawamoto to Swem, 7 August 1967.

29. Chelseth, interview.

30. Joseph L. Donovan, Secretary of State, *Minnesota Legislative Manual 1967–1968* (St. Paul: State of Minnesota), 154; "LeVander Makes 5 Top Appointments," *Duluth News Tribune*, 17 January 1967.

31. Leirfallom to Chapman, 1 September 1967, Minnesota Department of Conservation files, Minnesota Historical Society Archives.

32. John Kawamoto, memorandum to NPS Midwest Regional Director Fred Fagergren, 18 August 1987, Voyageurs National Park Archives. This memorandum regarded his field trip to meet with personnel from the Minnesota Department of Conservation.

33. Kawamoto to NPS Cooperative Activities Assistant Chief, 21 September 1967, Voyageurs National Park Archives.

34. Minnesota Department of Conservation, *A Summary Report: Voyageurs National Park Proposal*, prepared by Willard E. West and Roger S. Williams (St. Paul: Minnesota Department of Conservation, 1967).

35. Ibid., 69–76.

36. Ibid., 88.

37. NPS Planner Courtland Reid memorandum to Theodor Swem, Assistant Director, Cooperative Activities, 13 October 1967, Legislative and Congressional Affairs files, Department of the Interior, Washington, D.C.

38. "A Statement of Editorial Opinion." KDAL, Inc., 1 November 1967.

39. John Heritage, "Dayton Gives Timber Stock to Park Group," *Minneapolis Tribune*, 22 October 1967.

40. Letter to the editor, "Arrowhead Association Reiterates Park Stand," *International Falls Daily Journal,* 27 October 1967.

41. Leirfallom to LeVander, 27 September 1967, Minnesota Department of Conservation files, Minnesota Historical Society Archives.

42. State Senator Raymond Higgins at the Virginia conference on the Voyageurs National Park proposal, 28 November 1967, Governor Harold LeVander files, Minnesota Historical Society.

43. John Kawamoto, oral history interview by Voyageurs National Park Historian Mary Lou Pearson, 12 June 1979, Voyageurs National Park Archives.

44. Ronald A. Forestra, *America's National Parks and Their Keepers* (Washington, D.C.: Resources for the Future, 1984), 85. In 1964 Interior Secretary Udall appointed Hartzog to replace Conrad Wirth. With this appointment, Udall sought to bring the NPS under closer scrutiny of departmental leadership (meaning Udall and the assistant secretaries) where he felt the interests of a wider segment of the public could be considered in making policy choices. Udall felt that Hartzog understood this philosophy better than Wirth, who represented the earlier traditions of NPS administration.

45. "U.S. Official Predicts Park Soon," *Duluth News-Tribune,* 28 November 1967.

46. Senator Walter Mondale, telegram to Edwin Chapman, 28 November 1967, LeVander files, Minnesota Department of Conservation, Minnesota Historical Society Archives.

47. Voyagers National Park workshop transcript, 28 November 1967, Virginia, Minn., in the possession of Roger Williams, New Brighton, Minnesota, who was Governor LeVander's coordinator for the governor's interdepartmental committee on Voyageurs National Park.

48. Ibid.

49. Hartzog, memorandum to Theodor Swem, 30 November 1967, Voyageurs National Park Archives.

50. "LeVander Decides to Back National Park at Kabetogama," *Minneapolis Tribune,* 1 December 1967; Ted Smebakken, "Voyageurs Park Endorsement Marks Victory for Andersen," *Minneapolis Star,* 1 December 1967.

51. Smebakken, "Voyageurs Park Endorsement Marks Victory for Andersen."

52. "LeVander Praised on Park Site Action," *Minneapolis Tribune,* 2 December 1967.

53. Chelseth, letter to LeVander, 7 December 1967, LeVander files, Minnesota Historical Society Archives. The letter commends LeVander for endorsing Voyageurs.

54. Ibid. This memorandum encouraged the governor to seek the support of the Upper Great Lakes Regional Commission for the Voyageurs proposal. During the last half of the 1950s, the NPS, with the financial support of the Mellon Foundation, carried out sea and lakeshore studies for the purpose of making recommendations for protection and preservation of some of America's outstanding shore zones. One report, *Our Fourth Shore: Great Lakes Shoreline Recreation Area Survey* (1959), resulted in the establishment of three national lakeshore recreation areas along the shores of Lake Michigan and Lake Superior between 1966 and 1970: Pictured Rocks (1966) and Apostle Islands (1970) along Lake Superior's shore in Michigan and Wisconsin, and Indiana Dunes (1966) and Sleeping Bear Dunes (1970) along the Lake

Michigan shore in Indiana and the lower peninsula of Michigan. Barry Mackintosh, *The National Parks: Shaping the System* (Washington, D.C.: Division of Publications, National Park Service, U.S. Dept. of Interior, 1985).

55. Chelseth, memorandum to LeVander, 6 December 1967, LeVander file, Minnesota Historical Society Archives. The subject of this memorandum is the contents of a Blatnik bill authorizing Voyageurs National Park.

56. Chelseth, memorandum to LeVander, 6 December 1967, LeVander file, Minnesota Historical Society Archives. The memo recommends that the governor appoint an interdepartmental committee to coordinate efforts supporting Voyageurs.

57. Interdepartmental memorandum from J. Kimball Whitney, Minnesota Department of Conservation files, Minnesota Historical Society Archives. This memorandum is a report on a meeting held on December 26, 1967, with Durenberger, Herbst, Leirfallom, and others.

58. This group is not to be confused with the Citizens Council on Voyageurs National Park created by the state legislature in 1975 after Voyageurs National Park was established.

59. Voyageurs National Park Association, newsletter, February 1968, Minneapolis, Minn.

60. Voyageurs National Park Association, meeting minutes, 4 June 1970, author's files.

61. Editorial, "Forests and Parks," *Duluth News-Tribune*, 13 October 1967.

62. "Scored by Area GOP, LeVander Defends Park Stand," *International Falls Daily Journal*, 5 December 1967; E. J. Chilgren, letter to the editor, *St. Paul Dispatch*, 6 December 1967; editorial, "Big City Selfishness Basic to Demand for Kabetogama Peninsula," *Mesabi Daily News*, published in the *International Falls Daily Journal*, 27 November 1967.

63. Resolution by the International Falls, Minn., City Council opposing the establishment of Voyageurs National Park on the Kabetogama Peninsula, approved 11 December 1967. Northeast Minnesota Historical Center Archives, University of Minnesota-Duluth.

64. Editorial, "Is Boise Cascade Holding a Club?" *Minneapolis Tribune*, 13 December 1967.

65. *News Bulletin*, Superior National Forest, 28 December 1967, Duluth, Minn.; Samuel P. Hays, *Beauty, Health, and Permanence* (New York: Cambridge University Press, 1987), 124–25.

66. *News Bulletin*, 5.

6. The Introduction of Voyageurs National Park Legislation

1. LeVander to Blatnik, 8 January 1968, Voyageurs National Park Archives, International Falls, Minn.

2. "Park Responsibility Handed to Blatnik," *International Falls Daily Journal*, 12 January 1968.

3. "U.S. Rejects Two Park Pleas by LeVander," *Minneapolis Tribune*, 24 February 1968.

4. Ibid.

5. Wheelock Whitney and Wallace Dayton to business and civic leaders in the

Twin Cities area, 3 June 1968, Voyageurs National Park Association files, Minnesota Historical Society Archives, St. Paul.

6. Voyageurs National Park Association file #1374, Minnesota Historical Society Archives; Lloyd Brandt, conversations with author, 1980s and 1990s. The Minneapolis Chamber of Commerce helped launch the move for Voyageurs in April 1965 when it provided funds and leadership to help establish the VNPA. Lloyd Brandt, then the chamber's director of legislative affairs, assisted in the organizing of the VNPA and was a member of its first board of directors. He served for a time as its secretary and as president. Brandt said later that the Voyageurs project was one of several promoted by business interests in the Twin Cities area to help boost the lagging economy of the northeastern part of the state. Declines in the iron mining industry had contributed to a major loss of jobs across the entire region, and the taconite industry had only just begun to show promise.

7. The Duluth chapter of the Citizens Committee was organized and led by Jack Everett during the first two years of its existence. Everett was a tireless campaigner, calling on many resorts in the Rainy and Kabetogama Lakes area as well as on leaders of civic groups in Duluth and on the Iron Range. Other members of the Duluth committee were Bill Fayling, Glenn Maxham, Fran Skinner, Helen Seymore, "Joe" Goodsell, Dale Olsen, Henry Roberts, David Zentner, and Fred Witzig. Witzig and Zentner served as cochairs of the Duluth committee, 1969–70.

8. "Attitudes toward the Proposed Voyageurs National Park," survey conducted in the Eighth Congressional District of Minnesota by Mid-Continent Surveys, Minneapolis, Minn., 29 May 1968.

9. Bill Krueger, "A Statement of Editorial Opinion," KDAL-TV, Duluth, Minn., 3 April 1968 and 14 May 1968.

10. E. C. Pearson, ed., "Position Paper on the Proposed Voyageurs National Park" (Duluth: United Northern Sportsmen, 13 February 1968), author's files.

11. Ibid., 15; Kay Franklin and Norma Schaeffer, *Duel for the Dunes* (Urbana: University of Illinois Press, 1983), 189. The idea for a Land and Water Conservation Fund to help finance acquisition of park and recreation land was advanced by Secretary of the Interior Udall during the Kennedy administration. Funded largely by royalties from federal offshore oil-drilling leases, the LWCF provided Udall with a major source of revenue to carry out his goal of creating a "dynamic Park System," which would not only recognize the needs of the large western parks but also provide for establishment of parks closer to population concentrations. Voyageurs National Park and national lakeshores on Lake Superior and Lake Michigan—all authorized in the 1960s—benefited significantly from the LWCF.

12. Elmer L. Andersen, interview by author, Arden Hills, Minn., 23 October 1990.

13. "Management Plan: Crane Lake Recreation Area" (Duluth, Minn.: Superior National Forest, 1966), Superior National Forest files. Through approval of the Crane Lake Recreation Area Management Plan, Regional Forester George James officially established the Crane Lake Recreation Area on March 24, 1966.

14. John Wernham, speech before the Rotary and Kiwanis Clubs of Ely, Minn., 12 September 1968, Voyageurs National Park Association files, Minnesota Historical Society Archives.

15. Harold K. Steen, *The U.S. Forest Service: A History* (Seattle: University of Washington Press, 1976), 209.

16. House Committee on Interior and Insular Affairs, *Hearings on H.R. 10482*, 91st Cong., 1st sess., 16 and 17 July 1970, 265.

17. Roger Williams, memorandum summarizing his meeting observations at Crane Lake, 13 March 1968, Voyageurs National Park Archives.

18. Williams, memorandum, 13 March 1968; House Committee on Interior and Insular Affairs, *Hearings on H.R. 10482*, 16 and 17 July 1970.

19. "Blatnik May Offer Park Bill in April," *Minneapolis Tribune*, 15 February 1968.

20. Ibid.

21. Secretary of Agriculture Orville Freeman, statement before the House Sub-committee on National Parks and Recreation on H.R. 10951, S2515, to establish Redwood National Park, 21 May 1968, Governor Harold LeVander files, file 5566, Minnesota Historical Society Archives.

22. Roger Williams, memorandum to the Governor's Interdepartmental Com-mittee on Voyageurs National Park, 31 May 1968, LeVander files, Minnesota Histor-ical Society Archives.

23. Leirfallom, memorandum, 6 June 1968, LeVander files, Minnesota Historical Society Archives. The memorandum summarizes a meeting he held with George Amidon, Woodlands Manager for Boise Cascade Corporation, on June 4, 1968. The memorandum is marked "confidential."

24. Roger Williams and Archie Chelseth, interviews and conversations with author.

25. Andersen to Hartzog, 15 April 1968, Voyageurs National Park Association file P1374, Minnesota Historical Society Archives.

26. John Kawamoto, memorandum to NPS Regional Director Fred Fagergren recounting a telephone conversation with Elmer Andersen on 9 April 1968, undated, Voyageurs National Park Archives.

27. John Kawamoto, oral history interview by Voyageurs National Park Historian Mary Lou Pearson, 12 June 1979, 69–73, Voyageurs National Park Archives.

28. Kawamoto, interview, 69.

29. *A Master Plan for the Proposed Voyageurs National Park, Minnesota* (Wash-ington, D.C.: National Park Service, 1968), 13.

30. Kawamoto, interview, 73

31. "Blatnik Caught in Simmering Controversy over Voyageurs," *Duluth News-Tribune*, 14 July 1968. The Duluth newspaper carried a special report on Congress-man Blatnik's scheduling problem in its Sunday edition on July 14. The account was written by Robert Eisele of the newspaper's Washington bureau.

32. "Blatnik to Delay Offering Bill for Voyageurs Park," *Minneapolis Tribune*, 7 July 1968.

33. Williams to Oberstar, 11 July 1968, LeVander files, Minnesota Historical Soci-ety Archives.

34. "Crane Lake Club Opposes Area in Voyageurs Park," *Duluth News-Tribune*, 16 July 1968.

35. Ibid.

36. Editorial, *International Falls Daily Journal*, 16 July 1968.

37. "Voyageurs Park Proposal Ends Turbulent Ride to the Potomac," *Minneapo-lis Tribune*, 21 July 1968.

38. *Congressional Record*, 19 July 1968, A Bill to Establish a Voyageurs National Park, H.R. 18761, 90th Cong., 2nd sess., 114: 22279–82. Summary of a bill introduced

by Representative John Blatnik authorizing the establishment of Voyageurs National Park.

39. Larry and Joan Olson, Crane Lake, and Tim Watson, Kabetogama, resort owners, interviews by author, 21 and 22 August 2001.

40. Editorial, *Minneapolis Star,* 20 July 1968.

7. The Reintroduction of Park Legislation

1. Voyageurs National Park Association, *Voyageurs News,* December 1968, author's files.

2. Andersen to Lloyd Brandt, 17 December 1968, Voyageurs National Park Association files, Minnesota Historical Society Archives, St. Paul.

3. Chelseth to Governor LeVander's coordinating committee on Voyageurs National Park, 25 November 1968, Minnesota Department of Conservation files, Minnesota Historical Society Archives.

4. Andersen to Shemesh, 4 March 1969, Voyageurs National Park Association file P134, Box 1, Minnesota Historical Society Archives.

5. Higgins to LeVander, 2 May 1969, Voyageurs National Park Association file P134, Box 1, Minnesota Historical Society Archives.

6. Voyageurs National Park Association, executive committee meeting minutes, 2 May 1969, author's files.

7. House, Congressman Blatnik summarizing the provisions of HR 10482, a bill to authorize the establishment of Voyageurs National Park on the occasion of its reintroduction, 91st Cong., 1st sess., *Congressional Record* (23 April 1969), 3014.

8. Ibid.

9. Chelseth to LeVander, 2 May 1969, LeVander files, Minnesota Historical Society Archives. Chelseth wrote to LeVander as a member of the VNPA Board of Directors. In his letter he calls attention to sections of S.F. 2530 that if adopted, would be the death of the Voyageurs proposal. Chelseth left state government in early winter 1969 to be the administrative assistant to the publisher of the *Minneapolis Tribune.*

10. Chelseth to Andersen, 7 May 1969, LeVander files, Minnesota Historical Society Archives. Chelseth described the contents of implications of the proposed interim commission on the fate of the proposal for Voyageurs.

11. Luther J. Carter, "Walter J. Hickel Advocate of Economic Growth as Alaska's Governor Faces Tougher Job at Interior," *Science* 162 (December 1968): 1372.

12. "The Education of Wally Hickel," *Time* 94, 1 (1 August 1969): 42–44.

13. Luther J. Carter, "Hickel Controversy Points Up Environmental Quality Issue," *Science* 163 (11 January 1969): 455.

14. With any new administration comes pressure for changes in personnel at key positions in the several departments and bureaus. George Hartzog discloses in a book he wrote after he left office that when Hickel took over as secretary of the interior, he received requests to fire him. Chief among his "enemies" were Senators Clifford Hansen of Wyoming and Gordon Allott of Colorado. Both were influential and senior members of the Senate Interior and Insular Affairs Committee, which deals with parks and recreation matters. Hartzog learned early that a movement to

fire him was under way, and so he sought help from two individuals outside the department: William Penn Mott, who later became NPS director under Reagan, and Nathaniel Reed. Hickel had offered the job to each of them when he took over at Interior, but they turned him down. However, both endorsed Hartzog's retention as did several other influential "outsiders," and Hartzog was reappointed by President Nixon. George B. Hartzog Jr., *Battling for the National Parks* (Mt. Kisco, N.Y.: Moyer Bell, 1988), 183–90.

15. Voyageurs National Park Association, press release on the occasion of its annual meeting, 19 February 1969, author's files.

16. Albert Eisele, "Andersen, Blatnik Butt Heads over Voyageurs Park," *Duluth News-Tribune*, 9 March 1969.

17. Voyageurs National Park Association, executive committee meeting minutes, 14 March 1969, author's files.

18. Ibid.

19. LeVander to Blatnik, 25 March 1969, LeVander files, Minnesota Historical Society Archives.

20. Andersen to Blatnik, 8 April 1969, Voyageurs National Park Association files, Minnesota Historical Society Archives.

21. Richard Broderick, "Minnesotan of the Year—A Generous Spirit," *Minnesota Monthly*, December 1989, 53.

22. Voyageurs National Park Association, press release, 25 April 1969, author's files.

23. Shemesh to Voyageurs National Park Association executive committee members and local VNPA directors, 25 April 1969.

24. "Voyageurs Park Bill Chances Are Dim," *Minneapolis Tribune*, 31 May 1969.

25. Albert Eisele, "Blatnik Reintroduces Voyageurs Park Bill," *Duluth News-Tribune*, 24 April 1969.

26. Allan R. Sommarston in his doctoral dissertation commented on the hearings on April 19 and 20, 1968, by the House Subcommittee on Parks and Recreation on the proposal for North Cascades National Park in Washington: "The subcommittee was overwhelmed by the number of people [approximately 800] requesting to testify, which moved Representative Aspinal [*sic*], Chairman of the House Committee and Interior and Insular Affairs, to remark that 'he had never seen anything like it.'" Allan R. Sommarston, "Wild Land Preservation Crisis: The North Cascades Controversy" (Ph.D. diss., University of Washington, 1970), 135.

27. Snowmobiling, which was to become a major controversial issue after the park was established, was not even mentioned at the International Falls hearing.

28. House Subcommittee on Parks and Recreation of the Committee on Interior and Insular Affairs, *Hearings on H.R. 10482*, 91st Cong., 1st sess., 29 August 1969, 131–32.

29. Ibid., 37.

30. Richard O. Sielaff, Cecil H. Meyers, and Philip L. Friest, *The Economics of the Proposed Voyageurs National Park* (Duluth: published for the U.S. Department of the Interior, National Park Service by the University of Minnesota, Duluth, Division of Social Sciences, 1964).

31. House Subcommittee on Parks and Recreation, *Hearings on H.R. 10482*.

32. Statement by Hennepin County Municipal Court Judge Edwin P. Chapman, House Subcommittee on Parks and Recreation, *Hearings on H.R. 10482*, 162.

33. The reality twenty-five years later does not match the expectations of the 1960s. The spring 1995 edition of the AAA travel magazine featured ten national

parks as "relatively undiscovered parks" that offered "solitude along with the scenery." Yvette LaPierre, "A Place to Park," *Home and Away,* 16, 2 (March/April 1995): 14–19. Voyageurs was included in that group along with Apostle Islands National Lakeshore in northern Wisconsin. Significantly, both are situated in the more remote sections of the upper Great Lakes states. Since the early 1980s the NPS has been working to encourage visitation to lesser-known parks in order to spread park visitation more evenly among the parks and among the seasons. Its most aggressive attempt in this effort has been at Voyageurs, where a Tourism Development Task Force was organized with the participation of local residents to work on ways to stimulate visitation. "National Parks for a New Generation," report from the Conservation Foundation, Washington, D.C., 1985, 213.

34. Statement by Dr. Arnold Bolz, House Subcommittee on Parks and Recreation, *Hearings on H.R. 10482,* 68.

35. Sigurd Olson's statement prepared for the hearing did not reach the printing office in time to be included in the official record of the proceedings. Olson gave me a copy of the statement, and the sentiments expressed therein are similar to those presented by Olson at subsequent hearings and in public speeches on the subject.

36. Individuals representing the following organizations testified in favor of the park: VNPA and its Rainy Lake and Duluth Citizens Committee chapters, Minnesota Division of the Izaak Walton League, Democratic-Farmer-Labor Party, North Star Chapter of the Sierra Club, Midland Cooperatives, Inc., and the Greater Minneapolis Chamber of Commerce. The following organizations were represented by individuals opposing the park: Boise Cascade Corporation, Minnesota Forest Industries Association, Koochiching County Republican Committee, Minnesota Arrowhead Association, Minnesota Timber Producers Association, Crane Lake Commercial Club, and the Northland Multiple Use Association.

37. House Subcommittee on Parks and Recreation, *Hearings on H.R. 10482,* 10. Official position statement of Governor Harold LeVander on the proposed Voyageurs National Park in Minnesota, submitted to the House Subcommittee on Parks and Recreation for inclusion in the official record of the field hearings held in International Falls, Minn., on August 21, 1969; copy in author's files.

38. Statement by Representative Roy Taylor, House Subcommittee on Parks and Recreation, *Hearings on H.R. 10482,* 81.

39. Statement by NPS Director George Hartzog, Subcommittee on Parks and Recreation, *Hearings on North Cascades National Park,* 90th Cong., 2d sess., Washington, D.C., 1968, 248.

40. Statement by National Audubon Society, House Subcommittee on Parks and Recreation, *Hearings on H.R. 10482,* 81.

41. LeVander to Blatnik, 8 January 1968, Voyageurs National Park Archives; Hartzog to Blatnik, 19 February 1968, Voyageurs National Park Archives; LeVander to Blatnik, 9 March 1968, Voyageurs National Park Archives,.

42. Official position statement of Governor Harold LeVander on the proposed Voyageurs National Park, House Subcommittee on Parks and Recreation, *Hearings on H.R. 10482,* 10.

43. "Hunting Provision May Block Action on Voyageurs Park," *Minneapolis Tribune,* 22 August 1969.

44. "Hickel Suggests Recreation Area for Voyageurs," *Minneapolis Tribune,* 19 September 1969.

45. Ibid.

46. Mrs. Palmer K. Peterson to LeVander, 19 September 1969, Minnesota Department of Conservation files, Minnesota Historical Society Archives.

47. "Hickel Suggests New Idea for Kabetogama," *Duluth News-Tribune*, 19 September 1969.

48. Congress created the Bureau of the Budget in 1921 to assist the president in preparing an executive budget. When Nixon became president, he revamped the bureau and changed its name to Office of Management and Budget to reflect its expanded budget-managing role. The OMB's new director, Robert Mayo, was an experienced and competent bureaucrat who had worked in the Treasury Department for almost twenty years before coming to the Bureau of the Budget. Robert L. Limebury. *Government in America*, 3d ed. (New York: Little Brown and Co., 1986), 423, 518–19.

49. "Robert Mayo: Calling Signals on History's Biggest Budget," *U.S. News and World Report*, 19 January 1970.

50. Mayo to Aspinall, 19 September 1969, Minnesota Department of Conservation files, Minnesota Historical Society Archives.

51. "Voyageurs Park Called 'Dead'—Budget Cut Cited," *Minneapolis Tribune*, 20 September 1969.

52. Duane Hampton, "Opposition to National Parks," *Journal of Forest History* 21 (January 1981): 41.

53. LeVander files, Minnesota Department of Conservation files, Minnesota Historical Society Archives.

54. "Blatnik Reports Park Bill Dead for this Year," *Duluth News-Tribune*, 7 November 1969.

55. R. W. Hansberger to Nixon, 23 December 1969, Voyageurs National Park Archives.

56. William MacConnachie Jr. to LeVander, 31 October 1969, LeVander files, Minnesota Department of Conservation files, Minnesota Historical Society Archives.

57. Ibid.

58. F. A. Hjort, "Summary of the Senate Public Domain Committee Hearing on December 4, 1969" (National Park Service, 30 January 1970), Voyageurs National Park Archives.

59. "Interior Department Still Undecided on Voyageurs Park," *Duluth News-Tribune*, 26 November 1969.

60. Andersen to LeVander, 15 December 1969, LeVander files, Minnesota Department of Conservation files, Minnesota Historical Society Archives.

61. Andersen to Roger B. Morton, 30 December 1969, Voyageurs National Park Archives.

8. Deadlocks and Bottlenecks

1. Samuel P. Hays, "The Environmental Movement," *Journal of Forest History* 25 (1981): 1.

2. LeVander to Andersen, 6 January 1970, LeVander files, Minnesota Department of Conservation files, Minnesota Historical Society Archives, St. Paul.

3. Voyageurs National Park Association, executive committee meeting minutes, 22 January 1970.

4. Charles Stoddard to Rita Shemesh, 2 February 1970, LeVander files, Minnesota Department of Conservation files, Minnesota Historical Society Archives.

5. Shemesh to Charles Colson, 3 February 1970, author's files.

6. Shemesh to Clark MacGregor, 24 February 1970, author's files.

7. Shemesh to MacGregor, 23 April 1970, author's files.

8. George Rice, editorial, WCCO-TV, 24 April 1970.

9. Voyageurs National Park Association, press release on Elmer Andersen's speech to University of Minnesota students during Earth Day activities, 23 April 1970.

10. Boise Cascade's General Manager of Midwestern and Canadian Woodlands Division George Amidon to National Park Service Director Hartzog, 28 January 1970, Voyageurs National Park Archives, International Falls, Minn.

11. Andersen to W. S. Shaft, 13 January 1970, Voyageurs National Park Archives.

12. Voyageurs National Park Association, committee meeting minutes, 9 March 1970.

13. Ibid., 8 April 1970.

14. Ibid., 7 May 1970.

15. MacGregor to Shemesh, 4 May 1970, author's files. MacGregor's reference to poison was defined in a handwritten footnote at the bottom of his letter as "the poison of false information regarding my position and activities." The congressman had just begun a campaign for the Senate. His opponent was former Vice President Hubert Humphrey, and MacGregor was concerned that his activity on Voyageurs be characterized in a positive light.

16. Albert Quie to Shemesh, 11 May 1970, author's files.

17. Quie to Shemesh, 11 May 1970; Albert Eisele, "Lost: National Park Named Voyageurs," *Duluth News-Tribune*, 3 May 1970.

18. Blatnik to Shemesh, 27 May 1970, author's files.

19. Voyageurs National Park Association, meeting minutes, 4 June 1970.

20. LeVander to Douglas Nethercut of St. Paul, 15 June 1970, LeVander files, Minnesota Department of Conservation files, Minnesota Historical Society Archives.

21. Voyageurs National Park Association, committee meeting minutes, 4 June 1970.

22. Ibid.

23. *Summary Position Paper on H.R. 10482, A Bill to Authorize Establishment of Voyageurs National Park,* Minnesota Senate Public Domain Committee, O. A. Sundet, Chairman, 17 June 1970, Minnesota Department of Conservation files, Minnesota Historical Society Archives.

24. Leirfallom to Koll, 18 June 1970, Minnesota Department of Conservation files, Minnesota Historical Society Archives.

25. Leirfallom's real commitment to the Voyageurs project was always in question with some of LeVander's closest advisors. This was particularly true of those who helped LeVander shape his position on Voyageurs in the period from 1967 to 1969. Some thought Leirfallom originally supported the Crane Lake addition because it might serve to "kill the park." They were opposed to him testifying at major congressional hearings because they felt he might compromise the state's position on the park. They believed it was one thing for Leirfallom to cast doubt on

the wisdom of establishing a park on the Kabetogama Peninsula before a state senate committee hearing, but it was another to express such opinions at a congressional hearing.

26. This reticence to speak out on the park issue vanished in the winter and spring of 1971 when the state legislature took up the issue of donating school trust fund land to the NPS to fulfill a requirement in the authorizing legislation for Voyageurs. The park issue was clearly drawn in this debate.

9. Congressional Hearings

1. Trust fund lands were those received by grant from the federal government with a condition that receipts from the lands be used for certain specified purposes. In Minnesota, such funds were dedicated to education. Most "school" lands are located in the northeastern part of the state, with 51 percent in St. Louis and Koochiching Counties. Samuel T. Dana, *Minnesota Lands* (Washington, D.C.: American Forestry Association, 1960), 190.

2. House Subcommittee on National Parks and Recreation, *Hearings on a Proposal for Voyageurs National Park,* 91st Cong., 2d sess., 16 and 17 July 1970.

3. Ibid., 199.

4. Ibid., 210.

5. Ibid., 211.

6. John Kawamoto, oral history interview by Voyageurs National Park Historian Mary Lou Pearson, 12 June 1979, Voyageurs National Park Archives, 42, 43, 62.

7. This concern was no doubt heightened by Interior Secretary Udall's reorganization of the agency into three coequal branches—natural, historic, and recreational. Under this plan a number of new units representing diverse and varied habitats were coming into the system. Udall was also successful in persuading Congress to pass the Land and Water Conservation Fund Act, which provided funds for expansion of the system. Udall knew that many NPS veterans feared that the more deliberate and selective system of the past was being compromised and thus opposed the rapid expansion of the system. Nevertheless, Udall and others in the Kennedy and Johnson administrations opted for a more ambitious course for the National Park System. Kay Franklin and Norma Schaeffer, *Duel for the Dunes* (Urbana: University of Illinois Press, 1983), 189.

8. Kawamoto, interview, 42, 43, 62.

9. House Subcommittee, *Voyageurs National Park,* 230.

10. Ibid., 231.

11. Ibid.

12. Ibid., 219.

13. Ibid., 271–72.

14. Ibid., 275.

15. Since the park was established, other issues have been taken up by those who opposed the park, and many of these have been more troublesome and divisive than the Crane Lake addition.

16. House Subcommittee, *Voyageurs National Park,* 275–76.

17. Ibid., 276.

18. Ibid., 261.

19. Ibid.

20. Shemesh to Sigurd Olson, 6 August 1970, Sigurd Olson files, Minnesota Historical Society Archives, St. Paul.

21. House Subcommittee, *Voyageurs National Park,* 351–53.

22. Ibid., 358.

23. Ibid., 359.

24. Ibid., 367.

25. Ibid., 348.

26. Ibid., 356.

27. Shemesh to Olson, 6 August 1970.

28. House Subcommittee, *Voyageurs National Park,* 370–71.

29. Ibid.

30. Ibid.

31. Ibid., 175.

32. Ibid., 391.

33. Shemesh to Andersen, 12 August 1970, Olson files, Minnesota Historical Society Archives.

34. Lloyd Brandt to Wayne Aspinall, 14 August 1970, Legislative and Congressional Affairs Office, Department of the Interior files, Washington, D.C.

35. Harold LeVander to Roy Taylor, 5 September 1970, reproduced in VNPA executive committee meeting minutes, 9 September 1970.

10. Final Passage

1. Voyageurs National Park Association, executive committee meeting minutes, 10 September 1970.

2. Rita Shemesh to Voyageurs National Park Association executive committee, 14 September 1970, author's files.

3. Shemesh to John Blatnik, 15 September 1970, Voyageurs National Park Association records.

4. Voyageurs National Park Association, executive committee meeting minutes, 29 September 1970.

5. Albert Eisele, "John Blatnik, Power Politics and That Park," *Duluth News-Tribune,* 11 October 1970.

6. John Blatnik, interview with author, Washington, D.C., 13 March 1985.

7. Albert Eisele, "John Blatnik, Power Politics and That Park," *Duluth News-Tribune,* 11 October 1970.

8. Ibid.

9. Blatnik, interview.

10. Voyageurs National Park Association executive committee meeting minutes, 29 September 1970.

11. Several sources were used to compile the Interior Committee's actions on the markup of the Voyageurs legislation: *Duluth News-Tribune* and *Duluth Herald* articles on September 23 and 24, 1970; a memorandum from the director of the NPS Legislative and Cooperative Programs Division to the director of the NPS, Septem-

ber 24, 1970; files of the Legislative and Congressional Affairs Office, Department of the Interior, Washington, D.C.; VNPA executive committee meeting minutes for September 29, 1970; and the author's interview with Blatnik, 13 March 1985.

12. "House Panel Approves Voyageurs Park Bill," *Minneapolis Tribune*, 25 September 1970.

13. Shemesh to Alan Bible, 6 October 1970, Sigurd Olson files, Minnesota Historical Society Archives, St. Paul.

14. State legislators ran as conservatives and liberals at the time the park legislation was being considered. This practice was changed in 1974 when party labels were adopted: Independent Republican for conservatives, and Democratic-Farmer-Labor (DFL) for liberals.

15. The Minnesota Resource Commission was set up by statute and was composed of seven members of the house and seven members of the senate. The MRC did not speak for the Minnesota Legislature but was primarily a research and advisory agency.

16. Editorial, *Duluth News-Tribune*, 5 November 1970.

17. Shemesh to Walter Mondale, 19 November 1970, copy in author's files.

18. Senators present during the hearing sessions included Chairman Alan Bible (Nevada), Clinton Anderson (New Mexico), Mark Hatfield (Oregon), Clifford Hansen (Wyoming), and Frank Moss (Utah).

19. Senate Committee on Interior and Insular Affairs, *Hearings before the Subcommittee on Parks and Recreation on S. 1962 and H.R. 10482*, 91st Cong., 2d sess., 4 and 7 December 1970.

20. John Kawamoto, oral history interview by Voyageurs National Park Historian Mary Lou Pearson, 12 June 1979, Voyageurs National Park Archives, International Falls, Minn., 43–44.

21. "Council and Mayor Hassle over National Park," *International Falls Daily Journal*, 1 December 1970.

22. Senate Committee, *Hearings on S1962 and H.R. 10482*, 95.

23. "Miffed Senator Seen Blocking Voyageur Bill," *Duluth News-Tribune*, 5 December 1970.

24. Sigurd Olson to Senator Henry Jackson, telegram, 11 December 1970, Olson files, Minnesota Historical Society Archives. The eight conservation organizations Olson referred to included National Audubon Society, Federation of Western Outdoor Clubs, Friends of the Wilderness, Izaak Walton League, Sierra Club, The Wilderness Society, Voyageurs National Park Association, North Star Chapter of the Sierra Club, and the National Environmental Council.

25. "Andersen Boosts Voyageurs Park," *Duluth News-Tribune*, 15 December 1970; "Park Approval Will End Long Blatnik Fight," *Duluth News-Tribune*, 27 December 1970.

26. Elmer Andersen, interview with author, Arden Hills, Minn., 23 October 1990. Andersen's assessment of Mondale's and McCarthy's contributions during the rush for approval of Voyageurs in the Senate in December 1970 was quite correct. I could find only limited public support from Senator McCarthy in all the years the park proposal was before the people.

27. Ibid.

28. Ibid.

29. "Scott Fighting SST Filibuster," *New York Times,* 18 December 1970.

30. Public Law 91–661, 91st Cong., 2d sess. (8 January 1971). This legislation authorized the establishment of Voyageurs National Park.

31. Consensus statement on Voyageurs National Park by Governor Elmer L. Andersen, 27 June 1962, author's files.

11. The Final Step to Establishment

1. "County Informs Nixon of Park Opposition," *Duluth News-Tribune,* 6 January 1971.

2. Public Law 91–661, 91st Cong., 2d sess. (8 January 1971).

3. After the Voyageurs National Park bill, H.R. 10482, came over from the House, the Senate Committee on Interior and Insular Affairs reviewed the legislation and added several amendments, including the additional provision prohibiting the secretary of interior from purchasing any private lands until the state formally donated its land. The reasons for this provision were explained in its report to the full Senate. Senate Report No. 91–1513, 91st Cong., 1st sess., Calendar No. 1524, 15 December 1970.

4. "Most Favor Giving Voyageurs Land," *Minneapolis Tribune,* 10 February 1971.

5. "Governor to Submit Voyageurs' Proposal," *Minneapolis Tribune,* 10 January 1971.

6. Trust fund lands are those lands that were granted by the federal government to the states via the state Enabling Act of 1857 to be held in trust for a specified purpose. In Minnesota, the purpose was education. The School Trust Fund carried the stipulation that receipts from land sales or economic activity on school lands be invested in a permanent fund. In 1960, 51 percent of these lands were located in Koochiching and St. Louis Counties. Samuel T. Dana, *Minnesota Lands* (Washington D.C.: American Forestry Association, 1969), 190–91.

7. These figures were obtained from an undated document in the archives at Voyageurs National Park under the heading "Transfer of Lands." The document, prepared after the park was established, also included the amounts paid by the state to acquire the trust fund lands and the tax-forfeited lands acquired by the state from the counties for the appraised value of the lands. Lands in the Kabetogama State Forest were simply conveyed to the federal government as part of the donation.

8. Finlay Lewis, "Legislature to Seek Voyageurs Agreement," *Minneapolis Tribune,* 14 February 1971.

9. Ibid. Robert Herbst was the first commissioner of the newly created Minnesota Department of Natural Resources. He served briefly as deputy commissioner of the former Conservation Department and left to become executive director of the Izaak Walton League. He left that position to accept the leadership position in the new Department of Natural Resources.

10. "Voyageurs Park Land Bill Reaches Legislature," *International Falls Daily Journal,* 9 March 1971.

11. "Necessary Legislation to Make Voyageurs National Park a Reality," announcement at a special news conference of a major conservation project by Robert Herbst, commissioner of the Department of Natural Resources, 9 March 1971, author's files.

12. Ibid.

13. Statement by Elmer L. Andersen, president of the Voyageurs National Park Association, 9 March 1971, author's files. Ironically the day after transfer bills were filed, an article appeared in the *Minneapolis Tribune* referring to a speech made by a leading figure in the national environmental movement questioning the wisdom of the NPS for supporting the act authorizing Voyageurs National Park. Speaking at a natural resources conference in Portland, Oregon, Daniel Poole, president of the Wildlife Management Institute, complained that the park act authorized public use activities previously unacceptable in any of the other natural areas in the National Park System. Poole cited snowmobiling, power boating, and the use of seaplanes as examples of such activities. He saw this as a departure from NPS policy. In an interview after his talk, Poole observed that some appeals for national parks "are being promoted by political and economic interests and preservationists but for conflicting purposes." He also observed that some park proposals are sold on the basis of the tourism they will generate. "Voyageurs Terms Called Detrimental," *Minneapolis Tribune*, 10 March 1971.

14. Undated circular appealing for support of S.F. 1026 and H.F. 1337, the land transfer bills for Voyageurs National Park, prepared by the Izaak Walton League of America (Minnesota Division) for distribution at an annual outdoor sports show in Minneapolis.

15. Minnesota Resources Commission, *Voyageurs National Park Fact Book* (St. Paul: March 1971). Years later, U. W. Hella, former director of Minnesota State Parks and Recreation, shared the *Fact Book* with me and said that it provided information in a format that made it easy for legislators and staff personnel to be accurately informed on a number of topics germane to the debate on the park. It was regarded by legislators as a trusted source of information that dispelled rumors and prevented needless bickering. U. W. Hella, interview by author, St. Paul, Minn., October 23, 1990.

16. Thomas Newcome, letter to members of the Minnesota Legislature, 17 March 1971, cover letter for Minnesota Resources Commission, *Voyageurs National Park Fact Book*.

17. "Voyageurs Park Land Bill Reaches Legislature," *Duluth News-Tribune*, 9 March 1971.

18. Ibid.

19. "Most Favor Giving Voyageurs Land," Minnesota Poll in early February 1971, published in *Minneapolis Tribune*, 10 February 1971.

20. Rita Shemesh, memorandum to VNPA board members, 10 March 1971, author's files.

21. "State Measure Proposes Park at Kabetogama," *Duluth News-Tribune*, 18 March 1971.

22. Some of the witnesses appearing or providing statements in support of the legislation included Senate Majority Leader and chief sponsor of the land donation bill, Senator Holmquist; Elmer L. Andersen, president of the VNPA; former Governor Harold LeVander; Jack Everett, consulting geologist and first chair of the Duluth Chapter of the Citizens Committee for Voyageurs National Park; David Zentner, president of the Minnesota Division of the Izaak Walton League; Earnest Reusseau, president of the International Falls Chamber of Commerce; DNR Commissioner

Robert Herbst; David Roe, president of the Minnesota AFL-CIO; Dean McNeal, president of the Minneapolis Chamber of Commerce; Richard Thorpe, president of the North Star Chapter of the Sierra Club; U. W. Hella, director of Minnesota State Parks; Anton Sterle, president of the United Northern Sportsmen; John Kawamoto, planner in the Midwest Regional Office of the NPS; Judge Mark Abbott, International Falls; Archie Chelseth, VNPA; Erick Kendall and Ed Sletton, Minnesota Association of Cooperatives; William Dean, assistant director for Cooperative Programs in the Midwest Regional Office of the NPS; George Esslinger, International Falls; and Sam Morgan, attorney for the VNPA.

23. "Witnesses Testify for Voyageurs Park," *Minneapolis Tribune*, 19 March 1971.

24. "Voyageurs Backers Finish Testimony," *Duluth News-Tribune*, 30 March 1971.

25. Minnesota Resources Commission, *Voyageurs National Park Fact Book* (St. Paul: March 1971), XIX 1, 3.

26. Shemesh to VNPA board members, 30 March 1971, author's files.

27. Ibid.

28. Ibid.

29. Individuals and organizations testifying or filing statements with the Natural Resources and Environment Committee in opposition to S.F. 1026 authorizing the donation of state lands to the United States for Voyageurs National Park during the April 5 and 12 hearings included M. Russell Allen, executive secretary of the Minnesota Timber Producer's Association; Frank T. Frederickson, Woodlands Manager for Boise Cascade Corp.; Ed Chilgren, Northland Multiple Use Association; William W. Essling, spokesperson for the Boundary Waters Landowners Association; Hollis B. Ryan, Minnesota Arrowhead Association; Ray Higgins, former state senator from Duluth; Russell Daniels, president of the Crane Lake Area Association; James Makuski, resort owner. Einar Karlstrand, "Voyageurs Said Threat to State Forest Industries, *Duluth Herald*, 15 April 1971; "F. T. Frederickson Questions Fairness of Park Land Donation," *International Falls Daily Journal*, 4 April 1971; "Opponents of Park Ask Referendum," *Duluth News-Tribune*, 13 April 1971; Curt Bernd, DNR, to U. W. Hella, 6 April 1971, author's files; Erick Kendall, VNPA, "Summary of Voyageurs National Park April 12 Opposition Testimony at the State Senate Committee Hearing," author's files.

30. "F. T. Frederickson Questions Fairness of Park Land Donation," *International Falls Daily Journal*, 6 April 1971.

31. "Hansberger Urges Commission Instead of Park," *International Falls Daily Journal*, 14 April 1971.

32. Einar Karlstrand, "Holmquist Scored by Higgins over Voyageurs Stand," *Duluth News-Tribune*, 6 April 1971.

33. House Subcommittee on National Parks and Recreation, *Hearings on a Proposal for Voyageurs National Park*, 91st Cong., 2d sess., 16 and 17 July 1970, 260–61.

34. Karlstrand, "Holmquist Scored by Higgins over Voyageurs Stand."

35. Ibid.

36. Director U. W. Hella, Division of Parks and Recreation, Minnesota Department of Natural Resources to Minnesota State Senate's Natural Resources Subcommittees regarding establishment of Voyageurs National Park, 5 April 1971, author's files.

37. "LeVander Backs Voyageurs Park," *International Falls Daily Journal*, 18 March 1971.

38. "State Voyageurs Land Value Set," *Minneapolis Tribune,* 22 April 1971.

39. Einar Karlstrand, "Estimated Value of Land in Voyageurs Park Disputed," *Duluth News-Tribune,* April 1970.

40. "Senate Delays Vote on Voyageurs," *Duluth News-Tribune,* 23 April 1971.

41. William W. Essling, letter to the editor, *International Falls Daily Journal,* 23 April 1971.

42. "Fight Delays Voyageurs Action," *Minneapolis Tribune,* 23 April 1971.

43. Gene Lahammer, "Park Bill Causes Shouting Match in Senate Committee," *International Falls Daily Journal,* 22 April 1971.

44. Lahammer, "Park Bill Causes Shouting Match in Senate Committee"; "Fight Delays Voyageurs Action," *Minneapolis Tribune,* 23 April 1971.

45. Tom Mathews, "State Senators Block Voyageurs Park Plan," *St. Paul Pioneer Press,* 25 April 1971.

46. "1.4 Million Expected to Visit Voyageurs the First Year," *Duluth Herald,* 14 April 1971.

47. Mathews, "State Senators Block Voyageurs Park Plan."

48. Christopher Wren, "How to Wreck a National Park," *Look Magazine,* 16 June 1970, 77–80. This story appearing in a high-circulation national magazine in the 1970s describes how park rangers were trying to cope with the cars and crowds at Grand Teton National Park in summer 1970. George Hartzog, then director of the NPS, said it was not really people who clogged the parks but what they brought with them—cars, trailers, campers, and so on. Of course, Voyageurs, a water-based park, was not likely to have the vehicular problems that continued to confront the NPS in the more popular parks.

49. Bernie Shellum, "Voyageurs Bill Sent to Senate Subcommittee," *Minneapolis Tribune,* 25 April 1971.

50. Ibid.

51. "Park Bill Delay Held Message," *International Falls Daily Journal,* 26 April 1971.

52. Editorial, "Saving Voyageurs Park," *St. Paul Pioneer Press,* 28 April 1971.

53. Wayne Wangstad, "National Park Bill Is Revived," *St. Paul Dispatch,* 29 April 1971.

54. Tim Talle, "Key Senate Unit Passes Voyageurs Proposal," *Minneapolis Star,* 30 April 1971.

55. Robert Whereatt, "Voyageurs Bill Has Rough House Voyage," *St. Paul Pioneer Press,* 28 April 1971; Finlay Lewis, "National Park Bill Altered in House," *Minneapolis Tribune,* 28 April 1971.

56. Finlay Lewis, "House Committee Approves Bill for Voyageurs Park," *Minneapolis Tribune,* 30 April 1971.

57. Einar Karlstrand, "House Oks Voyageurs Bill," *Duluth News-Tribune,* 13 May 1971; Robert Whereatt, "Voyageurs Park Bill Is Passed by House," *St. Paul Pioneer Press,* 13 May 1971.

58. Einar Karlstrand, "Voyageurs Land Bill Sent to Senate Floor," *Duluth News-Tribune,* 12 May 1971.

59. Ibid.

60. Robert Franklin, "Senate Votes Voyageurs Park Bill," *Minneapolis Tribune,* 16 May 1971.

61. Lee Egerstrom, "Senate Gives Final OK to Voyageurs," *St. Paul Sunday Pioneer Press*, 16 May 1971.

62. "Amended Park Bill Sent to Governor," *Duluth News-Tribune*, 22 May 1971.

12. The Four Years to Establishment

1. Einar W. Karlstrand, "Voyageurs Bill Signed by Governor," *Duluth Herald*, 4 June 1971.

2. Ibid.

3. Barry Mackintosh, *The National Parks: Shaping the System* (Washington, D.C.: National Park Service, U.S. Department of the Interior, 1984).

4. George B. Hartzog Jr., *Battling for the National Parks* (Mt. Kisco, N.Y.: Moyer Bell, 1988), 79.

5. I consulted various chronologies of federal legislation, including Mackintosh, *The National Parks;* and Dwight F. Rettie, *Our National Park System* (Urbana, University of Illinois Press, 1995). Congress participated in this unprecedented expansion by passing the Wilderness Act in 1964; the Land and Water Conservation Act in 1964, which helped fund land acquisition in new units; the Wild and Scenic Rivers Act in 1968; the National Trails System Act in 1968; and the Environmental Policy Act in 1969, in addition to approving the sixty-nine new units.

6. Nine units were added to the National Park System in the Midwest alone in the six years 1965–71, including Herbert Hoover National Historic Site in Iowa, St. Croix National Scenic Riverway in Minnesota and Wisconsin, Apostle Islands National Lakeshore in Wisconsin, Sleeping Bear Dunes and Pictured Rocks National Lakeshores in Michigan, Lincoln Home National Historic Site in Illinois, George Rogers Clark National Historical Park and Indiana Dunes National Lakeshore in Indiana, and Voyageurs National Park in Minnesota.

7. Myrl Brooks, interview by Mary Lou Pearson, 11 July 1978, Voyageurs National Park Archives, International Falls, Minn.

8. "Project Manager Announced for Voyageurs National Park," *Minneapolis Tribune*, 13 June 1971.

9. Al McConagha, "Voyageurs Park Manager Gets His First Look," *Minneapolis Tribune*, 20 June 1971.

10. Brooks, interview, 4. Wendell Anderson and Rudy Perpich were elected governor and lieutenant governor, respectively, in 1970, and both were reelected in 1974. When Walter Mondale gave up his seat to become vice president, Governor Anderson, in the first year of his second term, resigned, elevating Perpich to governor. Perpich promptly appointed Anderson to fill the Senate seat vacated by Mondale.

11. Brooks, interview, 11.

12. Erik Kendall, "Voyageurs Park Now a Certainty," *Midland Cooperative*, reprinted in the *International Falls Daily Journal*, 16 June 1971.

13. "Park Service Plans Duluth Land Office," *Duluth News-Tribune*, 20 July 1971.

14. "IRS Clears Voyageur Problem," *Duluth News-Tribune*, 14 September 1971.

15. Elmer L. Andersen to Friends of Voyageurs National Park, August 1971, author's files.

16. "Transfer of School Lands to Park Challenged," *Minneapolis Tribune*, 11 August 1971.

17. "Voyageurs Decision Applauded," *Duluth News-Tribune,* 16 November 1971.

18. "Voyageurs National Park Appeal Denied," *Minneapolis Tribune,* 15 June 1972.

19. Dale Featherling, "Voyageurs Park Poses Problems in Planning," *Minneapolis Tribune,*" 8 August 1971.

20. Ibid.

21. Governor's Voyageurs National Park Management Committee, *Conference on Planning in the Voyageurs National Park Area: Proceedings,* sponsored by Governor's Voyageurs National Park Management Committee and Voyageurs National Park Association (International Falls, Minn.: Governor's Voyageurs National Park Management Committee, December 1973).

22. Arrowhead Regional Development Commission Executive Director Rudy Essala to State Planning Agency Director Peter Vanderpoel, 28 November 1975. The document that was transmitted was the *Subregional Plan for the Voyageurs Planning Area* (author's files).

23. Nina Helper, "County Board Hears about Park Peripheral Planning," *International Falls Daily Journal,* 5 April 1974.

24. NPS Midwest Region Chief of Cultural Resources F. A. Ketterson Jr. to Gregory Kinney, 7 May 1990, Voyageurs National Park Archives. This letter provides transfer dates for the inquiring Kinney, but no explanation for shifting back and forth between regions.

25. NPS Midwest Regional Director Merrill Beal to Minnesota Department of Natural Resources Commissioner Robert Herbst, 11 February 1976, Voyageurs National Park Archives.

26. Memorandum from Minnesota Department of Natural Resources Area Game Manager Jim Schneeweis to Supervisor Roger Holmes, 22 February 1972, Voyageurs National Park Archives.

27. Ibid.

28. Memorandum from Milt Stenlund to DNR Game Manager Roger Holmes, 28 February 1972, Voyageurs National Park Archives.

29. Memorandum from Stanley Hulett to Robert Herbst, 18 May 1972, Voyageurs National Park Archives.

30. Memorandum from Jim Schneeweis to Roger Holmes, 15 June 1972, Voyageurs National Park Archives.

31. "Park Project Chief Outlines Development and Management Plans," *International Falls Daily Journal,* 19 January 1972.

32. "Brooks Explains Goals of Voyageurs National Park," *Grand Rapids Review,* 20 April 1972.

33. "Operations Evaluation for Voyageurs National Park," NPS Northeast Region, Philadelphia, 25–27 June 1972, cover page, Voyageurs National Park Archives.

34. Ibid., 2.

35. Ibid., 6.

36. "Land Being Acquired for National Parks," *Duluth News-Tribune,* 21 January 1973. Just how significant the restrictions on land acquisition were for Voyageurs was shown in the article cited here. The story reviewed the land acquisition progress through 1972 for several new NPS units in Minnesota, Wisconsin, and Michigan. Apostle Islands National Lakeshore had appraised all of the unit's mainland area and twenty islands. Federal and state lands were acquired by donation. The process of acquisition and negotiation for purchase at Apostle Islands (established 1970)

went forward without the restrictions imposed at Voyageurs. The same was true for St. Croix National Scenic Riverway, which was established in 1969.

37. "Crumbling Hierarchy," editorial, *New York Times*, 14 September 1972.

38. "Land Transfer Hilights Governor's Park Tour," *Voyageurs National Park Association News*, 4 December 1972; Don Boxmeyer, "Voyageurs National Park Gets State Owned Lands," *St. Paul Pioneer Press*, 14 September 1972.

39. John Schweitzer, "National Park Management Goals Stress People, Education and Use," *International Falls Daily Journal*, 18 January 1973.

40. "Jim Blubaugh on Outdoors," *Duluth News-Tribune*, 18 August 1974.

41. Conservation Foundation, *National Parks for the Future* (Washington, D.C.: Conservation Foundation, 1972), 13.

42. "Jim Blubaugh on Outdoors," *Duluth News-Tribune*, 18 August 1974.

43. Minutes of the VNPA board meeting on August 14, 1974, 1, author's files.

44. "State Deeds Land for Voyageurs," *Duluth News-Tribune*, 13 December 1974.

45. Robert Herbst to George B. Hartzog, 13 April 1972, Voyageurs National Park Archives. Herbst's role in securing deletion of Black Bay was not forgotten by environmentalists, who testified against Herbst's nomination for assistant secretary of the interior in the Carter administration. Al McConagha, "Environmentalists Trying to Block Herbst Nomination," *Minneapolis Tribune*, 30 January 1977.

46. John A. Blatnik to George B. Hartzog, 30 October 1972, Voyageurs National Park Archives.

47. "DNR, Game Manager Back Change in Park for Area Duck Hunters," *International Falls Daily Journal*, 9 April 1974.

48. "Change in Boundary Supported," *Hibbing Daily Tribune*, 10 May 1974.

49. "Park Closing Confusing to Hunters," *International Falls Daily Journal*, 2 October 1974.

50. Memo from Bill Dean to Gary Tays, NPS Washington office, and Myrl Brooks, 18 July 1974, files in Office of Park Planning, Washington, D.C.

51. Jay Griggs, "Park Progress Outlined at Local Public Meeting," *International Falls Daily Journal*, 19 February 1975.

52. The Federal Register is a legal newspaper published every business day by the National Archives and Records Administration. It contains federal agency regulations, proposed rules and notices, executive orders, proclamations, and other presidential documents.

53. Myrl Brooks, interview by author, at Brooks's home outside Chattanooga, Tennessee, 17 April 1990.

54. Albert Eisele, "Voyageurs Park Becomes Reality," *Duluth News-Tribune*, 9 April 1975.

55. *The National Parks Index, 1985* (Washington, D.C.: National Park Service, Department of the Interior).

56. "Bill Would Establish Citizens Committee on Voyageurs Park," *International Falls Daily Journal*, 6 March 1975.

57. "House Unit OK's Citizens Panel on Voyageurs Park," *Duluth News-Tribune*, 19 March 1975.

58. Memo from NPS Midwest Regional Director Merrill D. Beal to Voyageurs National Park Project Manager Myrl Brooks, 4 April 1975, Voyageurs National Park Archives.

59. John Murrell, "Voyageurs Planning Debated," *Duluth News-Tribune*, 11 June 1975.

60. "Brooks Says People Misled on Park," *St. Paul Dispatch*, 30 June 1976.

61. Mary Lou Pearson, interview by author, 11 July 1978.

62. "Unit Suggests Voyageurs Park Changes," *Duluth News-Tribune*, 13 October 1975.

63. Memorandum from NPS Midwest Regional Director to Superintendents, Midwest Region, 11 November 1975, Voyageurs National Park Archives.

64. Memo from Voyageurs National Park Superintendent Myrl Brooks to Midwest Regional Director, 14 November 1975, Voyageurs National Park Archives.

65. "1975 Annual Report for Voyageurs National Park," submitted to Midwest Regional Director, 1976, Voyageurs National Park Archives.

66. Ibid.

67. Brooks, interview.

68. "1976 Annual Report for Voyageurs National Park," 1977, Voyageurs National Park Archives.

69. Hartzog, *Battling for the National Parks*, 79.

Bibliography

Archival Sources

Minnesota Historical Society Archives, St. Paul, Minnesota
LeVander, Harold. Papers.
Minnesota Department of Conservation. Records.
Oberholtzer, Ernest C. Interview. Interviewer unknown, Accession 9529.
Oberholtzer, Ernest C. Papers.
Olson, Sigurd. Papers.
Quetico-Superior Council. Records.
Voyageurs National Park Association. Records.

Superior National Forest Files, Duluth, Minnesota
Superior National Forest News Bulletin. Duluth, Minn., 28 December 1967.

U.S. Department of the Interior, Washington, D.C.
Legislative and Congressional Office. Records.
Office of Park Planning. Records.

Voyageurs National Park Archives, International Falls, Minnesota
Annual Reports for Voyageurs National Park, 1975–78.
Chronology on Voyageurs National Park, 1966.

Oral Histories

Voyageurs National Park
Amidon, George. Interview by Mary Lou Pearson. 12 July 1976.
Brooks, Myrl. Interview by Mary Lou Pearson. 11 July 1978.
Kawamoto, John. Interview by Mary Lou Pearson. 12 June 1979.

Books and Articles

Backes, David. "Wilderness Visions." *Forest and Conservation History* 35 (July 1991): 128–37.

Borchert, John R. *Atlas of Minnesota Resources and Settlement.* 3d ed. Minneapolis: University of Minnesota, Center for Urban and Regional Affairs, 1980.

———. *Minnesota's Changing Geography.* Minneapolis: University of Minnesota Press, 1959.

Broderick, Richard. "Minnesotan of the Year—A Generous Spirit," *Minnesota Monthly,* December 1989.

Brubaker, Sterling. *Rethinking the Federal Lands.* Washington, D.C.: Resources for the Future, 1984.

Carter, Luther J. "Walter J. Hickel Advocate of Economic Growth as Alaska's Governor Faces Tougher Job at Interior." *Science* 162 (December 1968).

———. "Hickel Controversy Points Up Environmental Quality Issue." *Science* 163 (January 1969).

Congressional Record. 90th Cong., 1st sess. (20 September 1967), 113: 26214–15.

Congressional Record. 90th Cong., 2d sess., 1968, 114: 22279–82.

Conservation Foundation, *National Parks for the Future.* Washington, D.C.: Conservation Foundation, 1972.

Dana, Samuel T. *Minnesota Lands.* Washington, D.C.: American Forestry Association, 1969.

Fitch, Edwin M., and John F. Shankland. *Bureau of Outdoor Recreation.* New York: Praeger Publishers, 1970.

Forestra, Ronald A. *America's National Parks and Their Keepers.* Washington, D.C.: Resources for the Future, 1984.

Franklin, Kay, and Norma Schaeffer. *Dual for the Dunes.* Urbana: University of Illinois Press, 1983.

Frome, Michael. *The Battle for Wilderness.* New York: Praeger Publishers, 1974.

Hampton, Duane. "Opposition to National Parks." *Journal of Forest History* 21 (1981).

Hartzog, George B., Jr. *Battling for the National Parks.* Mt. Kisco, N.Y.: Moyer Bell, 1988.

Hays, Samuel P. *Beauty, Health, and Permanence.* New York: Cambridge University Press, 1987.

———. "The Environmental Movement." *Journal of Forest History* 25 (1981).

Hella, U. W. *Quest for Excellence: A History of the Minnesota Council of Parks, 1954–1974.* St. Paul: Minnesota Parks Foundation, 1985.

LaPierre, Yvette. "A Place to Park." *Home and Away* 16, 2 (March/April 1995).

Leopold, A. Starker. "Wildlife Management in the National Parks." *Living Wilderness,* Spring 1963.

Limebury, Robert L. *Government in America.* 3d ed. New York: Little Brown and Co., 1986.

Mackintosh, Barry. *The National Parks: Shaping the System.* Washington, D.C.: National Park Service, U.S. Department of the Interior, 1984.

Mid-Continent Surveys. *Attitudes toward the Proposed Voyageurs National Park.* Minneapolis, 29 May 1968.

Minnesota Department of Conservation. *A Summary Report: Voyageurs National Park Proposal,* prepared by Willard E. West and Roger S. Williams. St. Paul: Minnesota Department of Conservation, 1967.

Minnesota Resources Commission. *Voyageurs National Park Fact Book.* St. Paul: March 1971.

National Park Service. "Proposed Voyageurs National Park." Revised draft. Omaha: National Park Service, September 1963.

———. *Proposed Voyageurs National Park.* Omaha: National Park Service, 1964.

———. *Proposed Voyageurs National Park.* Omaha: National Park Service, 1965.

———. *A Master Plan for the Proposed Voyageurs National Park, Minnesota.* Washington, D.C.: National Park Service, 1968.

Oberholtzer, Ernest C. "A University of the Wilderness." *American Forests* 35, 11 (November 1929): 692.

———. "Attention, Please for Quetico-Superior." *National Parks Magazine* 78 (July–September 1944): 15.

Paddock, Joe. *Keeper of the Wild: The Life of Ernest Oberholtzer.* St. Paul: Minnesota Historical Society Press, 2001.

Quetico-Superior Committee. *An International Peace Memorial Forest in the Quetico-Superior Country.* Chicago, 1948.

Reid, T. R. *Congressional Odyssey: The Saga of a Senate Bill.* San Francisco: W. H. Freeman, 1980.

Rettie, Dwight F. *Our National Park System: Caring for America's Greatest Natural and Historic Treasures.* Urbana, University of Illinois Press, 1995.

Runte, Alfred. *National Parks: The American Experience.* 2d. ed. Lincoln: University of Nebraska Press, 1987.

Searle, R. Newell. "Minnesota National Forest." *Minnesota History* 42 (1971): 249.

———. "Minnesota Forestry Comes of Age: Christopher C. Andrews, 1895–1911." *Forest History* 17, 2 (July 1973): 23–24.

———. *Saving Quetico-Superior: A Land Set Apart.* St. Paul: Minnesota Historical Society Press, 1977.

Sielaff, Richard O., Cecil H. Meyers, and Philip L. Friest. *The Economics of the Proposed Voyageurs National Park.* Duluth: published for the U.S. Department of the Interior, National Park Service by the University of Minnesota, Duluth, Division of Social Sciences, 1964.

Steen, Harold K. *The U.S. Forest Service: A History.* Seattle: University of Washington Press, 1976.

Stegner, Wallace. "The Best Idea We Ever Had." *Wilderness Magazine* Spring (1983): 4–13.

Treuer, Robert. *Voyageur Country: A Park in the Wilderness.* Minneapolis: University of Minnesota Press, 1979.

U.S. Congress. House. Committee on Interior and Insular Affairs. *Field Hearings on H.R. 10482 before the Subcommittee on Parks and Recreation.* 91st Cong., 1st sess., International Falls, Minn., 21 August 1969.

———. House. Subcommittee on National Parks and Recreation. *Hearings on a Proposal for Voyageurs National Park.* 91st Cong., 2d sess., 16 and 17 July 1970.

———. House. Committee on Interior and Insular Affairs. *Hearings on H.R 10482.* 91st Cong., 1st sess., 16 and 17 July 1970.

———. Senate. Committee on Interior and Insular Affairs. *Hearings before the Subcommittee on Parks and Recreation on S. 1962 and H.R. 10482.* 91st Cong., 2d sess., 4 and 7 December 1970.

———. Senate. Committee on Interior and Insular Affairs. Report No. 91–1513. 91st Cong., 2d sess. Calendar No. 1524, 15 December 1970.

White, J. Wesley. *Historical Sketches of the Quetico-Superior.* Duluth: Superior National Forest Service, U.S. Dept of Agriculture, 1968.

Wirth, Conrad. *Parks, Politics and People.* Norman: University of Oklahoma Press, 1980.

Witzig, Fred T. "The Crane Lake Issue in the Establishment of Voyageurs National Park." *Upper Midwest History* 3 (1983): 11.

Wren, Christopher. "How to Wreck a National Park." *Look Magazine* 16 (June 1970).

Index

Fred T. Witzig is professor emeritus of geography at the University of Minnesota, Duluth. His research and academic career have focused on environmental conservation and urban and regional planning. He has been a member of the Parks and Trails Council of Minnesota, the Voyageurs Region National Park Association, the Lake States Interpretive Association, and the Duluth City Planning Commission, where he received an award of excellence from the Minnesota Planning Association.

Elmer L. Andersen is one of Minnesota's leading political, business, and cultural figures. His autobiography, *A Man's Reach,* was published by the University of Minnesota Press in 2000. He lives in Arden Hills, Minnesota.